Principles of Information Security

Liam Lewis

WILLFORD PRESS

www.willfordpress.com

Published by Willford Press,
118-35 Queens Blvd., Suite 400,
Forest Hills, NY 11375, USA

ISBN: 978-1-64728-032-1

Cataloging-in-Publication Data

Principles of information security / Liam Lewis.
    p. cm.
Includes bibliographical references and index.
ISBN 978-1-64728-032-1
1. Computer networks--Security measures. 2. Computer security. 3. Data protection.
4. Information technology--Security measures. 5. Internet--Security measures.
I. Lewis, Liam.
TK5105.59 .P75 2022
005.8--dc23

For information on all Willford Press publications
visit our website at www.willfordpress.com

Table of Contents

Preface

This book is a culmination of my many years of practice in this field. I attribute the success of this book to my support group. I would like to thank my parents who have showered me with unconditional love and support and my peers and professors for their constant guidance.

The practice of protecting information by eliminating or reducing information risks is termed as information security. It is an important constituent of information risk management. It is primarily concerned with the prevention or reduction of the probability of inappropriate access, disclosure, use, disruption, destruction, modification, and recording. The key concepts related to information security are confidentiality, integrity and availability. Confidentiality ensures that information is not disclosed to unauthorized individuals or entities. Maintaining the accuracy and completeness of data over its entire lifecycle is termed as data integrity. Availability of information involves making it available whenever it is needed. This book is compiled in such a manner, that it will provide in-depth knowledge about the theory and principles of information security. It unfolds the innovative aspects of this field which will be crucial for the holistic understanding of the subject matter. This book will serve as a valuable source of reference for those interested in this field.

The details of chapters are provided below for a progressive learning:

Chapter – What is Information Security?

The practice of protecting information by reducing information risks is referred to as information security. It generally involves reducing the probability of unauthorized and inappropriate access. This chapter has been carefully written to provide an easy introduction to the varied facets of information security.

Chapter – Fundamental Concepts of Information Security

Some of the major concepts of information security are data confidentiality, data integrity, non-repudiation, electronic authentication and Parkerian hexad. The topics elaborated in this chapter will help in gaining a better perspective about these fundamental concepts of information security.

Chapter – Threats to Information Security

There are numerous threats that are dealt with under information security. Some of the major threats are cyber risk, security breach, data breach, data theft, data loss, malware, spyware, rootkit, keystroke logging, web shell, phishing, etc. This chapter discusses in detail these threats related to information security.

Chapter – Information Security Management

Information security management refers to the controls implemented by organizations to ensure that they are protecting the integrity and confidentiality of assets from threats and vulnerabilities. It involves the use of antivirus software and disk encryption. This chapter closely examines the key concepts of information security management.

Chapter – Cryptography

Cryptography refers to the study and practice of techniques to ensure secure communication in the presence of third parties known as adversaries. Some of the algorithms used in cryptography are cryptographic primitives and symmetric-key algorithm. The diverse aspects of cryptography have been carefully analyzed in this chapter.

Liam Lewis

1

What is Information Security?

The practice of protecting information by reducing information risks is referred to as information security. It generally involves reducing the probability of unauthorized and inappropriate access. This chapter has been carefully written to provide an easy introduction to the varied facets of information security.

Information System

Information system is an integrated set of components for collecting, storing, and processing data and for providing information, knowledge, and digital products. Business firms and other organizations rely on information systems to carry out and manage their operations, interact with their customers and suppliers, and compete in the marketplace. Information systems are used to run interorganizational supply chains and electronic markets. For instance, corporations use information systems to process financial accounts, to manage their human resources, and to reach their potential customers with online promotions. Many major companies are built entirely around information systems. These include eBay, a largely auction marketplace; Amazon, an expanding electronic mall and provider of cloud computing services; Alibaba, a business-to-business e-marketplace; and Google, a search engine company that derives most of its revenue from keyword advertising on Internet searches. Governments deploy information systems to provide services cost-effectively to citizens. Digital goods—such as electronic books, video products, and software—and online services, such as gaming and social networking, are delivered with information systems. Individuals rely on information systems, generally Internet-based, for conducting much of their personal lives: for socializing, study, shopping, banking, and entertainment.

As major new technologies for recording and processing information were invented over the millennia, new capabilities appeared, and people became empowered. The invention of the printing press by Johannes Gutenberg in the mid-15th century and the invention of a mechanical calculator by Blaise Pascal in the 17th century are but two examples. These inventions led to a profound revolution in the ability to record, process, disseminate, and reach for information and knowledge. This led, in turn, to even deeper changes in individual lives, business organization, and human governance.

The first large-scale mechanical information system was Herman Hollerith's census tabulator. Invented in time to process the 1890 U.S. census, Hollerith's machine represented a major step in automation, as well as an inspiration to develop computerized information systems.

One of the first computers used for such information processing was the UNIVAC I, installed at the U.S. Bureau of the Census in 1951 for administrative use and at General Electric in 1954 for commercial use. Beginning in the late 1970s, personal computers brought some of the advantages of information systems to small businesses and to individuals. Early in the same decade the Internet began its expansion as the global network of networks. In 1991 the World Wide Web, invented by Tim Berners-Lee as a means to access the interlinked information stored in the globally dispersed computers connected by the Internet, began operation and became the principal service delivered on the network. The global penetration of the Internet and the Web has enabled access to information and other resources and facilitated the forming of relationships among people and organizations on an unprecedented scale. The progress of electronic commerce over the Internet has resulted in a dramatic growth in digital interpersonal communications (via e-mail and social networks), distribution of products (software, music, e-books, and movies), and business transactions (buying, selling, and advertising on the Web). With the worldwide spread of smartphones, tablets, laptops, and other computer-based mobile devices, all of which are connected by wireless communicationnetworks, information systems have been extended to support mobility as the natural human condition.

As information systems enabled more diverse human activities, they exerted a profound influence over society. These systems quickened the pace of daily activities, enabled people to develop and maintain new and often more-rewarding relationships, affected the structure and mix of organizations, changed the type of products bought, and influenced the nature of work. Information and knowledge became vital economic resources. Yet, along with new opportunities, the dependence on information systems brought new threats. Intensive industry innovation and academic research continually develop new opportunities while aiming to contain the threats.

Components of Information Systems

The main components of information systems are computer hardware and software, telecommunications, databases and data warehouses, human resources, and procedures. The hardware, software, and telecommunications constitute information technology (IT), which is now ingrained in the operations and management of organizations.

Computer Hardware

Today throughout the world even the smallest firms, as well as many households, own or lease computers. Individuals may own multiple computers in the form of smartphones, tablets, and other wearable devices. Large organizations typically employ distributed computer systems, from powerful parallel-processing servers located in data centres to widely dispersed personal computers and mobile devices, integrated into the organizational information systems. Sensors are becoming ever more widely distributed throughout the physical and biological environment to gather data and, in many cases, to effect control via devices known as actuators. Together with the peripheral equipment—such as magnetic or solid-state storage disks, input-output devices, and telecommunications gear—these constitute the hardware of information systems. The cost of hardware has steadily and rapidly decreased, while processing speed and storage capacity have increased vastly. This development has been occurring under Moore's law: the power of the microprocessors at the heart of computing devices has been doubling approximately every 18 to 24 months. However, hardware's use of electric power and its environmental impact are concerns being addressed by designers. Increasingly, computer and storage services are delivered from the cloud—from shared facilities accessed over telecommunications networks.

Computer Software

Computer software falls into two broad classes: system software and application software. The principal system software is the operating system. It manages the hardware, data and program files, and other system resources and provides means for the user to control the computer, generally via a graphical user interface (GUI). Application software is programs designed to handle specific tasks for users. Smartphone apps became a common way for individuals to access information systems. Other examples include general-purpose application suites with their spreadsheet and word-processing programs, as well as "vertical" applications that serve a specific industry segment—for instance, an application that schedules, routes, and tracks package deliveries for an overnight carrier. Larger firms use licensed applications developed and maintained by specialized software companies, customizing them to meet their specific needs, and develop other applications in-house or on an outsourced basis. Companies may also use applications delivered as software-as-a-service (SaaS) from the cloud over the Web. Proprietary software, available from and supported by its vendors, is being challenged by open-source software available on the Web for free use and modification under a license that protects its future availability.

Telecommunications

Telecommunications are used to connect, or network, computer systems and portable and wearable devices and to transmit information. Connections are established via wired or wireless media. Wired technologies include coaxial cable and fibre optics. Wireless technologies, predominantly based on the transmission of microwaves and radio waves, support mobile computing. Pervasive information systems have arisen with the computing devices embedded in many different physical objects. For example, sensors such as radio frequency identification devices (RFIDs) can be attached to products moving through the supply chain to enable the tracking of their location and the monitoring of their condition. Wireless sensor networks that are integrated into the Internet can produce massive amounts of data that can be used in seeking higher productivity or in monitoring the environment.

Various computer network configurations are possible, depending on the needs of an organization. Local area networks (LANs) join computers at a particular site, such as an office building or an academic campus. Metropolitan area networks (MANs) cover a limited densely populated area and are the electronic infrastructure of "smart cities." Wide area networks(WANs) connect widely distributed data centres, frequently run by different organizations. Peer-to-peer networks, without a centralized control, enable broad sharing of content. The Internet is a network of networks, connecting billions of computers located on every continent. Through networking, users gain access to information resources, such as large databases, and to other individuals, such as coworkers, clients, friends, or people who share their professional or private interests. Internet-type services can be provided within an organization and for its exclusive use by various intranets that are accessible through a browser; for example, an intranet may be deployed as an access portal to a shared corporate document base. To connect with business partners over the Internet in a private and secure manner, extranets are established as so-called virtual private networks (VPNs) by encrypting the messages.

A massive "Internet of things" has emerged, as sensors and actuators have been widely distributed in the physical environment and are supplying data, such as acidity of a square yard of soil, the speed of a driving vehicle, or the blood pressure of an individual. The availability of such information enables a rapid reaction when necessary as well as sustained decision making based on processing of the massive accumulated data.

Extensive networking infrastructure supports the growing move to cloud computing, with the information-system resources shared among multiple companies, leading to utilization efficiencies and freedom in localization of the data centres. Software-defined networking affords flexible control of telecommunications networks with algorithms that are responsive to real-time demands and resource availabilities.

Databases and Data Warehouses

Many information systems are primarily delivery vehicles for data stored in databases. A database is a collection of interrelated data organized so that individual records or groups of records can be retrieved to satisfy various criteria. Typical examples of databases include employee records and product catalogs. Databases support the operations and management functions of an enterprise. Data warehouses contain the archival data, collected over time, that can be mined for information in order to develop and market new products, serve the existing customers better, or reach out to potential new customers. Anyone who has ever purchased something with a credit card—in person, by mail order, or over the Web—is included within such data collections.

Massive collection and processing of the quantitative, or structured, data, as well as of the textual data often gathered on the Web, has developed into a broad initiative known as "big data." Many benefits can arise from decisions based on the facts reflected by big data. Examples include evidence-based medicine, economy of resources as a result of avoiding waste, and recommendations of new products (such as books or movies) based on a user's interests. Big data enables innovative business models. For example, a commercial firm collects the prices of goods by crowdsourcing (collecting from numerous independent individuals) via smartphones around the world. The aggregated data supplies early information on price movements, enabling more responsive decision making than was previously possible.

The processing of textual data—such as reviews and opinions articulated by individuals on social networks, blogs, and discussion boards—permits automated sentiment analysis for marketing, competitive intelligence, new product development, and other decision-making purposes.

Human Resources and Procedures

Qualified people are a vital component of any information system. Technical personnel include development and operations managers, business analysts, systems analysts and designers, database administrators, programmers, computer security specialists, and computer operators. In addition, all workers in an organization must be trained to utilize the capabilities of information systems as fully as possible. Billions of people around the world are learning about information systems as they use the Web.

Procedures for using, operating, and maintaining an information system are part of its documentation. For example, procedures need to be established to run a payroll program, including when to run it, who is authorized to run it, and who has access to the output. In the autonomous computing initiative, data centres are increasingly run automatically, with the procedures embedded in the software that controls those centres.

Types of Information Systems

Information systems support operations, knowledge work, and management in organizations. (The overall structure of organizational information systems is shown in the figure.) Functional information systems that support a specific organizational function, such as marketing or production, have been supplanted in many cases by cross-functional systems built to support complete business processes, such as order processing or employee management. Such systems can be more effective in the development and delivery of the firm's products and can be evaluated more closely with respect to the business outcomes. The information-system categories described here may be implemented with a great variety of application programs.

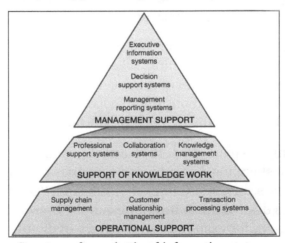

Structure of organizational information systems

Information systems consist of three layers: operational support, support of knowledge work, and management support. Operational support forms the base of an information system and contains various transaction processing systems for designing, marketing, producing, and delivering products and services. Support of knowledge work forms the middle layer; it contains subsystems for sharing information within an organization. Management support, forming the top layer, contains subsystems for managing and evaluating an organization's resources and goals.

Operational Support and Enterprise Systems

Transaction processing systems support the operations through which products are designed, marketed, produced, and delivered. In larger organizations, transaction processing is frequently accomplished with large integrated systems known as enterprise systems. In this case, the information systems that support various functional units—sales and marketing, production, finance, and human resources—are integrated into an enterprise resource planning (ERP) system, the principal kind of enterprise system. ERP systems support the value chain—that is, the entire sequence of activities or processes through which a firm adds value to its products. For example, an individual or another business may submit a custom order over the Web that automatically initiates just-in-time production to the customer's specifications through an approach known as mass customization. This involves sending orders from the customers to the firm's warehouses and perhaps to suppliers to deliver input materials just in time for a batched custom production run. Financial accounts are updated accordingly, and delivery logistics and billing are initiated.

Along with helping to integrate a firm's own value chain, transaction processing systems can also serve to integrate the overall supply chain of which the organization is a part. This includes all firms involved in designing, producing, marketing, and delivering the goods and services—from raw materials to the final delivery of the product. A supply chain management (SCM) system manages the flow of products, data, money, and information throughout the entire supply chain, which starts with the suppliers of raw materials, runs through the intermediate tiers of the processing companies, and ends with the distributors and retailers. For example, purchasing an item at a major retail store generates more than a cash register receipt: it also automatically sends a restocking order to the appropriate supplier, which in turn may call for orders to the supplier's suppliers. With an SCM system, suppliers can also access a retailer's inventory database over the Web to schedule efficient and timely deliveries in appropriate quantities.

The third type of enterprise system, customer relationship management (CRM), supports dealing with the company's customers in marketing, sales, service, and new product development. A CRM system gives a business a unified view of each customer and its dealings with that customer, enabling a consistent and proactive relationship. In cocreation initiatives, the customers may be involved in the development of the company's new products.

Many transaction processing systems support electronic commerce over the Internet. Among these are systems for online shopping, banking, and securities trading. Other systems deliver information, educational services, and entertainment on demand. Yet other systems serve to support the search for products with desired attributes (for example, keyword search on search engines), price discovery (via an auction, for example), and delivery of digital products (such as software, music, movies, or greeting cards). Social network sites, such as Facebook and LinkedIn, are a powerful tool for supporting customer communities and individuals as they articulate opinions, evolve new ideas, and are exposed to promotional messages. A growing array of specialized services and information-based products are offered by various organizations on the Web, as an infrastructure for electronic commerce has emerged on a global scale.

Transaction processing systems accumulate the data in databases and data warehouses that are necessary for the higher-level information systems. Enterprise systems also provide software modules needed to perform many of these higher-level functions.

Support of Knowledge Work

A large proportion of work in an information society involves manipulating abstract information and knowledge (understood in this context as an organized and comprehensivestructure of facts, relationships, theories, and insights) rather than directly processing, manufacturing, or delivering tangible materials. Such work is called knowledge work. Three general categories of information systems support such knowledge work: professional support systems, collaboration systems, and knowledge management systems.

Professional Support Systems

Professional support systems offer the facilities needed to perform tasks specific to a given profession. For example, automotive engineers use computer-aided engineering (CAE) software together with virtual reality systems to design and test new models as electronic prototypes for fuel efficiency, handling, and passenger protection before producing physical prototypes, and later they use CAE in the design and analysis of physical tests. Biochemists use specialized three-dimensional modeling software to visualize the molecular structure and probable effect of new drugs before investing in lengthy clinical tests. Investment bankers often employ financial software to calculate the expected rewards and potential risks of various investment strategies. Indeed, specialized support systems are now available for most professions.

Collaboration Systems

The main objectives of collaboration systems are to facilitate communication and teamwork among the members of an organization and across organizations. One type of collaboration system, known as a workflow system, is used to route relevant documents automatically to all appropriate individuals for their contributions.

Development, pricing, and approval of a commercial insurance policy is a process that can benefit from such a system. Another category of collaboration systems allows different individuals to work simultaneously on a shared project. Known as groupware, such systems accomplish this by allowing controlled shared access, often over an intranet, to the work objects, such as business proposals, new designs, or digital products in progress. The collaborators can be located anywhere in the world, and, in some multinational companies, work on a project continues 24 hours a day.

Other types of collaboration systems include enhanced e-mail and videoconferencing systems, sometimes with telepresence using avatars of the participants. Yet another type of collaboration software, known as wiki, enables multiple participants to add and edit content. (Some online encyclopaedias are produced on such platforms.) Collaboration systems can also be established on social network platforms or virtual life systems. In the open innovationinitiative, members of the public, as well as existing and potential customers, can be drawn in, if desired, to enable the cocreation of new products or projection of future outcomes.

Knowledge Management Systems

Knowledge management systems provide a means to assemble and act on the knowledge accumulated throughout an organization. Such knowledge may include the texts and images contained in patents, design methods, best practices, competitor intelligence, and similar sources, with the elaboration and commentary included. Placing the organization's documents and communications in an indexed and cross-referenced form enables rich search capabilities. Numerous application programs, such as Microsoft's SharePoint, exist to facilitate the implementation of such systems. Organizational knowledge is often tacit, rather than explicit, so these systems must also direct users to members of the organization with special expertise.

Management Support

A large category of information systems comprises those designed to support the management of an organization. These systems rely on the data obtained by transaction processing systems, as well as on data and information acquired outside the organization (on the Web, for example) and provided by business partners, suppliers, and customers.

Management Reporting Systems

Information systems support all levels of management, from those in charge of short-term schedules and budgets for small work groups to those concerned with long-term plans and budgets for the entire organization. Management reporting systems provide routine, detailed, and voluminous information reports specific to each manager's areas of responsibility. These systems are typically used by first-level supervisors. Generally, such reports focus on past and present activities, rather than projecting future performance. To prevent information overload, reports may be automatically sent only under exceptional circumstances or at the specific request of a manager.

Decision Support Systems and Business intelligence

All information systems support decision making, however indirectly, but decision support systems are expressly designed for this purpose. As these systems are increasingly being developed to analyze massive collections of data (known as big data), they are becoming known as business intelligence, or business analytics, applications. The two principal varieties of decision support systems are model-driven and data-driven.

In a model-driven decision support system, a preprogrammed model is applied to a relatively limited data set, such as a sales database for the present quarter. During a typical session, an analyst or sales manager will conduct a dialog with this decision support system by specifying a number of what-if scenarios. For example, in order to establish a selling price for a new product, the sales manager may use a marketing decision support system. It contains a model relating various factors—the price of the product, the cost of goods, and the promotion expense in various media—to the projected sales volume over the first five years on the market. By supplying different product prices to the model, the manager can compare predicted results and select the most profitable selling price.

The primary objective of data-driven business intelligence systems is to analyze large pools of data, accumulated over long periods of time in data warehouses, in a process known as data mining. Data mining aims to discover significant patterns, such as sequences (buying a new house, followed by a new dinner table), clusters, and correlations (large families and van sales), with which decisions can be made. Predictive analytics attempts to forecast future outcomes based on the discovered trends. Data-driven decision support systems include a variety of statistical models and may rely on various artificial intelligence techniques, such as expert systems, neural networks, and machine learning. In addition to mining numeric data, text mining is conducted on large aggregates of unstructured data, such as the contents of social media that include social networks, wikis, blogs, and microblogs. As used in electronic commerce, for example, text mining helps in finding buying trends, targeting advertisements, and detecting fraud.

An important variety of decision support systems enables a group of decision makers to work together without necessarily being in the same place at the same time. These group decision systems include software tools for brainstorming and reaching consensus.

Another category, geographic information systems, can help analyze and display data by using digitized maps. Digital mapping of various regions is a continuing activity of numerous business firms. Such data visualization supports rapid decision making. By looking at a geographic distribution of mortgage loans, for example, one can easily establish a pattern of discrimination.

Executive Information Systems

Executive information systems make a variety of critical information readily available in a highly summarized and convenient form, typically via a graphical digital dashboard. Senior managers characteristically employ many informal sources of information, however, so that formal, computerized information systems are only of partial assistance. Nevertheless, this assistance is important for the chief executive officer, senior and executive vice presidents, and the board of directors to monitor the performance of the company, assess the business environment, and develop strategic directions for the future. In particular, these executives need to compare their organization's performance with that of its competitors and investigate general economic trends in regions or countries. Often individualized and relying on multiple media formats, executive information systems give their users an opportunity to "drill down" from summary information to increasingly focused details.

Acquiring Information Systems and Services

Information systems are a major corporate asset, with respect both to the benefits they provide and to their high costs. Therefore, organizations have to plan for the long term when acquiring information systems and services that will support business initiatives. At the same time, firms have to be responsive to emerging opportunities. On the basis of long-term corporate plans and the requirements of various individuals from data workers to top management, essential applications are identified and project priorities are set. For example, certain projects may have to be carried out immediately to satisfy a new government reporting regulation or to interact with a new customer's information system. Other projects may be given a higher priority because of their strategic role or greater expected benefits.

Once the need for a specific information system has been established, the system has to be acquired. This is generally done in the context of the already existing information systems architecture of the firm. The acquisition of information systems can either involve external sourcing or rely on internal development or modification. With today's highly developed IT industry, companies tend to acquire information systems and services from specialized vendors. The principal tasks of information systems specialists involve modifying the applications for their employer's needs and integrating the applications to create a coherentsystems architecture for the firm. Generally, only smaller applications are developed internally. Certain applications of a more personal nature may be developed by the end users themselves.

Acquisition from External Sources

There are several principal ways to acquire an information system from outside the organization. Many firms have resorted to outsourcing their information systems. Outsourcing entails transferring the major components of the firm's systems and operations—such as data centres, telecommunications, and software development and maintenance—to a specialized company that provides its services under long-term contracts specifying the service levels (that is, the scope and the quality of service to be provided). In some cases the outsourcing entails moving the services abroad—i.e., offshoring in pursuit of the cost or expertise advantages. Responsibility for the acquisition of new applications then falls to the outside company. In other cases the company may outsource just the development or maintenance of their information systems, with the outside company being a systems developer.

Cloud computing is increasingly being adopted as a source of information services. It offers on-demand access via the Internet to services furnished by a provider that runs data centres with the necessary software and other resources. The services can be provided at one of three levels: as the infrastructure for running existing applications, as the platform for developing new applications, or as software-as-a-service (SaaS) to be used by the firm over the network. In particular, SaaS has become a cost-effective way to use enterprise systems. Generally, cloud computing is provided by external vendors, although some firms implement their own private clouds in order to share resources that employees can access over the network from a variety of devices, often including smartphones. Scalability and avoidance of capital expenditures are notable advantages of public clouds; the partial loss of control is a drawback.

Companies may choose to acquire an application by leasing a proprietary package from a vendor under a license and having the software customized internally or externally by the vendor or another outside contractor. Enterprise systems are generally leased in this way. An alternative is to deploy an open-source application, whose program code is free and open for all to modify under a different type of license that enforces the openness of the application in perpetuity. Generally, the costs of the use of open-source software include the technical support from specialized vendors.

Internal Information Systems Development

When an information system is developed internally by an organization, one of two broad methods is used: life-cycle development or rapid application development (RAD).

The same methods are used by software vendors, which need to provide more general, customizable systems. Large organizational systems, such as enterprise systems, are generally developed and maintained through a systematic process, known as a system life cycle, which consists of six stages: feasibility study, system analysis, system design, programming and testing, installation, and operation and maintenance. The first five stages are system development proper, and the last stage is the long-term exploitation. Following a period of use (with maintenance as needed), the information system may be either phased out or upgraded. In the case of a major upgrade, the system enters another development life cycle.

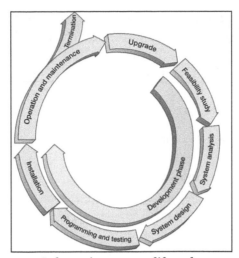

Information systems life cycle.

The development phase of the life cycle for an information system consists of a feasibility study, system analysis, system design, programming and testing, and installation. Following a period of operation and maintenance, typically 5 to 10 years, an evaluation is made of whether to terminate or upgrade the system.

The principal objective of a feasibility study is to determine whether the system is desirable on the basis of long-term plans, strategic initiatives, and a cost-benefit analysis. System analysisprovides a detailed answer to the question, What will the new system do? The next stage, system design, results in an extensive blueprint for how the new system will be organized. During the programming and testing stage, the individual software modules of the system are developed, tested, and integrated into a coherent operational system. Further levels of testing ensure continuing quality control. Installation includes final testing of the system in the work environment and conversion of organizational operations to the new system, integrating it with other systems already in place. The later stages of development include such implementation activities as training users and modifying the organizational processes in which the system will be used.

Life-cycle development is frequently faulted for its long development times and voluminous documentation requirements—and, in some instances, for its failure to fulfill the user's requirements at the end of the long development road.

Increasingly, life-cycle development is being replaced by RAD. In various RAD methodologies a prototype—a preliminary working version of an application—is built quickly and inexpensively, albeit imperfectly. This prototype is turned over to the users, their reactions are collected, suggested modifications are incorporated, and successive prototype versions eventually evolve into the complete system. Formal processes for the collaboration between system developers and users, such as joint applications development (JAD), have been introduced by some firms. Sometimes RAD and life-cycle development are combined: a prototype is produced to determine user requirements during the initial system analysis stage, after which life-cycle development takes over. A version of RAD known as agile development aims to dispense with the notion of a prototype: an initial version of the system is built, released to users, and then subject to frequent modifications as needs arise.

Industrial methods of software production and reuse have been implemented in systems development. Thus, reusable software components are developed, tested, and catalogued to be deployed as parts of future information systems. A particularly important method of component-based development is the use of Web services, which are software objects that deliver a specific function (such as looking up a customer's order in a database) and can be stitched together into interorganizational information systems enabling business partners to cooperate.

After an installed system is handed over to its users and operations personnel, it will almost invariably be modified extensively over its useful life in a process known as system maintenance. A large system will typically be used and maintained for some 5 to 10 years or even longer. Most maintenance is to adjust the system to the organization's changing needs and to new equipment and other software, but inevitably some maintenance involves correcting design errors and exterminating software "bugs" as they are discovered.

Managing Information Systems

For an organization to use its information services to support its operations or to innovate by launching a new initiative, those services have to be part of a well-planned infrastructure of core resources. The specific systems ought to be configured into a coherent architecture to deliver the necessary information services. Many organizations rely on outside firms—that is, specialized IT companies—to deliver some, or even all, of their information services. If located in-house, the management of information systems can be decentralized to a certain degree to correspond to the organization's overall structure.

Information System Infrastructure and Architecture

A well-designed information system rests on a coherent foundation that supports responsive change—and, thus, the organization's agility—as new business or administrative initiativesarise. Known as the information system infrastructure, the foundation consists of core telecommunications networks, databases and data warehouses, software, hardware, and procedures managed by various specialists. With business globalization, an organization's infrastructure often crosses many national boundaries. Establishing and maintaining such a complex infrastructure requires extensive planning and consistent implementation to handle strategic corporate initiatives, transformations, mergers, and acquisitions. Information system infrastructure should be established in order to create meaningful options for future corporate development.

When organized into a coherent whole, the specific information systems that support operations, management, and knowledge work constitute the system architecture of an organization. Clearly, an organization's long-term general strategic plans must be considered when designing an information system infrastructure and architecture.

Organization of Information Services

Information services of an organization are delivered by an outside firm, by an internal unit, or by a combination of the two. Outsourcing of information services helps with such objectives as cost savings, access to superior personnel, and focusing on core competencies.

An information services unit is typically in charge of an organization's information systems. When the systems are largely outsourced, this unit is of a limited size and concentrates on aligning the systems with the corporate competitive strategy and on supervising the outside company's services. When information services are provided in-house and centralized, this unit is responsible for planning, acquiring, operating, and maintaining information systems for the entire organization. In decentralized structures, however, the central unit is responsible only for planning and maintaining the infrastructure, while business and administrative specialists supervise systems and services for their own units. A variety of intermediate organizational forms are possible.

In many organizations, information systems are headed by a chief information officer (CIO) or a chief technology officer (CTO). The activities of information services are usually supervised by a steering committee consisting of the executives representing various functional units of the organization. Steering committees set the priorities for the development of future systems. In the organizations where information systems play a strategic role, boards of directors need to be involved in their governance. a vital responsibility of an information services unit is to ensure uninterrupted service and integrity of the systems and information in the face of many security threats.

Information Systems Security

Information systems security is responsible for the integrity and safety of system resources and activities. Most organizations in developed countries are dependent on the secure operation of their information systems. In fact, the very fabric of societies often depends on this security. Multiple infrastructural grids—including power, water supply, and health care—rely on it. Information systems are at the heart of intensive care units and air traffic control systems. Financial institutions could not survive a total failure of their information systems for longer than a day or two. Electronic funds transfer systems (EFTS) handle immense amounts of money that exist only as electronic signals sent over the networks or as spots on storage disks. Information systems are vulnerable to a number of threats and require strict controls, such as continuing countermeasures and regular audits to ensure that the system remains secure.

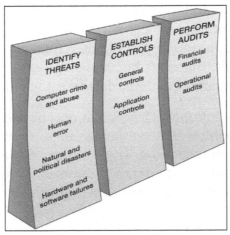

Information systems security measures.

The first step in creating a secure information system is to identify threats. Once potential problems are known, the second step, establishing controls, can be taken. Finally, the third step consists of audits to discover any breach of security.

Although instances of computer crime and abuse receive extensive media attention, human error is estimated to cause greater losses in information systems operation. Disasters such as earthquakes, floods, and fires are the particular concern of disaster recovery planning, which is a part of a corporate business continuity plan. A contingency scheme is also necessary to cover the failure of servers, telecommunications networks, or software.

Computer Crime and Abuse

Computer crime—illegal acts in which computers are the primary tool—costs the world economy many billions of dollars annually. Computer abuse does not rise to the level of crime, yet it involves unethical use of a computer. The objectives of the so-called hacking of information systems include vandalism, theft of consumer information, governmental and commercial espionage, sabotage, and cyberwar. Some of the more widespread means of computer crime include phishing and planting of malware, such as computer viruses and worms, Trojan horses, and logic bombs.

Phishing involves obtaining a legitimate user's login and other information by subterfuge via messages fraudulently claiming to originate with a legitimate entity, such as a bank or government office. A successful phishing raid to obtain a user's information may be followed by identity theft, an impersonation of the user to gain access to the user's resources.

Computer viruses are a particularly common form of attack. These are program instructions that are able not only to perform malicious acts but also to insert copies of themselves into other programs and thus spread to other computer systems. Similar to viruses, worms are complete computer programs that replicate and propagate through telecommunications networks. Because of their ability to spread rapidly and widely, viruses and worms can inflict immense damage. The damage can be in the form of tampering with system operation, theft of large volumes of data (e.g., credit card numbers), known as data breach, or denial of service by overloading systems with a barrage of spurious requests.

In a Trojan horse attack, the malefactor conceals unauthorized instructions within an authorized program. A logic bomb consists of hidden instructions, often introduced with the Trojan horse technique, that stay dormant until a specific event occurs, at which time the instructions are activated. In one well-known case, in 1985 a programmer at an insurance company in Fort Worth, Texas, placed a logic bomb in his company's human resources system; when he was fired and his name was deleted from the company's employee database, the entire database was erased.

Once a system connected to the Internet is invaded, it may be used to take over many others and organize them into so-called botnets that can launch massive attacks against other systems to steal information or sabotage their operation. There is a growing concern that, in the "Internet of things," computer-controlled devices such as refrigerators or TV sets may be deployed in botnets. The variety of devices makes them difficult to control against malware.

Information Systems Controls

To ensure secure and efficient operation of information systems, an organization institutes a set of procedures and technological measures called controls. Information systems are safeguarded through a combination of general and application controls.

General controls apply to information system activities throughout an organization. The most important general controls are the measures that control access to computer systems and the information stored there or transmitted over telecommunications networks. General controls include administrative measures that restrict employees' access to only those processes directly relevant to their duties. As a result, these controls limit the damage that any individual employee or employee impersonator can do. Fault-tolerant computer systems installed in critical environments, such as in hospital information systems or securities marketplaces, are designed to control and isolate problems so that the system can continue to function. Backup systems, often in remote locations, may be activated in the case of failure of the primary information system.

Application controls are specific to a given application and include such measures as validating input data, logging the accesses to the system, regularly archiving copies of various databases, and ensuring that information is disseminated only to authorized users.

Securing Information

Controlling access to information systems became profoundly more difficult with the spread of wide area networks (WANs) and, in particular, the Internet. Users, as well as interlopers, may access systems from any unattended computer within an organization or from virtually anywhere over the Internet. As a security measure, each legitimate user has a unique name and a regularly changed password. Another security measure is to require some form of physical authentication, such as an object (a physical token or a smart card) or a personal characteristic (fingerprint, retinal pattern, hand geometry, or signature). Many systems combine these types of measures—such as automatic teller machines, which rely on a combination of a personal identification number (PIN) and an identification card. Security measures placed between an organization's internal networks and the Internet are known as firewalls. These combinations of hardware and software continually filter the incoming, and often outgoing, data traffic.

A different way to prohibit access to information is via data encryption, which has gained particular importance in electronic commerce. Public key encryption is used widely in such commerce. To ensure confidentiality, only the intended addressee has the private key needed to decrypt messages that have been encrypted with the addressee's public key. Furthermore, authentication of both parties in an electronic transaction is possible through the digital certificates issued to both parties by a trusted third party and the use of digital signatures—an additional code attached to the message to verify its origin. A type of antitampering code can also be attached to a message to detect corruption. Similar means are available to ensure that parties to an electronic transaction cannot later repudiate their participation. Some messages require additional attributes. For example, a payment in electronic cash is a type of message, with encryption used to ensure the purchaser's anonymity, that acts like physical cash.

To continually monitor information systems, intrusion detection systems are used. They detect anomalous events and log the information necessary to produce reports and to establish the source and the nature of the possible intrusion. More active systems also attempt to prevent the intrusion upon detection in real time.

Information Systems Audit

The effectiveness of an information system's controls is evaluated through an information systems audit. An audit aims to establish whether information systems are safeguarding corporate assets, maintaining the integrity of stored and communicated data, supporting corporate objectives effectively, and operating efficiently. It is a part of a more general financial audit that verifies an organization's accounting records and financial statements. Information systems are designed so that every financial transaction can be traced. In other words, an audit trail must exist that can establish where each transaction originated and how it was processed. Aside from financial audits, operational audits are used to evaluate the effectiveness and efficiency of information systems operations, and technological audits verify that information technologies are appropriately chosen, configured, and implemented.

Impacts of Information Systems

Computerized information systems, particularly since the arrival of the Web and mobile computing, have had a profound effect on organizations, economies, and societies, as well as on individuals whose lives and activities are conducted in these social aggregates.

Organizational Impacts of Information Systems

Essential organizational capabilities are enabled or enhanced by information systems. These systems provide support for business operations; for individual and group decision making; for innovation through new product and process development; for relationships with customers, suppliers, and partners; for pursuit of competitive advantage; and, in some cases, for the business model itself (e.g., Google). Information systems bring new options to the way companies interact and compete, the way organizations are structured, and the way workplaces are designed. In general, use of Web-based information systems can significantly lower the costs of communication among workers and firms and cost-effectively enhance the coordination of supply chains or webs. This has led many organizations to concentrate on their core competencies and to outsource other parts of their value chain to specialized companies. The capability to communicate information efficiently within a firm has led to the deployment of flatter organizational structures with fewer hierarchical layers.

Nevertheless, information systems do not uniformly lead to higher profits. Success depends both on the skill with which information systems are deployed and on their use being combined with other resources of the firm, such as relationships with business partners or superior knowledge in the industrial segment.

The use of information systems has enabled new organizational structures. In particular, so-called virtual organizations have emerged that do not rely on physical offices and standard organizational charts. Two notable forms of virtual organizations are the network organization and the cluster organization.

In a network organization, long-term corporate partners supply goods and services through a central hub firm. Together, a network of relatively small companies can present the appearance of a large corporation. Indeed, at the core of such an organization may be nothing more than a single entrepreneur supported by only a few employees. Thus, network organization forms a flexible ecosystem of companies, whose formation and work is organized around Web-based information systems.

In a cluster organization, the principal work units are permanent and temporary teams of individuals with complementary skills. Team members, who are often widely dispersed around the globe, are greatly assisted in their work by the use of Web resources, corporate intranets, and collaboration systems. Global virtual teams are able to work around the clock, moving knowledge work electronically "to follow the sun." Information systems delivered over mobile platforms have enabled employees to work not just outside the corporate offices but virtually anywhere. "Work is the thing we do, not the place we go to" became the slogan of the emerging new workplace. Virtual workplaces include home offices, regional work centres, customers' premises, and mobile offices of people such as insurance adjusters. Employees who work in virtual workplaces outside their company's premises are known as teleworkers.

The role of consumers has changed, empowered by the Web. Instead of being just passive recipients of products, they can actively participate with the producers in the cocreation of value. By coordinating their collective work using information systems, individuals created such products as open-source software and online encyclopaedias. The value of virtual worlds and massively multiplayer online games has been created largely by the participants. The electronic word-of-mouth in the form of reviews and opinions expressed on the Web can make or break products. In sponsored cocreation, companies attract their customers to generate and evaluate ideas, codevelop new products, and promote the existing goods and services. Virtual customer communities are created online for these purposes.

Information Systems in the Economy and Society

Along with the global transportation infrastructure, network-based information systems have been a factor in the growth of international business and corporations. A relationship between the deployment of information systems and higher productivity has been shown in a number of industries when these systems complement other corporate resources. Electronic commerce has moved many relationships and transactions among companies and individuals to the Internet and the Web, with the resulting expansion of possibilities and efficiencies. The development of the Internet-based ecosystem—accompanied by the low cost of hardware and telecommunications, the availability of open-source software, and the mass global access to mobile phones—has led to a flowering of entrepreneurial activity and the emergence to prominence and significant market value of numerous firms based on new business models. Among the examples are electronic auction firms, search engine firms, electronic malls, social network platforms, and online game companies. Because of the vast opportunities for moving work with data, information, and knowledge in electronic form to the most cost-effective venue, a global redistribution of work has been taking place.

As the use of information systems became pervasive in advanced economies and societies at large, several societal and ethical issues moved into the forefront. The most important are issues of individual privacy, property rights, universal access and free speech, information accuracy, and quality of life.

Individual privacy hinges on the right to control one's personal information. While invasion of privacy is generally perceived as an undesirable loss of autonomy, government and business organizations do need to collect data in order to facilitate administration and exploit sales and marketing opportunities. Electronic commerce presents a particular challenge to privacy, as personal information is routinely collected and potentially disseminated in a largely unregulated manner.

The ownership of and control over the personal profiles, contacts, and communications in social networks are one example of a privacy issue that awaits resolution through a combination of market forces, industry self-regulation, and possibly government regulation. Preventing invasions of privacy is complicated by the lack of an international legal standard.

Intellectual property, such as software, books, music, and movies, is protected, albeit imperfectly, by patents, trade secrets, and copyrights. However, such intangible goods can be easily copied and transmitted electronically over the Web for unlawful reproduction and use. Combinations of legal statutes and technological safeguards, including antipiracy encryption and electronic watermarks, are in place, but much of the abuse prevention relies on the ethicsof the user. The means of protection themselves, such as patents, play a great role in the information society. However, the protection of business methods (e.g., Amazon's patenting of one-click ordering) is being questioned, and the global enforcement of intellectual property protection encounters various challenges.

Access to information systems over the Web is necessary for full participation in modern society. In particular, it is desirable to avoid the emergence of digital divides between nations or regions and between social and ethnic groups. Open access to the Web as a medium for human communication and as a repository for shared knowledge is treasured. Indeed, many people consider free speech a universal human right and the Internet and Web the most widely accessible means to exercise that right. Yet, legitimate concerns arise about protecting children without resorting to censorship. Technological solutions, such as software that filters out pornography and inappropriate communications, are partially successful.

Of concern to everyone is the accuracy and security of information contained in databases and data warehouses—whether in health and insurance data, credit bureau records, or government files—as misinformation or privileged information released inappropriately can adversely affect personal safety, livelihood, and everyday life. Individuals must cooperate in reviewing and correcting their files, and organizations must ensure appropriate security, access to, and use of such files.

Information systems have affected the quality of personal and working lives. In the workplace, information systems can be deployed to eliminate tedious tasks and give workers greater autonomy, or they can be used to thoughtlessly eliminate jobs and subject the remaining workforce to pervasive electronic surveillance. Consumers can use the Web for shopping, networking, and entertainment—but at the risk of contending with spam (unsolicited e-mail), interception of credit card numbers, and attack by computer viruses.

Information systems can expand participation of ordinary citizens in government through electronic elections, referendums, and polls and also can provide electronic access to government services and information—permitting, for instance, electronic filing of taxes, direct deposit of government checks, and viewing of current and historical government documents. More transparent and beneficial government operations are possible by opening the data collected by and about governments to public scrutiny in a searchable and easy-to-use form. With the Web, the public sphere of deliberation and self-organization can expand and give voice to individuals. However, information systems have also conjured Orwellian images of government surveillance and business intrusion into private lives. It remains for society to harness the power of information systems by strengthening legal, social, and technological means.

With the exponentially growing power of computers, driven by Moore's law, and the development of ever more-sophisticated software—in particular, systems deploying the techniques of artificial intelligence (AI)—job markets and professions have been affected. Flexible and inexpensive robotics reduces some opportunities in the labour markets. Cognitive computing, with systems relying on AI techniques—such as computer learning, pattern recognition in multiple media, and massive amounts of stored information—emerged as a competitor to human professionals.

The emergence of the "on-demand economy," enabled by information system platforms, has raised concerns about the quality of jobs. Providing instant access to services, such as transportation, the platforms (for example, Uber and Lyft) connect the service suppliers, usually individuals, with those seeking the service. Although claimed to erode stable workplaces, such business models offer flexibility, a larger measure of independence to the suppliers, and convenience to the demanders.

Information Security

Information security is a set of strategies for managing the processes, tools and policies necessary to prevent, detect, document and counter threats to digital and non-digital information. Infosec responsibilities include establishing a set of processes that will protect information assets regardless of how the information is formatted or whether it is in transit, is being processed or is at rest in storage.

Information security has become a continuing concern in all areas of an Information system. Security is neither a product nor a software; it is a discipline that needs to be taken into consideration in any organizational decision. It is indeed true that there is no such thing as a completely secure system. But it is also correct that by increasing the security measures that protect the assets, we are making the system a much more difficult target for intruders, which, in turn, reduces the chances of becoming a victim when the right security technologies are in place.

Goals for Security

Security is required to achieve four main goals:

S. no	Goal	Threat
1	Confidentiality	Exposure to Data
2	Integrity	Alteration to Data
3	Availability	Denial of Service
4	Authenticity	Attacks by viruses

Confidentiality: This means secret data must remain confidential. This means that if somebody wants some data to be available to certain people, then the operating system must make that data available to those particular people, with no one else allowed to see that data. It prevents unauthorized disclosure of secured information.

Integrity: This means restricting unauthorized modification of secured information. Unauthorized users must not be allowed to modify the data without the owner's permission. Data modification includes not only changing or deleting data, but also removing data or adding false data to change its behavior.

Availability: This means nobody can disturb the system to make it unusable. It assures that the system works promptly, and that service is not denied to authorized users. This is to restrict unauthorized users by withholding information, causing a denial of service to authorized users.

Authenticity: This means the system must able to verify the identity of users. Users can login to the system by providing a combination of username and password, or matching any other security parameters.

Protection of Assets

Security is about the protection of assets. For this reason, we must first identify the organizational assets. Information system assets can be categorized as:

Assets	Availability	Secrecy	Integrity/Authenticity
Hardware	Equipment gone bad. Denial of services.	-	-
Software	Programs can be deleted, altered, etc. Denying access to users	An unauthorized copy of software is made.	A program can be modified to fail or change its behavior
Data	Files are deleted. Denial of access to users.	An unauthorized reading of data is made.	Existing files are modified or deleted, and new files are added.
Communication Lines	Data is deleted	Data can be read. Network traffic is analyzed	Data is modified, delayed, or false data is added.

Hardware: Includes CPUs, motherboards, hard disks, CD-ROMs, etc., and all other physical devices. Threats can be accidental or deliberate damage to equipment.

Software: Includes operating system, utilities, applications, etc. Several distinct threats need to be considered. Software can be deleted, altered, or changed in behavior.

Data: Includes files and other forms of data. Unauthorized persons can read, modify, or delete data.

Communication Lines: Includes cables and other network communication media. Data in transfer can be read, modified, or deleted.

Distinguishing the Attackers

In security literature, people who try to gain unauthorized access to information systems, whether for commercial or non-commercial purposes, are known as intruders, generally referred as hackers or crackers. They act in two different ways: passive and active. The former just wants to read files or data for which they are not permitted, while the latter is more dangerous, wanting to make unauthorized changes to data.

Some common types of intruders are:

1. Casual prying by non-technical users: People who want to read other people's e-mails or files while they are connected on shared devices.

2. Snooping by insiders: Highly skilled people likes developers, students, or other technical persons, who consider it a personal challenge to break the security of a computer system.

3. Determined attempts to make money: Some developers or others personnel working in banking societies attempt to steal money from their organizations.

4. Attempts at secret military or government data: This is considered to be very serious crime. This category involves attempts made by competing foreign countries to gain a country's information for the purpose of national defense, attacks, etc.

Types of Threats

Insider Attacks

Logic Bombs: These are code embedded in a program that is set to explode when certain conditions are met. The conditions used to trigger the bomb can be the presence or absence of certain files, a particular day or date, a particular user running the application, etc. Once triggered, a bomb may alter or delete data or sometimes entire files, causing a machine halt or dealing some other damage. For example, if a developer is fired, the logic bomb will trigger upon not receiving his daily password to a certain portion of code, or when any other set of conditions are satisfied.

Trap Doors: These are login programs written by developers to gain unauthorized access. For example, a developer could add code to a login program to allow anyone using a particular login name (like "student"), no matter the password. If this code is inserted into a working program, the login succeeds by entering the login name as "student" with any password or with a blank password.

Login Spoofing: This is a technique of collecting other users' passwords. In this method, a false login interface that seems identical to the real thing (which would normally be connected to a safe server) is mounted on an actual login screen. When the user enters their user ID and password, this information is stored in an intruder's database. Then the dummy login shell is destroyed, and the actual login screen will start asking login parameters again. Most—probably all—users think they have made a mistake in the entering ID or password. They never know about the spoof, and will enter their credentials again and successfully login into the system. Because of this, a login screen will be presented after pressing CTRL+ALT+DEL in most systems.

Outsider Attacks

Trojan Horses: Can look like useful software applications but has hidden malware contained within it. To spread it across networks, it is attached to games, etc., which attract people to eagerly download it. The malware then does whatever it is designed for, such as deleting, modifying, or encrypting files. It can also search for credit card numbers, passwords, or other useful data. Moreover, it will restart automatically when the machine is rebooted and runs in the background. The bottom line is it does not require the author's involvement; the victim does all the necessary things to infect themselves.

Virus: A program that infects other programs and makes copies of itself, which can spread across the whole file system and take temporary control of operating system. Then a fresh copy of virus is attached to uninfected files when they comes in contact. It can spread from computer to computer when files are shared.

Worm: A worm is a program that replicates itself and sends copies from computer to computer across the network connections. Upon arrival, the worm may be activated and propagates again to perform unwanted functions. It is used as an e-mail virus.

Zombie: A program that secretly takes over an Internet connected computer and uses it to launch attacks that are difficult to trace back to the zombie creators. It is used in denial-of-service attacks against web servers.

Spyware: Software that is loaded onto a PC and runs in the background, causing infections without user's knowledge.

Adware: An advertisement that is integrated into software. It can result in pop-up ads or redirection of the browser to a commercial site. It also changes the home page of a browser to its redirecting link.

Root kit: A set of tools used to gain root level access after breaking computer security. Root kits can contain any of above malicious software, like virus, worms, spyware, etc.

Protective Measures

The ideal solution to all these threats is to prevent any of the threats from entering the system. Though prevention can fail, it can at least help reduce the number of successful attacks. The next best approach is:

- Detection: Determine whether an infection has occurred. If so, locate the infection.

- Identification: Once it is detected, identify the specific threat that has infected a program.

- Removal: After the specific virus has been identified, remove all the traces of the threat from the   infected systems so that it cannot spread further to other systems.

All these approaches give rise to some ways that a system can be designed and implemented to increase its security. It is always advisable to have multiple layers of security, so that if one of them is not enough, there are still others capable of defending the system. The defenses are not really hierarchical, but still occur in the following categories:

Firewall: A firewall is a software or hardware appliance that filters the information that flows from an Internet connection into the network or computer system. If an incoming packet of data is flagged by the filters, it is not allowed to pass through.

Antivirus: Firewalls try to keep intruders away from systems, but they fail in some situations when threats try to hide from them. In such cases, an antivirus is used to detect and remove malicious software. Sometimes it can be just scanner, or a remover, or both. A scanner examines the behavior and location of files, etc., thereby detecting the threat, while the remover removes the virus.

Intrusion Detection: Intrusion detection (ID) gathers and analyzes information within a computer system or network to identify security breaches, which include both intrusions (attacks from outside the organization) and misuse (attacks from within the organization). It periodically scans threats to contribute to the security of a computer system or network.

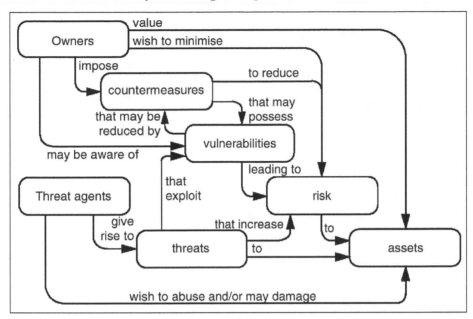

All of these basic security concepts can be linked together to calculate the security risk to stored data or data that is being transferred. Asset owners are always worried about their assets being attacked by intruders, as these attackers could cause vulnerabilities using their threats. Therefore, counter security protection can be laid out to increase security or reducing the risk of data being compromised.

2
Fundamental Concepts of Information Security

Some of the major concepts of information security are data confidentiality, data integrity, non-repudiation, electronic authentication and Parkerian hexad. The topics elaborated in this chapter will help in gaining a better perspective about these fundamental concepts of information security.

Data Confidentiality

Data confidentiality is about protecting data against unintentional, unlawful, or unauthorized access, disclosure, or theft.

Confidentiality has to do with the privacy of information, including authorizations to view, share, and use it. Information with low confidentiality concerns may be considered "public" or otherwise not threatening if exposed beyond its intended audience. Information with high confidentiality concerns is considered secret and must be kept confidential to prevent identity theft, compromise of accounts and systems, legal or reputational damage, and other severe consequences.

Examples of data with high confidentiality concerns include:

- Social Security numbers, which must remain confidential to prevent identity theft.

- Passwords, which must remain confidential to protect systems and accounts.

Consider the following when managing data confidentiality:

- To whom data can be disclosed.

- Whether laws, regulations, or contracts require data to remain confidential.

- Whether data may only be used or released under certain conditions.

- Whether data is sensitive by nature and would have a negative impact if disclosed.

- Whether data would be valuable to those who aren't permitted to have it (e.g., hackers).

When managing data confidentiality, follow these guidelines:

- Encrypt Sensitive Files

Encryption is a process that renders data unreadable to anyone except those who have the appropriate password or key. By encrypting sensitive files (by using file passwords, for example), one can protect them from being read or used by those who are not entitled to do either.

- Manage data access

Controlling confidentiality is, in large part, about controlling who has access to data. Ensuring that access is only authorized and granted to those who have a "need to know" goes a long way in limiting unnecessary exposure. Users should also authenticate their access with strong passwords and, where practical, two-factor authentication. Periodically review access lists and promptly revoke access when it is no longer necessary.

- Physically secure devices and paper documents

Controlling access to data includes controlling access of all kinds, both digital and physical. Protect devices and paper documents from misuse or theft by storing them in locked areas. Never leave devices or sensitive documents unattented in public locations.

- Securely dispose of data, devices, and paper records

When data is no longer necessary for University-related purposes, it must be disposed of appropriately.

  - Sensitive data, such as Social Security numbers, must be securely erased to ensure that it cannot be recovered and misused.

  - Devices that were used for University-related purposes or that were otherwise used to store sensitive information should be destroyed or securely erased to ensure that their previous contents cannot be recovered and misused.

  - Paper documents containing sensitive information should be shredded rather than dumped into trash or recycling bins.

- Manage data acquisition

When collecting sensitive data, be conscious of how much data is actually needed and carefully consider privacy and confidentiality in the acquisition process. Avoid acquiring sensitive data unless absolutely necessary; one of the best ways to reduce confidentiality risk is to reduce the amount of sensitive data being collected in the first place.

- Manage data utilization

Confidentiality risk can be further reduced by using sensitive data only as approved and as necessary. Misusing sensitive data violates the privacy and confidentiality of that data and of the individuals or groups the data represents.

- Manage devices

Computer management is a broad topic that includes many essential security practices. By protecting devices, one can also protect the data they contain. Follow basic cybersecurity hygiene by using anti-virus software, routinely patching software, whitelisting applications, using device passcodes, suspending inactive sessions, enabling firewalls, and using whole-disk encryption.

Data Integrity

Data integrity is the maintenance of, and the assurance of the accuracy and consistency of, data over its entire life-cycle, and is a critical aspect to the design, implementation and usage of any system which stores, processes, or retrieves data. The term is broad in scope and may have widely different meanings depending on the specific context – even under the same general umbrella of computing. It is at times used as a proxy term for data quality, while data validation is a pre-requisite for data integrity. Data integrity is the opposite of data corruption. The overall intent of any data integrity technique is the same: ensure data is recorded exactly as intended (such as a database correctly rejecting mutually exclusive possibilities,) and upon later retrieval, ensure the data is the same as it was when it was originally recorded. In short, data integrity aims to prevent unintentional changes to information. Data integrity is not to be confused with data security, the discipline of protecting data from unauthorized parties.

Any unintended changes to data as the result of a storage, retrieval or processing operation, including malicious intent, unexpected hardware failure, and human error, is failure of data integrity. If the changes are the result of unauthorized access, it may also be a failure of data security. Depending on the data involved this could manifest itself as benign as a single pixel in an image appearing a different color than was originally recorded, to the loss of vacation pictures or a business-critical database, to even catastrophic loss of human life in a life-critical system.

Integrity Types

Physical Integrity

Physical integrity deals with challenges associated with correctly storing and fetching the data itself. Challenges with physical integrity may include electromechanical faults, design flaws, material fatigue, corrosion, power outages, natural disasters, acts of war and terrorism, and other special environmental hazards such as ionizing radiation, extreme temperatures, pressures and g-forces. Ensuring physical integrity includes methods such as redundant hardware, an uninterruptible power supply, certain types of RAID arrays, radiation hardened chips, error-correcting memory, use of a clustered file system, using file systems that employ block level checksums such as ZFS, storage arrays that compute parity calculations such as exclusive or or use a cryptographic hash function and even having a watchdog timer on critical subsystems.

Physical integrity often makes extensive use of error detecting algorithms known as error-correcting codes. Human-induced data integrity errors are often detected through the use of simpler checks and algorithms, such as the Damm algorithm or Luhn algorithm. These are used to maintain data integrity after manual transcription from one computer system to another by a human intermediary (e.g. credit card or bank routing numbers). Computer-induced transcription errors can be detected through hash functions.

In production systems, these techniques are used together to ensure various degrees of data integrity. For example, a computer file system may be configured on a fault-tolerant RAID array, but might not provide block-level checksums to detect and prevent silent data corruption. As another example, a database management system might be compliant with the ACID properties, but the RAID controller or hard disk drive's internal write cache might not be.

Logical Integrity

This type of integrity is concerned with the correctness or rationality of a piece of data, given a particular context. This includes topics such as referential integrity and entity integrity in a relational database or correctly ignoring impossible sensor data in robotic systems. These concerns involve ensuring that the data "makes sense" given its environment. Challenges include software bugs, design flaws, and human errors. Common methods of ensuring logical integrity include things such as a check constraints, foreign key constraints, program assertions, and other run-time sanity checks.

Both physical and logical integrity often share many common challenges such as human errors and design flaws, and both must appropriately deal with concurrent requests to record and retrieve data, the latter of which is entirely a subject on its own.

Databases

Data integrity contains guidelines for data retention, specifying or guaranteeing the length of time data can be retained in a particular database. To achieve data integrity, these rules are consistently and routinely applied to all data entering the system, and any relaxation of enforcement could cause errors in the data. Implementing checks on the data as close as possible to the source of input (such as human data entry), causes less erroneous data to enter the system. Strict enforcement of data integrity rules results in lower error rates, and time saved troubleshooting and tracing erroneous data and the errors it causes to algorithms.

Data integrity also includes rules defining the relations a piece of data can have, to other pieces of data, such as a *Customer* record being allowed to link to purchased *Products*, but not to unrelated data such as *Corporate Assets*. Data integrity often includes checks and correction for invalid data, based on a fixed schema or a predefined set of rules. An example being textual data entered where a date-time value is required. Rules for data derivation are also applicable, specifying how a data value is derived based on algorithm, contributors and conditions. It also specifies the conditions on how the data value could be re-derived.

Types of Integrity Constraints

Data integrity is normally enforced in a database system by a series of integrity constraints or rules. Three types of integrity constraints are an inherent part of the relational data model: entity integrity, referential integrity and domain integrity.

- Entity integrity concerns the concept of a primary key. Entity integrity is an integrity rule which states that every table must have a primary key and that the column or columns chosen to be the primary key should be unique and not null.

- Referential integrity concerns the concept of a foreign key. The referential integrity rule states that any foreign-key value can only be in one of two states. The usual state of affairs is that the foreign-key value refers to a primary key value of some table in the database. Occasionally, and this will depend on the rules of the data owner, a foreign-key value can be null. In this case, we are explicitly saying that either there is no relationship between the objects represented in the database or that this relationship is unknown.

- Domain integrity specifies that all columns in a relational database must be declared upon a defined domain. The primary unit of data in the relational data model is the data item. Such data items are said to be non-decomposable or atomic. A domain is a set of values of the same type. Domains are therefore pools of values from which actual values appearing in the columns of a table are drawn.

- User-defined integrity refers to a set of rules specified by a user, which do not belong to the entity, domain and referential integrity categories.

If a database supports these features, it is the responsibility of the database to ensure data integrity as well as the consistency model for the data storage and retrieval. If a database does not support these features, it is the responsibility of the applications to ensure data integrity while the database supports the consistency model for the data storage and retrieval.

Having a single, well-controlled, and well-defined data-integrity system increases:

- Stability (one centralized system performs all data integrity operations).

- Performance (all data integrity operations are performed in the same tier as the consistency model).

- Re-usability (all applications benefit from a single centralized data integrity system).

- Maintainability (one centralized system for all data integrity administration).

Modern databases support these features, and it has become the de facto responsibility of the database to ensure data integrity. Companies, and indeed many database systems, offer products and services to migrate legacy systems to modern databases.

Examples:

An example of a data-integrity mechanism is the parent-and-child relationship of related records. If a parent record owns one or more related child records all of the referential integrity processes are handled by the database itself, which automatically ensures the accuracy and integrity of the data so that no child record can exist without a parent (also called being orphaned) and that no parent loses their child records. It also ensures that no parent record can be deleted while the parent record owns any child records. All of this is handled at the database level and does not require coding integrity checks into each application.

File Systems

Various research results show that neither widespread filesystems (including UFS, Ext, XFS, JFS and NTFS) nor hardware RAID solutions provide sufficient protection against data integrity problems. Some filesystems (including Btrfs and ZFS) provide internal data and metadata checksumming that is used for detecting silent data corruption and improving data integrity. If a corruption is detected that way and internal RAID mechanisms provided by those filesystems are also used, such filesystems can additionally reconstruct corrupted data in a transparent way. This approach allows improved data integrity protection covering the entire data paths, which is usually known as end-to-end data protection.

Data Integrity as Applied to Various Industries

- The U.S. Food and Drug Administration has created draft guidance on data integrity for the pharmaceutical manufacturers required to adhere to U.S. Code of Federal Regulations 21 CFR Parts 210–212. Outside the U.S., similar data integrity guidance has been issued by the United Kingdom (2015), Switzerland (2016), and Australia (2017).

- Various standards for the manufacture of medical devices address data integrity either directly or indirectly, including ISO 13485, ISO 14155, and ISO 5840.

- Consumer healthcare companies producing over-the-counter therapies must also put safeguards in place to manage data integrity. In addition to compliance with FDA regulations, there is a significant risk to brand and reputation.

- In early 2017, the Financial Industry Regulatory Authority (FINRA), noting data integrity problems with automated trading and money movement surveillance systems, stated it would make "the development of a data integrity program to monitor the accuracy of the submitted data" a priority. In early 2018, FINRA said it would expand its approach on data integrity to firms' "technology change management policies and procedures" and Treasury securities reviews.

- Other sectors such as mining and product manufacturing are increasingly focusing on the importance of data integrity in associated automation and production monitoring assets.

- Cloud storage providers have long faced significant challenges ensuring the integrity or provenance of customer data and tracking violations.

Electronic Authentication

Electronic authentication is the process of establishing confidence in user identities electronically presented to an information system. Digital authentication or e-authentication may be used synonymously when referring to the authentication process that confirms or certifies a person's identity and works. When used in conjunction with an electronic signature, it can provide evidence whether data received has been tampered with after being signed by its original sender. In a time where fraud and identity theft has become rampant, electronic authentication can be a more secure method of verifying that a person is who they say they are when performing transactions online.

There are various e-authentication methods that can be used to authenticate a user's identify ranging from a password to higher levels of security that utilize multifactor authentication (MFA). Depending on the level of security used, the user might need to prove his or her identity through the use of security tokens, challenge questions or being in possession of a certificate from a third-party certificate authority that attests to their identity.

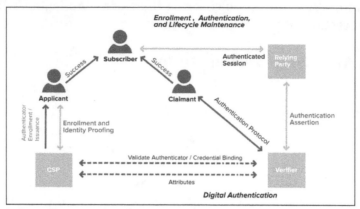

Digital enrollment and authentication reference process by the American
National Institute of Standards and Technology (NIST).

The American National Institute of Standards and Technology (NIST) has developed a generic electronic authentication model that provides a basic framework on how the authentication process is accomplished regardless of jurisdiction or geographic region. According to this model, the enrollment process begins with an individual applying to a Credential Service Provider (CSP). The CSP will need to prove the applicant's identity before proceeding with the transaction. Once the applicant's identity has been confirmed by the CSP, he or she receives the status of "subscriber", is given an authenticator, such as a token and a credential, which may be in the form of a username.

The CSP is responsible for managing the credential along with the subscriber's enrollment data for the life of the credential. The subscriber will be tasked with maintaining the authenticators. An example of this is when a user normally uses a specific computer to do their online banking. If he or she attempts to access their bank account from another computer, the authenticator will not be present. In order to gain access, the subscriber would need to verify their identity to the CSP, which might be in the form of answering a challenge question successfully before being given access.

Authentication Factors

There are three generally accepted factors that are used to establish a digital identity for electronic authentication, including:

- Knowledge factor, which is something that the user knows, such as a password, answers to challenge questions, ID numbers or a PIN.

- Possession factor, which is something that the user has, such as mobile phone, PC or token.

- Biometric factor, which is something that the user is, such as his or her fingerprints, eye scan or voice pattern.

Out of the three factors, the biometric factor is the most convenient and convincing to prove an individual's identity. However, having to rely on this sole factor can be expensive to sustain. Although having their own unique weaknesses, by combining two or more factors allows for reliable authentication. It is always recommended to use multifactor authentication for that reason.

Methods

Authentication systems are often categorized by the number of factors that they incorporate. The three factors often considered as the cornerstone of authentication are: Something you know (for example, a password) Something you have (for example, an ID badge or a cryptographic key) Something you are (for example, a voice print, thumb print or other biometric)

Multifactor authentication is generally more secure than single-factor authentication. But, some multi-factor authentication approaches are still vulnerable to cases like man-in-the-middle attacks and Trojan attacks. Common methods used in authentication systems are summarized below.

Token

A sample of token.

Tokens generically are something the claimant possesses and controls that may be used to authenticate the claimant's identity. In e-authentication, the claimant authenticates to a system or application over a network. Therefore, a token used for e-authentication is a secret and the token must be protected. The token may, for example, be a cryptographic key, that is protected by encrypting it under a password. An impostor must steal the encrypted key and learn the password to use the token.

Passwords and PIN-based Authentication

Passwords and PINs are categorized as "something you know" method. A combination of numbers, symbols, and mixed cases are considered to be stronger than all-letter password. Also, the adoption of Transport Layer Security (TLS) or Secure Socket Layer (SSL) features during the information transmission process will as well create an encrypted channel for data exchange and to further protect information delivered. Currently, most security attacks target on password-based authentication systems.

Public-key Authentication

This type of authentication has two parts. One is a public key, the other is a private key. A public key is issued by a Certification Authority and is available to any user or server. A private key is known by the user only.

Symmetric-key Authentication

The user shares a unique key with an authentication server. When the user sends a randomly generated message (the challenge) encrypted by the secret key to the authentication server, if the message can be matched by the server using its shared secret key, the user is authenticated. When implemented together with the password authentication, this method also provides a possible solution for two-factor authentication systems.

SMS-based authentication

Biometric authentication.

The user receives password by reading the message in the cell phone, and types back the password to complete the authentication. Short Message Service (SMS) is very effective when cell phones are commonly adopted. SMS is also suitable against man-in-the-middle (MITM) attacks, since the use of SMS does not involve the Internet.

Biometric Authentication

Biometric authentication is the use of unique physical attributes and body measurements as the intermediate for better identification and access control. Physical characteristics that are often used for authentication include fingerprints, voice recognition, face, recognition, and iris scans because all of these are unique to every individual separately. Traditionally, Biometric Authentication based on token-based identification systems, such as passport, and nowadays becomes one of the most secure identification systems to user protections. A new technological innovation which provides a wide variety of either behavioral or physical characteristics which are defining the proper concept of Biometric Authentication.

Digital Identity Authentication

Digital identity authentication refers to the combined use of device, behavior, location and other data, including email address, account and credit card information, to authenticate online users in real time.

Electronic Credentials

Paper credentials are documents that attest to the identity or other attributes of an individual or entity called the subject of the credentials. Some common paper credentials include passports, birth certificates, driver's licenses, and employee identity cards. The credentials themselves are authenticated in a variety of ways: traditionally perhaps by a signature or a seal, special papers and inks, high quality engraving, and today by more complex mechanisms, such as holograms, that make the credentials recognizable and difficult to copy or forge. In some cases, simple possession of the credentials is sufficient to establish that the physical holder of the credentials is indeed the subject of the credentials. More commonly, the credentials contain biometric information such as the subject's description, a picture of the subject or the handwritten signature of the subject that can be used to authenticate that the holder of the credentials is indeed the subject of the credentials. When these paper credentials are presented in-person, authentication biometrics contained in those credentials can be checked to confirm that the physical holder of the credential is the subject.

Electronic identity credentials bind a name and perhaps other attributes to a token. There are a variety of electronic credential types in use today, and new types of credentials are constantly being created (eID, electronic voter ID card, biometric passports, bank cards, etc.) At a minimum, credentials include identifying information that permits recovery of the records of the registration associated with the credentials and a name that is associated with the subscriber.

Verifiers

In any authenticated on-line transaction, the verifier is the party that verifies that the claimant has possession and control of the token that verifies his or her identity. A claimant authenticates his or her identity to a verifier by the use of a token and an authentication protocol. This is called Proof of Possession (PoP). Many PoP protocols are designed so that a verifier, with no knowledge of the token before the authentication protocol run, learns nothing about the token from the run. The verifier and CSP may be the same entity, the verifier and relying party may be the same entity or they may all three be separate entities. It is undesirable for verifiers to learn shared secrets unless they are a part of the same entity as the CSP that registered the tokens. Where the verifier and the relying party are separate entities, the verifier must convey the result of the authentication protocol to the relying party. The object created by the verifier to convey this result is called an assertion.

Authentication Schemes

There are four types of authentication schemes: local authentication, centralized authentication, global centralized authentication, global authentication and web application (portal).

When using a local authentication scheme, the application retains the data that pertains to the user's credentials. This information is not usually shared with other applications. The onus is on the user to maintain and remember the types and number of credentials that are associated with the service in which they need to access. This is a high risk scheme because of the possibility that the storage area for passwords might become compromised.

Using the central authentication scheme allows for each user to use the same credentials to access various services. Each application is different and must be designed with interfaces and the ability to interact with a central system to successfully provide authentication for the user. This allows the user to access important information and be able to access private keys that will allow him or her to electronically sign documents.

Using a third party through a global centralized authentication scheme allows the user direct access to authentication services. This then allows the user to access the particular services they need.

The most secure scheme is the global centralized authentication and web application (portal). It is ideal for E-Government use because it allows a wide range of services. It uses a single authentication mechanism involving a minimum of two factors to allow access to required services and the ability to sign documents.

Authentication and Digital Signing Working Together

Often, authentication and digital signing are applied in conjunction. In advanced electronic signatures, the signatory has authenticated and uniquely linked to a signature. In the case of a qualified electronic signature as defined in the eIDAS-regulation, the signer's identity is even certified by a qualified trust service provider. This linking of signature and authentication firstly supports the probative value of the signature – commonly referred to as non-repudiation of origin. The protection of the message on the network-level is called non-repudiation of emission. The authenticated sender and the message content are linked to each other. If a 3rd party tries to change the message content, the signature loses validity.

Characteristics Biometric Authentication

Homogenization and Decoupling

Biometric authentication can be defined by many different procedures and sensors which are being used to produce security. Biometric can be separated into physical or behavioral security. Physical protection is based on identification through fingerprint, face, hand, iris, etc. On the other hand, behavioral safety is succeeded by keystroke, signature, and voice. The main point is that all of these different procedures and mechanism that exist, produce the same homogeneous result, namely the security of the system and users. When thinking of the decoupling of hardware, the hardware is not coded in the same form by digitization which directly makes decoupling more difficult. Because of unlinkability and irreversibility of biometric templates, this technology can secure user authentication.

Digital Traces

Biometric authentication has a substantial impact on digital traces. For example when the user decides to use his fingerprint to protect his data on his smartphone, then the system memorizes the input so it will be able to be re-used again. During this procedure and many other similar applications proves that the digital trace is vital and exist on biometric authentication.

Connectivity

Another characteristic of biometric authentication is that it combines different components such as security tokens with computer systems to protect the user. Another example is the connection between devices, such as camera and computer systems to scan the user's retina and produce new ways of security. So biometric authentication could be defined by connectivity as long it connects different applications or components and through these users are getting connected and can work under the same roof and especially on a safe environment on the cyber world.

Reprogrammable and Smart

As new kinds of cybercrime are appearing, the ways of authentication must be able to adapt. This adaptation means that it is always ready for evolution and updating, and so it will be able to protect the users at any time. At first biometric authentication started in the sampler form of user's access and defining user profiles and policies. Over time the need of biometric authentication became more complex, so cybersecurity organizations started reprogramming their products/technology from simple personal user's access to allow interoperability of identities across multiple solutions. Through this evolution, business value also rises.

Risk Assessment

When developing electronic systems, there are some industry standards requiring United States agencies to ensure the transactions provide an appropriate level of assurance. Generally, servers adopt the US' Office of Management and Budget's (OMB's) E-Authentication Guidance for Federal Agencies (M-04-04) as a guideline, which is published to help federal agencies provide secure electronic services that protect individual privacy. It asks agencies to check whether their transactions require e-authentication, and determine a proper level of assurance.

It established four levels of assurance:

Assurance Level 1: Little or no confidence in the asserted identity's validity. Assurance Level 2: Some confidence in the asserted identity's validity. Assurance Level 3: High confidence in the asserted identity's validity. Assurance Level 4: Very high confidence in the asserted identity's validity.

Determining Assurance Levels

The OMB proposes a five-step process to determine the appropriate assurance level for their applications:

- Conduct a risk assessment, which measures possible negative impacts.

- Compare with the five assurance levels and decide which one suits this case.

- Select technology according to the technical guidance issued by NIST.

- Confirm the selected authentication process satisfies requirements.

- Reassess the system regularly and adjust it with changes.

The required level of authentication assurance are assessed through the factors below:

- Inconvenience, distress, or damage to standing or reputation.

- Financial loss or agency liability.

- Harm to agency programs or public interests.

- Unauthorized release of sensitive information.

- Personal safety; and/or civil or criminal violations.

Determining Technical Requirements

National Institute of Standards and Technology (NIST) guidance defines technical requirements for each of the four levels of assurance in the following areas:

- Tokens are used for proving identity. Passwords and symmetric cryptographic keys are private information that the verifier needs to protect. Asymmetric cryptographic keys have a private key (which only the subscriber knows) and a related public key.

- Identity proofing, registration, and the delivery of credentials that bind an identity to a token. This process can involve a far distance operation.

- Credentials, tokens, and authentication protocols can also be combined together to identify that a claimant is in fact the claimed subscriber.

- An assertion mechanism that involves either a digital signature of the claimant or is acquired directly by a trusted third party through a secure authentication protocol.

Guidelines and Regulations

Triggered by the growth of new cloud solutions and online transactions, person-to-machine and machine-to-machine identities play a significant role in identifying individuals and accessing information. According to the Office of Management and Budget in the U.S, more than $70 million was spent on identity management solutions in both 2013 and 2014.

Governments use e-authentication systems to offer services and reduce time people traveling to a government office. Services ranging from applying for visas to renewing driver's licenses can all be achieved in a more efficient and flexible way. Infrastructure to support e-authentication is regarded as an important component in successful e-government. Poor coordination and poor technical design might be major barriers to electronic authentication.

In several countries there has been established nationwide common e-authentication schemes to ease the reuse of digital identities in different electronic services. Other policy initiatives have included the creation of frameworks for electronic authentication, in order to establish common levels of trust and possibly interoperability between different authentication schemes.

US

E-authentication is a centerpiece of the United States government's effort to expand electronic government, or e-government, as a way of making government more effective and efficient and easier to access. The e-authentication service enables users to access government services online using log-in IDs (identity credentials) from other web sites that both the user and the government trust.

E-authentication is a government-wide partnership that is supported by the agencies that comprise the Federal CIO Council. The United States General Services Administration (GSA) is the lead agency partner. E-authentication works through an association with a trusted credential issuer, making it necessary for the user to log into the issuer's site to obtain the authentication credentials. Those credentials or e-authentication ID are then transferred the supporting government web site causing authentication. The system was created in response a December 16, 2003 memorandum was issued through the Office of Management and Budget (Memorandum M04-04 Whitehouse). That memorandum updates the guidance issued in the *Paperwork Elimination Act* of 1998, 44 U.S.C. 3504 and implements section 203 of the E-Government Act, 44 U.S.C.

NIST provides guidelines for digital authentication standards and does away with most knowledge-based authentication methods. A stricter standard has been drafted on more complicated passwords that at least 8 characters long or passphrases that are at least 64 characters long.

Europe

In Europe, eIDAS provides guidelines to be used for electronic authentication in regards to electronic signatures and certificate services for website authentication. Once confirmed by the issuing Member State, other participating States are required to accept the user's electronic signature as valid for cross border transactions.

Under eIDAS, electronic identification refers to a material/immaterial unit that contains personal identification data to be used for authentication for an online service. Authentication is referred to as an electronic process that allows for the electronic identification of a natural or legal person. A trust service is an electronic service that is used to create, verify and validate electronic signatures, in addition to creating, verifying and validating certificates for website authentication.

Article 8 of eIDAS allows for the authentication mechanism that is used by a natural or legal person to use electronic identification methods in confirming their identity to a relying party. Annex IV provides requirements for qualified certificates for website authentication.

Russia

E-authentication is a centerpiece of the Russia government's effort to expand e-government, as a way of making government more effective and efficient and easier for the Russian people to access. The e-authentication service enables users to access government services online using log-in IDs (identity credentials) they already have from web sites that they and the government trust.

Other Applications

Apart from government services, e-authentication is also widely used in other technology and industries. These new applications combine the features of authorizing identities in traditional database and new technology to provide a more secure and diverse use of e-authentication.

Mobile Authentication

Mobile authentication is the verification of a user's identity through the use a mobile device. It can be treated as an independent field or it can also be applied with other multifactor authentication schemes in the e-authentication field.

For mobile authentication, there are five levels of application sensitivity from Level 0 to Level 4. Level 0 is for public use over a mobile device and requires no identity authentications, while level 4 has the most multi-procedures to identify users. For either level, mobile authentication is relatively easy to process. Firstly, users send a one-time password (OTP) through offline channels. Then, a server identifies the information and makes adjustment in the database. Since only the user has the access to a PIN code and can send information through their mobile devices, there is a low risk of attacks.

E-commerce Authentication

In the early 1980s, electronic data interchange (EDI) systems was implemented, which was considered as an early representative of E-commerce. But ensuring its security is not a significant issue since the systems are all constructed around closed networks. However, more recently, business-to-consumer transactions have transformed. Remote transacting parties have forced the implementation of E-commerce authentication systems.

Generally speaking, the approaches adopted in E-commerce authentication are basically the same as e-authentication. The difference is E-commerce authentication is a more narrow field that focuses on the transactions between customers and suppliers. A simple example of E-commerce authentication includes a client communicating with a merchant server via the Internet. The merchant server usually utilizes a web server to accept client requests, a database management system to manage data and a payment gateway to provide online payment services.

Perspectives

To keep up with the evolution of services in the digital world, there is continued need for security mechanisms. While passwords will continued to be used, it is important to rely on authentication mechanisms, most importantly multifactor authentication. As the usage of e-signatures continues to significantly expand throughout the United States, the EU and throughout the world, there is expectation that regulations such as eIDAS will eventually be amended to reflect changing conditions along with regulations in the United States.

Non-repudiation

Non-repudiation usually applies to cases of a formal contract, a communication, or the transfer of data. Its aim is to ensure that an individual or organization bound by the terms of a contract, or the parties involved in a particular communication or document transfer are unable to deny the authenticity of their signatures on the contract documents, or that they were the originator of a particular message or transfer.

Classic analog examples of non-repudiation methods would include the signatures and documentation associated with a registered mail delivery (where by signing, the recipient is unable to deny having received that court summons from the utilities company), or the recorded presence of witnesses to the signing of a legal document or treaty.

Beyond Authenticity

Clearly, non-deniability in a communications or data transfer context cannot be achieved if the true identities of both parties to the dialog cannot be confirmed. So some reliable means of authenticating these parties has to be put in place. These methods might range from the Kerberos authentication protocol used to validate procedures on most operating systems to a simple Message Authentication Code.

But authenticity by itself isn't enough to guarantee non-deniability. For example, the SSL or TLS authentication protocols used for internet communications can provide an assurance that a given client system is "talking" to its intended server, but there's no fool-proof method of recording a session which the client could present in the case of a legal dispute with the service provider – which would introduce the element of non-repudiation into the data transfer.

So one can have authenticity/authentication without non-repudiation. But the reverse is not the case. Non-repudiation cannot be achieved without the identities of the concerned parties first having been established beyond reasonable doubt – in other words, authenticity has to be a part of the mix. But it's not all of it.

Non-repudiation Principles

Non-repudiation requires the creation of artifacts which may be used to dispute the claims of an entity or organization that denies being the originator of an action or communication. These artifacts consist of:

- An identity.

- The authentication of that identity.

- Tangible evidence connecting the identified party to a particular communication or action.

Non-repudiation Techniques

For email transmission, non-repudiation typically involves using methods designed to ensure that a sender can't deny having sent a particular message, or that a message recipient can't deny having received it. Techniques would include email tracking.

Cryptographic hash functions may be used to establish the integrity of transmitted documents. No encryption keys are involved, and strong hash functions are designed to be irreversible. Moreover, they're designed to avoid collision, which occurs in the rare cases where two separate documents give rise to the same hash value.

Taking this a stage further is HMAC, a technique used to provide data authentication and integrity through the hashing of a document and its transmission with a shared encryption key.

However, the very fact that the key is a shared one means that this method lacks non-repudiation.

Digital Signatures

A digital signature is used to introduce the qualities of uniqueness and non-deniability to internet communications. Each certificate is digitally signed by a trusted Certificate Authority or CA, and its hash value is encrypted with a private key also held by that same trusted CA.

The sender of a message can use a private key to encrypt the hash of the document – giving its digital signature, which is attached to the document as it's sent. At the other end, the recipient may decrypt the digital signature using a public key. By calculating the hash value of the document and comparing it with the document's decrypted digital signature (which is also the hash value of the document), the two may be compared to confirm that they match.

With this match established, the recipient is able to confirm who the sender of the message actually is, and which particular message was actually sent. Digital signatures ensure that a document or message has actually been signed by the person who claims to have signed it. In addition, a digital signature can only be created by one person – so that person can't later deny having been the originator of the transmission.

Repudiation Attacks

When a system or application doesn't include protocols or controls for tracking and logging the actions of its users, the system may be manipulated by malicious intruders, who can forge the identifying credentials of new actions, which can't be denied with certainty.

In a repudiation attack of this type, erroneous data may be fed into log files, the authoring information of actions on the system may be altered, and general data manipulation or spoofing may occur.

Parkerian Hexad

Donn B. Parker, one of the information security specialists of repute, brought out some alternate perspectives of the properties of information security. In addition to the three properties specified through the CIA triad, he brought out three more descriptors or properties, namely, possession, authenticity, and utility, thus forming a hexad known as the Parkerian Hexad. The Parkerian Hexad also groups confidentiality and possession, integrity and authenticity, availability and utility, pairs together as these are related.

The definitions provided by the Parkerian Hexad for the six properties or descriptors are as follows:

- "Confidentiality" is defined as the "quality or state of being private or secret; known only to a limited few."

- "Possession or Control" is defined as "a state of having in or taking into one's control or holding at one's disposal; actual physical control of property by one who holds for himself, as distinguished from custody; something owned or controlled."

- "Integrity" is defined as "unimpaired or unmarred condition; soundness; entire correspondence with an original condition; the quality or state of being complete or undivided; material wholeness."

- "Authenticity" is defined as "authoritative, valid, true, real, genuine, or worthy of acceptance or belief by reason of conformity to fact and reality."

- "Availability" is defined as "capable of use for the accomplishment of a purpose, immediately usable, accessible, may be obtained."

- "Utility" is defined as "useful, fitness for some purpose."

The Parkerian Hexad describes "confidentiality" as a little different from the traditional definition of "confidentiality" that is provided by U.S.Code/NIST. This hexad considers "possession" as an important element which may impact confidentiality. The "possession" of confidential information can sometimes lead to such threats like blackmail, extortion, sabotage, or destruction. Similarly, proprietary and personal information considered by traditional definition to be confidential may in fact be confidential or not confidential, depending upon the nature of the information or timing of the information divulgence.

Six properties of information security.

The Parkerian Hexad describes "integrity" as a little different from the traditional definition of "integrity" that is provided by U.S.Code/NIST. This hexad doesn't consider "authenticity" as a part of "integrity" and as a different property, which has to do with the validity or genuineness of the information than the unimpaired condition of the information. Again here, "non-repudiation" is considered a different aspect than "integrity" and as related to "authenticity" as it refers to validity or genuineness of the information.

Parkerian hexad considers "availability" along with "utility" as information even if available is of use only if it is usable or has utility. It differs from the traditional definition in that "availability" has nothing to do with "reliable access".

References

- Ford, Matthew (23 Feb 2005). "Identity Authentication and 'E-Commerce'". Warwick, Journal of Information Law &Technology. Retrieved 3 November 2015

- Confidentiality, data, security: udel.edu, Retrieved 12 August, 2019

- Zafar, F.; Khan, A.; Malik, S.U.R.; et al. (2017). "A survey of cloud computing data integrity schemes: Design challenges, taxonomy and future trends". Computers & Security. 65 (3): 29–49. Doi:10.1016/j.cose.2016.10.006

- What-is-non-repudiation: finjan.com, Retrieved 12 May, 2019

- Priyadharshini, B.; Parvathi, P. (2012). "Data integrity in cloud storage". Proceedings from the 2012 International Conference on Advances in Engineering, Science and Management. ISBN 9788190904223

- Parkerian-hexad, computer-science, 26648: ebrary.net, Retrieved 1 January, 2019

- Turner, Dawn M. "Understanding Non-Repudiation of Origin and Non-Repudiation of Emission". Cryptomathic. Retrieved 9 January 2017

3

Threats to Information Security

There are numerous threats that are dealt with under information security. Some of the major threats are cyber risk, security breach, data breach, data theft, data loss, malware, spyware, rootkit, keystroke logging, web shell, phishing, etc. This chapter discusses in detail these threats related to information security.

Cyber Risk

Cyber risk is commonly defined as exposure to harm or loss resulting from breaches of or attacks on information systems. However, this definition must be broadened. A better, more encompassing definition is "the potential of loss or harm related to technical infrastructure or the use of technology within an organization." Events covered by this more comprehensive definition can be categorized in multiple ways. One is intent. Events may be the result of deliberately malicious acts, such as a hacker carrying out an attack with the aim of compromising sensitive information, but they may also be unintentional, such as user error that makes a system temporarily unavailable. Risk events may come from sources outside the organization, such as cybercriminals or supply chain partners, or sources inside the organization such as employees or contractors.

Combining these two dimensions leads us to a practical framework for inventorying and categorizing cyber risks:

- Internal Malicious: Deliberate acts of sabotage, theft or other malfeasance committed by employees and other insiders. For example, a disgruntled employee deleting key information before they leave the organization.

- Internal Unintentional: Acts leading to damage or loss stemming from human error committed by employees and other insiders. For example, in 2013, NASDAQ experienced internal technology issues that caused backup systems to fail.

- External Malicious: The most publicized cyber risk; pre-meditated attacks from outside parties, including criminal syndicates, hacktivists and nation states. Examples include network infiltration and extraction of intellectual property, and denial-of-service (DoS) attacks that cause system availability issues, business interruptions, or interfere with the proper performance of connected devices such as medical devices or industrial systems.

- External Unintentional: Similar to the internal unintentional, these cause loss or damage to business, but are not deliberate. For example, a third party partner experiencing technical issues can impact system availability, as can natural disasters.

Security Breach

A security breach occurs when an intruder gains unauthorized access to an organization's protected systems and data. Cybercriminals or malicious applications bypass security mechanisms to reach restricted areas. A security breach is an early-stage violation that can lead to things like system damage and data loss.

Types of Security Breaches

Attackers can initiate different types of security breaches. Here are three big ones:

- Viruses,

- Spyware,

- Malware.

Cybercriminals often use malicious software to break in to protected networks. Viruses, spyware, and other types of malware often arrive by email or from downloads from the internet.

For instance, one might receive an email with an attached text, image, or audio file. Opening that attachment could infect the computer. Or one might download an infected program from the internet. In that case, the computer would become infected when one open or run the malicious program. If it's a virus, it could spread to other computers on the network.

Impersonation of an Organization

Cybercriminals sometimes can create a gap in security by sending a bogus, but convincing email to an employee of an organization. The email is made to appear like it's from an executive with an urgent request for, say, employment records, log-in information, or other sensitive data. Eager to fill the request, the employee may email back the information — putting it in the hands of cybercriminals.

This tactic is known as phishing — or spearfishing, if the email is highly targeted to a specific person.

The attacks often target the financial industry, with the goal of accessing financial accounts. Or a phishing email may target one, as an account holder. One might receive an urgent email saying, there's been an attempt to access the bank account, so click on this link and log-in now. But the link is fake, and the log-in information goes straight to fraudsters.

Denial of Service Attacks

A denial-of-service attack is capable of crashing websites. Hackers can make a website — or a computer — unavailable by flooding it with traffic. DDoS attacks are considered security breaches because they can overwhelm an organization's security devices and its ability to do business. DDoS attacks often target government or financial websites. The motive can be activism, revenge, or extortion. During an attack, anyone who has legitimate business with an organization — like one — will be unable to access the website.

But these three examples are just a start. There are other types of security breaches. Cybercriminals can also exploit software bugs or upload encryption software onto a network to initiate ransomware attacks — in essence, demanding a ransom in exchange for the encryption key. Or intrusions may occur inside an organization, with employees seeking to access or steal information for financial gain.

Difference between Security Breach and Data Breach

The terms security breach and data breach are sometimes used interchangeably, but they're two different things. It's usually a question of order. A security breach happens first. A data breach may follow. One exception: A company may negligently expose data. That's considered a data breach.

A security breach occurs when an unauthorized party bypasses security measures to reach protected areas of a system. It can put the intruder within reach of valuable information — company accounts, intellectual property, the personal information of customers that might include names, addresses, Social Security numbers, and credit card information.

If a cybercriminal steals confidential information, a data breach has occurred. Personally identifiable information is often sold on the dark web and can be used to commit crimes such as identity theft.

Yahoo Security Breach

The Yahoo security breach began with a spear-phishing email sent in early 2014. A Yahoo company employee clicked on a link, giving hackers access to the company's network. Three Yahoo breaches in total gave cybercriminals access to 3 billion user accounts. Yahoo announced the first breach in 2016.

Exposed user account information included names, birth dates, phone numbers, security questions, and passwords that were weakly encrypted. Keep in mind, some people use the same password — a dangerous practice — on multiple accounts. This could give cybercriminals access to other accounts. Some stolen information reportedly has been sold on the dark web.

Equifax Security Breach

The data breach at Equifax, one of the nation's largest credit reporting companies, exposed the personal information of more than 145 million Americans.

Cybercriminals exploited a website application vulnerability. Unauthorized access to data occurred from between May and July 2017. Equifax announced the cybersecurity incident on September 7, 2017.

Hackers accessed personally identifiable information that included names, Social Security numbers, birth dates, addresses, and, in some cases, driver's license numbers. The breach arguably increased the risk of identity theft for millions of Americans.

Facebook Security Breach

Facebook, in September 2018, announced an attack on its computer network. The personal information of nearly 29 million users was exposed. Cybercriminals exploited three software flaws in Facebook's system.

Hackers were able to break into user accounts that included those of Facebook CEO Mark Zuckerberg and Chief Operating Officer Sheryl Sandberg.

Protective Measures

The personal information is in a lot of places, including with government agencies, healthcare providers, financial institutions, and stores.

There's not much one can do to prevent a security breach at any of those places. But one can do some things to help protect the self before and after a breach occurs. Here are some examples:

- Create strong, secure passwords: That means using uppercase and lowercase letters, as well as non-sequential numbers and special characters.

- Use different passwords on different accounts: If one account is compromised, cybercriminals won't be able to easily access the other accounts.

- Use secure websites: Look for "https" in the web address. It indicates a secure, encrypted connection.

- Protect Social Security number: Provide the SSN only when it's absolutely required. Ask about providing a different form of identification.

- Install updates: Always update the computers and mobile devices with the latest versions of operating systems and applications. Updates sometimes contain patches for security vulnerabilities.

- Stay informed: If one do business with a company that's had a data breach, find out what information was taken and how it could affect one. Companies sometimes set up a website to keep consumers informed.

- Be watchful: Monitor online and monthly financial account statements to make sure the transactions are legitimate.

- Sign up for credit reports: Regularly check the credit reports to make sure an imposter hasn't opened credit cards, loans, or other accounts in the name.

- Consider credit services: Credit freezes, credit monitoring, and identity theft protection services can help one keep track of the information.

Steps to Help Defend against a Security Breach

Helping to defend theself against a security breach boils down to taking three steps — one before, one during, and one after a breach occurs.

- Plan ahead: The personal information has value to help protect it by sharing as little as possible. Guard key identifiers like the Social Security Number. Consider the tradeoffs of providing the personal data to organizations, computer app makers, and social media platforms. Read privacy policies and seek assurances that the data will be protected.

- Be proactive: When a security breach happens, it's important to know what personal data was exposed and what one should do to help protect theself. This might include changing passwords on the accounts, freezing the credit reports, and considering an identity theft protection service to help manage any fallout.

- Follow up. Here's the thing: If the personal information is stolen, one could face the consequences in the short or long term. One might detect suspicious charges on a credit account soon afterward. That might be easy to spot and take care of. But often stolen information doesn't appear for sale on the dark web until months or years after a data breach. Regularly checking the credit reports or enlisting the help of an identity theft protection service can help spot some problems as they arise.

Data Breach

A data breach is a confirmed incident in which sensitive, confidential or otherwise protected data has been accessed and/or disclosed in an unauthorized fashion. Data breaches may involve personal health information (PHI), personally identifiable information (PII), trade secrets or intellectual property.

Common data breach exposures include personal information, such as credit card numbers, Social Security numbers and healthcare histories, as well as corporate information, such as customer lists, manufacturing processes and software source code. If anyone who is not specifically authorized to do so views such data, the organization charged with protecting that information is said to have suffered a data breach. If a data breach results in identity theft and/or a violation of government or industry compliance mandates, the offending organization may face fines or other civil litigation.

Data Breach Causes

A familiar example of a data breach is an attacker hacking into a corporate website and stealing sensitive data out of a database. However, not all breaches are so dramatic. If an unauthorized hospital employee views a patient's health information on a computer screen over the shoulder of an authorized employee, that also constitutes a data breach. Data breaches can be brought about by weak passwords, missing software patches that are exploited or lost or stolen laptop computers and mobile devices. Users connecting to rogue wireless networks that capture login credentials or other sensitive information in transit can also lead to unauthorized exposures. Social engineering especially attacks carried out via email phishing can lead to users providing their login credentials directly to attackers or through subsequent malware infections. Criminals can then use the credentials they obtained to gain entry to sensitive systems and records access which often goes undetected for months, if not indefinitely. Threat actors can also target third-party business partners in order to gain access to large organizations; such incidents typically involve hackers compromising less secure businesses to obtain access to the primary target.

While hackers and cybercriminals often cause data breaches, there are also incidents where enterprises or government agencies inadvertently expose sensitive or confidential data on the internet. These incidents are typically known as *accidental data breaches*, and they usually involve organizations misconfiguring cloud services or failing to implement the proper access controls, such as password requirements for public-facing web services or applications.

Preventing Data Breaches

There is no one security product or control that can prevent data breaches. The most reasonable means for preventing data breaches involve commonsense security practices. This includes well-known security basics, such as conducting ongoing vulnerability and penetration testing, applying proven malware protection, using strong passwords/passphrases and consistently applying the necessary software patches on all systems. While these steps will help prevent intrusions into an environment, information security (infosec) experts also encourage encrypting sensitive data, whether it is stored inside an on-premises network or third-party cloud service. In the event of a successful intrusion into the environment, encryption will prevent threat actors from accessing the actual data.

Additional measures for preventing breaches, as well as minimizing their impact, include well-written security policies for employees and ongoing security awareness training to promote those policies and educate employees. Such policies may include concepts such as the principle of least privilege (POLP), which gives employees the bare minimum of permissions and administrative rights to perform their duties. In addition, organizations should have an incident response plan (IRP) that can be implemented in the event of an intrusion or breach; an IRP typically includes a formal process for identifying, containing and quantifying a security incident.

Notable Data Breaches

Most data breaches occur in the banking industry, followed by the healthcare sector and the public sector, according to a 2019 Verizon Data Breach Investigations Report (DBIR). The study included incidents reported from Nov. 1, 2017 to Oct. 31, 2018, and was based on data from 41,686 security incidents and 2,013 data breaches provided by 73 data sources, both public and private entities, spanning 86 countries.

In the financial services industry, 927 incidents were reported with 207 cased of confirmed data disclosure. In heathcare, where most of the breaches were attributed to internal actors, 466 incidents were reported with 304 confirmed cases of data disclosure. And in the public sector, where 79 percent of breaches were blamed on state-affiliated actors (i.e., government spies), there were 23,399 incidents and 330 with confirmed data disclosure.

There have been several major data breaches of both large enterprises and government agencies in recent years. In 2013, retail giant Target Corporation disclosed it had suffered a major data breach that exposed customer names and credit card information. The company initially announced that 40 million customers were affected by the breach but later raised that number to 110 million. An internal investigation into the matter revealed the initial intrusion point was a third-party business partner that had been breached; the threat actors then used the business partner's credentials to access Target's network and then spread point-of-sale (POS) malware to the company's POS systems. The Target data breach led to several lawsuits from customers, state governments and credit card companies, which resulted in the company paying tens of millions of dollars in legal settlements. In addition, the company's CEO and CIO both resigned in the wake of the breach.

In late 2014, Sony Pictures Entertainment's corporate network was shut down when threat actors that had previously breached the company executed malware that disabled workstations and servers. A hacker group known as Guardians of Peace claimed responsibility for the data breach; the group leaked unreleased films that had been stolen from Sony's network, as well as confidential emails from company executives. The company later pulled from movie theaters the 2014 comedy *The Interview*, which featured the assassination of a fictional version of North Korean leader Kim Jong-un, prior to its premiere after the hackers issued vague threats. Cybersecurity experts and the U.S. government later attributed the data breach to the North Korean government.

Yahoo suffered a massive data breach in 2013, though the company didn't discover the incident until 2016 when it began investigating another, separate security incident. Initially, Yahoo announced that more than 1 billion email accounts were affected in the breach; exposed user data included names, email addresses, telephone numbers and dates of birth, as well as hashed passwords (using the MD5 algorithm) and some encrypted or unencrypted security questions and answers. Following a full investigation into the 2013 data breach, Yahoo disclosed that the incident affected all of the company's 3 billion email accounts. Yahoo also discovered a second major breach that occurred in 2014 that affected 500 million email accounts; the company found that threat actors had gained access to its corporate network and minted authentication cookies that allowed them to access email accounts without passwords. Following a criminal investigation into the 2014 breach, the U.S. Department of Justice indicted four men, including two Russian Federal Security Service agents, in connection with the hack.

The U.S. Office of Personnel Management (OPM) announced in 2015 that it had been breached by threat actors, giving up the personal information and government records of more than 21 million current and former federal employees. The exposed data included personal information, such as Social Security numbers and dates of birth, while the government records included SF-86 forms for security clearance, as well as some fingerprint scans. The authorities reported the hackers obtained credentials from a federal contractor and then used those credentials to access the OPM's network. The data breach led to the resignations of both the agency's director and its CIO. Later that year, the Chinese government announced it had arrested and charged several Chinese nationals for the breach. In 2017, the FBI arrested another Chinese national who authorities claimed was responsible for the malware used in the OPM data breach.

Data Theft

Data theft is a growing phenomenon primarily caused by system administrators and office workers with access to technology such as database servers, desktop computers and a growing list of handheld devices capable of storing digital information, such as USB flash drives, iPods and even digital cameras. Since employees often spend a considerable amount of time developing contacts and confidential and copyrighted information for the company they work for, they may feel they have some right to the information and are inclined to copy and/or delete part of it when they leave the company, or misuse it while they are still in employment. They can be sold and bought and then used by criminals and criminal organizations. Alternatively, an employee may choose to deliberately abuse trusted access to information for the purpose of exposing misconduct by the employer; From the perspective of the society such an act of whistleblowing can be seen as positive and is in certain situations protected by law in some jurisdictions, such as the USA.

A common scenario is where a sales person makes a copy of the contact database for use in their next job. Typically, this is a clear violation of their terms of employment.

Notable acts of data theft include those by leaker Chelsea Manning and self-proclaimed whistleblowers Edward Snowden and Hervé Falciani.

Data Theft Methods

The phrase data theft is actually a misnomer, since unlike theft the typical data theft methods typically do not deprive the owner of their data, but rather create an additional, unauthorized copy.

Thumbsucking

Thumbsucking, similar to podslurping, is the intentional or undeliberate use of a portable USB mass storage device, such as a USB flash drive (or "thumbdrive"), to illicitly download confidential data from a network endpoint.

A USB flash drive was allegedly used to remove without authorization highly classified documents about the design of U.S. nuclear weapons from a vault at Los Alamos.

The threat of thumbsucking has been amplified for a number of reasons, including the following:

- The storage capacity of portable USB storage devices has increased.

- The cost of high-capacity portable USB storage devices has decreased.

- Networks have grown more dispersed, the number of remote network access points has increased and methods of network connection have expanded, increasing the number of vectors for network infiltration.

Investigating Data Theft

Techniques to investigate data theft include stochastic forensics, digital artifact analysis (especially of USB drive artifacts), and other computer forensics techniques.

Data Loss

Data loss is an error condition in information systems in which information is destroyed by failures or neglect in storage, transmission, or processing. Information systems implement backup and disaster recovery equipment and processes to prevent data loss or restore lost data.

Data loss is distinguished from data unavailability, which may arise from a network outage. Although the two have substantially similar consequences for users, data unavailability is temporary, while data loss may be permanent. Data loss is also distinct from data breach, an incident where data falls into the wrong hands, although the term data loss has been used in those incidents.

Types

- Procedural

- Intentional Action

  ◦ Intentional deletion of a file or program.

- Unintentional Action

  ◦ Accidental deletion of a file or program.

  ◦ Misplacement of CDs or Memory sticks.

  ◦ Administration errors.

  ◦ Inability to read unknown file format.

- Failure

  ◦ Power failure, resulting in data in volatile memory not being saved to permanent memory.

  ◦ Hardware failure, such as a head crash in a hard disk.

  ◦ A software crash or freeze, resulting in data not being saved.

  ◦ Software bugs or poor usability, such as not confirming a file delete command.

  ◦ Business failure (vendor bankruptcy), where data is stored with a software vendor using Software-as-a-service and SaaS data escrow has not been provisioned.

  ◦ Data corruption, such as file system corruption or database corruption.

- Disaster

  ◦ Natural disaster, earthquake, flood, tornado, etc.

  ◦ Fire.

- Crime

  ◦ Theft, hacking, SQL injection, sabotage, etc.

  ◦ A malicious act, such as a worm, virus, hacker or theft of physical media.

Studies show hardware failure and human error are the two most common causes of data loss, accounting for roughly three quarters of all incidents. Another cause of data loss is a natural disaster, which is a greater risk dependant on where the hardware is located. While the probability of data loss due to natural disaster is small, the only way to prepare for such an event is to store backup data in a separate physical location. As such, the best backup plans always include at least one copy being stored off-site.

Cost

The cost of a *data loss event* is directly related to the value of the data and the length of time that it is unavailable yet needed. For an enterprise in particular, the definition of cost extends beyond the financial and can also include time. Consider:

- The cost of continuing without the data.

- The cost of recreating the data.

- The cost of notifying users in the event of a compromise.

Prevention

The frequency of data loss and the impact can be greatly mitigated by taking proper precautions, those of which necessary can vary depending on the type of data loss. For example, multiple power circuits with battery backup and a generator only protect against power failures, though using an Uninterruptable Power Supply can protect drive against sudden power spikes. Similarly, using a journaling file system and RAID storage only protect against certain types of software and hardware failure.

For hard disk drives, which are a physical storage medium, ensuring minimal vibration and movement will help protect against damaging the components internally, as can maintaining a suitable drive temperature.

Regular data backups are an important asset to have when trying to recover after a data loss event, but they do not prevent user errors or system failures. As such, a data backup plan needs to be established and run in unison with a disaster recovery plan in order to lower risk.

Data Recovery

Media that's suffered a catastrophic electronic failure requires data recovery in order to salvage its contents.

Data recovery is often performed by specialized commercial services that have developed often proprietary methods to recover data from physically damaged media. Service costs at data recovery labs are usually dependent on type of damage and type of storage medium, as well as the required security or cleanroom procedures.

File system corruption can frequently be repaired by the user or the system administrator. For example, a deleted file is typically not immediately overwritten on disk, but more often simply has its entry deleted from the file system index. In such a case, the deletion can be easily reversed.

Successful recovery from data loss generally requires implementation of an effective backup strategy. Without an implemented backup strategy, recovery requires reinstallation of programs and regeneration of data. Even with an effective backup strategy, restoring a system to the precise state it was in prior to the Data Loss Event is extremely difficult. Some level of compromise between granularity of recoverability and cost is necessary. Furthermore, a Data Loss Event may not be immediately apparent. An effective backup strategy must also consider the cost of maintaining the ability to recover lost data for long periods of time.

A highly effective backup system would have duplicate copies of every file and program that were immediately accessible whenever a Data Loss Event was noticed. However, in most situations, there is an inverse correlation between the value of a unit of data and the length of time it takes to notice the loss of that data. Taking this into consideration, many backup strategies decrease the granularity of restorability as the time increases since the potential Data Loss Event. By this logic, recovery from recent Data Loss Events is easier and more complete than recovery from Data Loss Events that happened further in the past.

Recovery is also related to the type of Data Loss Event. Recovering a single lost file is substantially different from recovering an entire system that was destroyed in a disaster. An effective backup regimen has some proportionality between the magnitude of Data Loss and the magnitude of effort required to recover. For example, it should be far easier to restore the single lost file than to recover the entire system.

Initial Steps upon Data Loss

If data loss occurs, a successful recovery must ensure that the deleted data is not over-written. For this reason — one should avoid all write operations to the affected storage device. This includes not starting the system to which the affected device is connected. This is because many operating systems create temporary files in order to boot, and these may overwrite areas of lost data — rendering it unrecoverable. Viewing web pages has the same effect — potentially overwriting lost files with the temporary HTML and image files created when viewing a web page. File operations such as copying, editing, or deleting should also be avoided.

Upon realizing data loss has occurred, it is often best to shut down the computer and remove the drive in question from the unit. Re-attach this drive to a secondary computer with a write blocker device and then attempt to recover lost data. If possible, create an image of the drive in order to establish a secondary copy of the data. This can then be tested on, with recovery attempted, abolishing the risk of harming the source data.

Malware

Malware is any software intentionally designed to cause damage to a computer, server, client, or computer network. Malware does the damage after it is implanted or introduced in some way into a target's computer and can take the form of directly executable code, scripts, so-called "active content" (Microsoft Windows), and other forms of data. Some kinds of malware are largely referred to in the media as computer viruses, worms, Trojan horses, ransomware, spyware, adware, and scareware, among other terms. Malware has a malicious intent, acting against the interest of the computer user—and so does not include software that causes unintentional harm due to some deficiency, which is typically described as a software bug.

Programs officially supplied by companies can be considered malware if they secretly act against the interests of the computer user. For example, at one point Sony music Compact discs silently installed a rootkit on purchasers' computers running Microsoft Windows with the intention of preventing illicit copying; but which also reported on users' listening habits, and unintentionally created extra security vulnerabilities.

One strategy for protecting against malware is to prevent the harmful software from gaining access to the target computer. For this reason, antivirus software, firewalls and other strategies are used to help protect against the introduction of malware, in addition to checking for the presence of malware and malicious activity and recovering from attacks.

Purposes

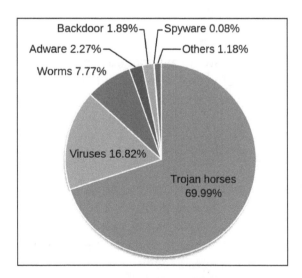

Many early infectious programs, including the first Internet Worm, were written as experiments or pranks. Today, malware is used by both black hat hackers and governments, to steal personal, financial, or business information.

Malware is sometimes used broadly against government or corporate websites to gather guarded information, or to disrupt their operation in general. However, malware can be used against individuals to gain information such as personal identification numbers or details, bank or credit card numbers, and passwords.

Since the rise of widespread broadband Internet access, malicious software has more frequently been designed for profit. Since 2003, the majority of widespread viruses and worms have been designed to take control of users' computers for illicit purposes. Infected "zombie computers" can be used to send email spam, to host contraband data such as child pornography, or to engage in distributed denial-of-service attacks as a form of extortion.

Programs designed to monitor users' web browsing, display unsolicited advertisements, or redirect affiliate marketing revenues are called spyware. Spyware programs do not spread like viruses; instead they are generally installed by exploiting security holes. They can also be hidden and packaged together with unrelated user-installed software. The Sony BMG rootkit was intended to preventing illicit copying; but also reported on users' listening habits, and unintentionally created extra security vulnerabilities.

Ransomware affects an infected computer system in some way, and demands payment to bring it back to its normal state. For example, programs such as CryptoLocker encrypt files securely, and only decrypt them on payment of a substantial sum of money.

Some malware is used to generate money by click fraud, making it appear that the computer user has clicked an advertising link on a site, generating a payment from the advertiser. It was estimated in 2012 that about 60 to 70% of all active malware used some kind of click fraud, and 22% of all ad-clicks were fraudulent.

In addition to criminal money-making, malware can be used for sabotage, often for political motives. Stuxnet, for example, was designed to disrupt very specific industrial equipment. There have been politically motivated attacks that have spread over and shut down large computer networks, including massive deletion of files and corruption of master boot records, described as "computer killing". Such attacks were made on Sony Pictures Entertainment and Saudi Aramco.

Infectious Malware

The best-known types of malware, viruses and worms, are known for the manner in which they spread, rather than any specific types of behavior. A computer virus is software that embeds itself in some other executable software (including the operating system itself) on the target system without the user's knowledge and consent and when it is run, the virus is spread to other executables. On the other hand, a *worm* is a stand-alone malware software that *actively* transmits itself over a network to infect other computers. These definitions lead to the observation that a virus requires the user to run an infected software or operating system for the virus to spread, whereas a worm spreads itself.

Concealment

These categories are not mutually exclusive, so malware may use multiple techniques.

Viruses

A computer virus is software usually hidden within another seemingly innocuous program that can produce copies of itself and insert them into other programs or files, and that usually performs a harmful action (such as destroying data). An example of this is a PE infection, a technique, usually used to spread malware, that inserts extra data or executable code into PE files.

Screen-locking Ransomware

'Lock-screens', or screen lockers is a type of "cyber police" ransomware that blocks screens on Windows or Android devices with a false accusation in harvesting illegal content, trying to scare the victims into paying up a fee. Jisut and SLocker impact Android devices more than other lock-screens, with Jisut making up nearly 60 percent of all Android ransomware detections.

Trojan Horses

A Trojan horse is a harmful program that misrepresents itself to masquerade as a regular, benign program or utility in order to persuade a victim to install it. A Trojan horse usually carries a hidden destructive function that is activated when the application is started.

Trojan horses are generally spread by some form of social engineering, for example, where a user is duped into executing an e-mail attachment disguised to be unsuspicious, (e.g., a routine form to be filled in), or by drive-by download. Although their payload can be anything, many modern forms act as a backdoor, contacting a controller which can then have unauthorized access to the affected computer. While Trojan horses and backdoors are not easily detectable by themselves, computers may appear to run slower due to heavy processor or network usage.

Unlike computer viruses and worms, Trojan horses generally do not attempt to inject themselves into other files or otherwise propagate themselves.

In spring 2017 Mac users were hit by the new version of Proton Remote Access Trojan (RAT) trained to extract password data from various sources, such as browser auto-fill data, the Mac-OS keychain, and password vaults.

Rootkits

Once malicious software is installed on a system, it is essential that it stays concealed, to avoid detection. Software packages known as *rootkits* allow this concealment, by modifying the host's operating system so that the malware is hidden from the user. Rootkits can prevent a harmful process from being visible in the system's list of processes, or keep its files from being read.

Some types of harmful software contain routines to evade identification and/or removal attempts, not merely to hide themselves. An early example of this behavior is recorded in the Jargon File tale of a pair of programs infesting a Xerox CP-V time sharing system:

> "Each ghost-job would detect the fact that the other had been killed, and would start a new copy of the recently stopped program within a few milliseconds. The only way to kill both ghosts was to kill them simultaneously (very difficult) or to deliberately crash the system".

Backdoors

A backdoor is a method of bypassing normal authentication procedures, usually over a connection to a network such as the Internet. Once a system has been compromised, one or more backdoors may be installed in order to allow access in the future, invisibly to the user.

The idea has often been suggested that computer manufacturers preinstall backdoors on their systems to provide technical support for customers, but this has never been reliably verified. It was reported in 2014 that US government agencies had been diverting computers purchased by those considered "targets" to secret workshops where software or hardware permitting remote access by the agency was installed, considered to be among the most productive operations to obtain access to networks around the world. Backdoors may be installed by Trojan horses, worms, implants, or other methods.

Evasion

Since the beginning of 2015, a sizable portion of malware utilizes a combination of many techniques designed to avoid detection and analysis. From the more common, to the least common:

- Evasion of analysis and detection by fingerprinting the environment when executed.

- Confusing automated tools' detection methods: This allows malware to avoid detection by technologies such as signature-based antivirus software by changing the server used by the malware.

- Timing-based evasion: This is when malware runs at certain times or following certain actions taken by the user, so it executes during certain vulnerable periods, such as during the boot process, while remaining dormant the rest of the time.

- Obfuscating internal data so that automated tools do not detect the malware.

An increasingly common technique (2015) is adware that uses stolen certificates to disable anti-malware and virus protection; technical remedies are available to deal with the adware.

Nowadays, one of the most sophisticated and stealthy ways of evasion is to use information hiding techniques, namely stegomalware.

Vulnerability

- In this context, and throughout, what is called the "system" under attack may be anything from a single application, through a complete computer and operating system, to a large network.

- Various factors make a system more vulnerable to malware:

Security Defects in Software

Malware exploits security defects (security bugs or vulnerabilities) in the design of the operating system, in applications (such as browsers, e.g. older versions of Microsoft Internet Explorer supported by Windows XP), or in vulnerable versions of browser plugins such as Adobe Flash Player, Adobe Acrobat or Reader, or Java SE. Sometimes even installing new versions of such plugins does not automatically uninstall old versions. Security advisories from plug-in providers announce security-related updates. Common vulnerabilities are assigned CVE IDs and listed in the US National Vulnerability Database. Secunia PSI is an example of software, free for personal use, that will check a PC for vulnerable out-of-date software, and attempt to update it.

Malware authors target bugs, or loopholes, to exploit. A common method is exploitation of a buffer overrun vulnerability, where software designed to store data in a specified region of memory does not prevent more data than the buffer can accommodate being supplied. Malware may provide data that overflows the buffer, with malicious executable code or data after the end; when this payload is accessed it does what the attacker, not the legitimate software, determines.

Insecure Design or User Error

Early PCs had to be booted from floppy disks. When built-in hard drives became common, the operating system was normally started from them, but it was possible to boot from another boot device if available, such as a floppy disk, CD-ROM, DVD-ROM, USB flash drive or network. It was common to configure the computer to boot from one of these devices when available. Normally none would be available; the user would intentionally insert, say, a CD into the optical drive to boot the computer in some special way, for example, to install an operating system. Even without booting, computers can be configured to execute software on some media as soon as they become available, e.g. to autorun a CD or USB device when inserted.

Malware distributors would trick the user into booting or running from an infected device or medium. For example, a virus could make an infected computer add autorunnable code to any USB stick plugged into it. Anyone who then attached the stick to another computer set to autorun from USB would in turn become infected, and also pass on the infection in the same way. More generally, any device that plugs into a USB port - even lights, fans, speakers, toys, or peripherals such as a digital microscope - can be used to spread malware. Devices can be infected during manufacturing or supply if quality control is inadequate.

This form of infection can largely be avoided by setting up computers by default to boot from the internal hard drive, if available, and not to autorun from devices. Intentional booting from another device is always possible by pressing certain keys during boot.

Older email software would automatically open HTML email containing potentially malicious JavaScript code. Users may also execute disguised malicious email attachments. The *2018 Data Breach Investigations Report* by Verizon, cited by CSO Online, states that emails are the primary method of malware delivery, accounting for 92% of malware delivery around the world.

Over-privileged users and Over-privileged Code

In computing, privilege refers to how much a user or program is allowed to modify a system. In poorly designed computer systems, both users and programs can be assigned more privileges than they should be, and malware can take advantage of this. The two ways that malware does this is through overprivileged users and overprivileged code.

Some systems allow all users to modify their internal structures, and such users today would be considered over-privileged users. This was the standard operating procedure for early microcomputer and home computer systems, where there was no distinction between an *administrator* or *root*, and a regular user of the system. In some systems, non-administrator users are over-privileged by design, in the sense that they are allowed to modify internal structures of the system. In some environments, users are over-privileged because they have been inappropriately granted administrator or equivalent status.

Some systems allow code executed by a user to access all rights of that user, which is known as over-privileged code. This was also standard operating procedure for early microcomputer and home computer systems. Malware, running as over-privileged code, can use this privilege to subvert the system. Almost all currently popular operating systems, and also many scripting applications allow code too many privileges, usually in the sense that when a user executes code, the system allows that code all rights of that user. This makes users vulnerable to malware in the form of e-mail attachments, which may or may not be disguised.

Use of the Same Operating System

- Homogeneity can be a vulnerability: For example, when all computers in a network run the same operating system, upon exploiting one, one worm can exploit them all: In particular, Microsoft Windows or Mac OS X have such a large share of the market that an exploited vulnerability concentrating on either operating system could subvert a large number of systems. Introducing diversity purely for the sake of robustness, such as adding Linux computers, could increase short-term costs for training and maintenance. However, as long as all the nodes are not part of the same directory service for authentication, having a few diverse nodes could deter total shutdown of the network and allow those nodes to help with recovery of the infected nodes. Such separate, functional redundancy could avoid the cost of a total shutdown, at the cost of increased complexity and reduced usability in terms of single sign-on authentication.

Anti-malware Strategies

As malware attacks become more frequent, attention has begun to shift from viruses and spyware protection, to malware protection, and programs that have been specifically developed to combat malware:

Anti-virus and Anti-malware Software

A specific component of anti-virus and anti-malware software, commonly referred to as an on-access or real-time scanner, hooks deep into the operating system's core or kernel and functions in a manner similar to how certain malware itself would attempt to operate, though with the user's informed permission for protecting the system. Any time the operating system accesses a file, the on-access scanner checks if the file is a 'legitimate' file or not. If the file is identified as malware by the scanner, the access operation will be stopped, the file will be dealt with by the scanner in a pre-defined way (how the anti-virus program was configured during/post installation), and the user will be notified. This may have a considerable performance impact on the operating system, though the degree of impact is dependent on how well the scanner was programmed. The goal is to stop any operations the malware may attempt on the system before they occur, including activities which might exploit bugs or trigger unexpected operating system behavior.

Anti-malware programs can combat malware in two ways:

1. They can provide real time protection against the installation of malware software on a computer. This type of malware protection works the same way as that of antivirus protection in that the anti-malware software scans all incoming network data for malware and blocks any threats it comes across.

2. Anti-malware software programs can be used solely for detection and removal of malware software that has already been installed onto a computer. This type of anti-malware software scans the contents of the Windows registry, operating system files, and installed programs on a computer and will provide a list of any threats found, allowing the user to choose which files to delete or keep, or to compare this list to a list of known malware components, removing files that match.

Real-time protection from malware works identically to real-time antivirus protection: the software scans disk files at download time, and blocks the activity of components known to represent malware. In some cases, it may also intercept attempts to install start-up items or to modify browser settings. Because many malware components are installed as a result of browser exploits or user error, using security software (some of which are anti-malware, though many are not) to "sandbox" browsers (essentially isolate the browser from the computer and hence any malware induced change) can also be effective in helping to restrict any damage done.

Examples of Microsoft Windows antivirus and anti-malware software include the optional Microsoft Security Essentials (for Windows XP, Vista, and Windows 7) for real-time protection, the Windows Malicious Software Removal Tool (now included with Windows (Security) Updates on "Patch Tuesday", the second Tuesday of each month), and Windows Defender (an optional download in the case of Windows XP, incorporating MSE functionality in the case of Windows 8 and later). Additionally, several capable antivirus software programs are available for free download from the Internet (usually restricted to non-commercial use). Tests found some free programs to be competitive with commercial ones. Microsoft's System File Checker can be used to check for and repair corrupted system files.

Some viruses disable System Restore and other important Windows tools such as Task Manager and Command Prompt. Many such viruses can be removed by rebooting the computer, entering Windows safe mode with networking, and then using system tools or Microsoft Safety Scanner.

Hardware implants can be of any type, so there can be no general way to detect them.

Website Security Scans

As malware also harms the compromised websites (by breaking reputation, blacklisting in search engines, etc.), some websites offer vulnerability scanning. Such scans check the website, detect malware, may note outdated software, and may report known security issues.

"Air Gap" Isolation or "Parallel Network"

As a last resort, computers can be protected from malware, and infected computers can be prevented from disseminating trusted information, by imposing an "air gap" (i.e. completely disconnecting them from all other networks). However, malware can still cross the air gap in some situations. For example, removable media can carry malware across the gap. In December 2013 researchers in Germany showed one way that an apparent air gap can be defeated.

"AirHopper", "BitWhisper", "GSMem" and "Fansmitter" are four techniques introduced by researchers that can leak data from air-gapped computers using electromagnetic, thermal and acoustic emissions.

Grayware

Grayware is a term applied to unwanted applications or files that are not classified as malware, but can worsen the performance of computers and may cause security risks.

It describes applications that behave in an annoying or undesirable manner, and yet are less serious or troublesome than malware. Grayware encompasses spyware, adware, fraudulent dialers, joke programs, remote access tools and other unwanted programs that may harm the performance of computers or cause inconvenience. The term came into use around 2004.

Another term, potentially unwanted program (PUP) or potentially unwanted application (PUA), refers to applications that would be considered unwanted despite often having been downloaded by the user, possibly after failing to read a download agreement. PUPs include spyware, adware, and fraudulent dialers. Many security products classify unauthorised key generators as grayware, although they frequently carry true malware in addition to their ostensible purpose.

Trojan Horse

In computing, a Trojan horse, or Trojan, is any malware which misleads users of its true intent.

Trojans are generally spread by some form of social engineering, for example where a user is duped into executing an e-mail attachment disguised to appear not suspicious, (e.g., a routine form to be filled in), or by clicking on some fake advertisement on social media or anywhere else. Although their payload can be anything, many modern forms act as a backdoor, contacting a controller which can then have unauthorized access to the affected computer. Trojans may allow an attacker to access users' personal information such as banking information, passwords, or personal identity. It can also delete a user's files or infect other devices connected to the network. Ransomware attacks are often carried out using a Trojan.

Unlike computer viruses and worms, Trojans generally do not attempt to inject themselves into other files or otherwise propagate themselves.

Malicious Uses

Trojan Viruses, in this way, may require interaction with a malicious controller (not necessarily distributing the Trojan) to fulfil their purpose. It is possible for those involved with Trojans to scan computers on a network to locate any with a Trojan installed, which the hacker can then control.

Some Trojans take advantage of a security flaw in older versions of Internet Explorer and Google Chrome to use the host computer as an anonymizer proxy to effectively hide Internet usage, enabling the controller to use the Internet for illegal purposes while all potentially incriminating evidence indicates the infected computer or its IP address. The host's computer may or may not show the internet history of the sites viewed using the computer as a proxy. The first generation of anonymizer Trojan horses tended to leave their tracks in the page view histories of the host computer. Later generations of the Trojan tend to "cover" their tracks more efficiently. Several versions of Sub7 have been widely circulated in the US and Europe and became the most widely distributed examples of this type of Trojan.

In German-speaking countries, spyware used or made by the government is sometimes called *govware*. Govware is typically a Trojan software used to intercept communications from the target computer. Some countries like Switzerland and Germany have a legal framework governing the use of such software. Examples of govware Trojans include the Swiss MiniPanzer and MegaPanzer and the German "state trojan" nicknamed R2D2. German govware works by exploiting security gaps unknown to the general public and accessing smartphone data before it becomes encrypted via other applications.

Due to the popularity of botnets among hackers and the availability of advertising services that permit authors to violate their users' privacy, Trojans are becoming more common. According to a survey conducted by BitDefender from January to June 2009, "Trojan-type malware is on the rise, accounting for 83% of the global malware detected in the world." Trojans have a relationship with worms, as they spread with the help given by worms and travel across the internet with them. BitDefender has stated that approximately 15% of computers are members of a botnet, usually recruited by a Trojan infection.

Computer Virus

A computer virus is a type of malware that, when executed, replicates itself by modifying other computer programs and inserting its own code. When this replication succeeds, the affected areas are then said to be "infected" with a computer virus.

Virus writers use social engineering deceptions and exploit detailed knowledge of security vulnerabilities to initially infect systems and to spread the virus. The vast majority of viruses target systems running Microsoft Windows, employing a variety of mechanisms to infect new hosts, and often using complex anti-detection/stealth strategies to evade antivirus software. Motives for creating viruses can include seeking profit (e.g., with ransomware), desire to send a political message, personal amusement, to demonstrate that a vulnerability exists in software, for sabotage and denial of service, or simply because they wish to explore cybersecurity issues, artificial life and evolutionary algorithms.

Computer viruses currently cause billions of dollars' worth of economic damage each year, due to causing system failure, wasting computer resources, corrupting data, increasing maintenance costs, stealing personal information etc. In response, free, open-source antivirus tools have been developed, and an industry of antivirus software has cropped up, selling or freely distributing virus protection to users of various operating systems. As of 2005, even though no currently existing antivirus software was able to uncover all computer viruses (especially new ones), computer security researchers are actively searching for new ways to enable antivirus solutions to more effectively detect emerging viruses, before they have already become widely distributed.

The term "virus" is also misused by extension to refer to other types of malware. "Malware" encompasses computer viruses along with many other forms of malicious software, such as computer "worms", ransomware, spyware, adware, trojan horses, keyloggers, rootkits, bootkits, malicious Browser Helper Object (BHOs), and other malicious software. The majority of active malware threats are actually trojan horse programs or computer worms rather than computer viruses. The term computer virus, coined by Fred Cohen in 1985, is a misnomer. Viruses often perform some type of harmful activity on infected host computers, such as acquisition of hard disk space or central processing unit (CPU) time, accessing and stealing private information (e.g., credit card numbers, Debit card numbers, phone numbers, names, email addresses, passwords, Bank Information, House Addresses, etc), corrupting data, displaying political, humorous or threatening messages on the user's screen, spamming their e-mail contacts, logging their keystrokes, or even rendering the computer useless. However, not all viruses carry a destructive "payload" and attempt to hide themselves—the defining characteristic of viruses is that they are self-replicating computer programs which modify other software without user consent.

Operations and Functions

Parts

A viable computer virus must contain a search routine, which locates new files or new disks which are worthwhile targets for infection. Secondly, every computer virus must contain a routine to copy itself into the program which the search routine locates. The three main virus parts are:

Infection Mechanism

Infection mechanism (also called 'infection vector'), is how the virus spreads or propagates. A virus typically has a search routine, which locates new files or new disks for infection.

Trigger

The trigger, which is also known as a logic bomb, is the compiled version that could be activated any time within an executable file when the virus is run that determines the event or condition for the malicious "payload" to be activated or delivered such as a particular date, a particular time, particular presence of another program, capacity of the disk exceeding some limit, or a double-click that opens a particular file.

Payload

The "payload" is the actual body or data that performs the actual malicious purpose of the virus. Payload activity might be noticeable (e.g., because it causes the system to slow down or "freeze"), as most of the time the "payload" itself is the harmful activity, or some times non-destructive but distributive, which is called Virus hoax.

Phases

Virus phases is the life cycle of the computer virus, described by using an analogy to biology. This life cycle can be divided into four phases:

Dormant Phase

The virus program is idle during this stage. The virus program has managed to access the target user's computer or software, but during this stage, the virus does not take any action. The virus will eventually be activated by the "trigger" which states which event will execute the virus, such as a date, the presence of another program or file, the capacity of the disk exceeding some limit or the user taking a certain action (e.g., double-clicking on a certain icon, opening an e-mail, etc.). Not all viruses have this stage.

Propagation Phase

The virus starts propagating, that is multiplying and replicating itself. The virus places a copy of itself into other programs or into certain system areas on the disk. The copy may not be identical to the propagating version; viruses often "morph" or change to evade detection by IT professionals and anti-virus software. Each infected program will now contain a clone of the virus, which will itself enter a propagation phase.

Triggering Phase

A dormant virus moves into this phase when it is activated, and will now perform the function for which it was intended. The triggering phase can be caused by a variety of system events, including a count of the number of times that this copy of the virus has made copies of itself.

Execution Phase

This is the actual work of the virus, where the "payload" will be released. It can be destructive such as deleting files on disk, crashing the system, or corrupting files or relatively harmless such as popping up humorous or political messages on screen.

Infection Targets and Replication Techniques

Computer viruses infect a variety of different subsystems on their host computers and software. One manner of classifying viruses is to analyze whether they reside in binary executables (such as .EXE or .COM files), data files (such as Microsoft Word documents or PDF files), or in the boot sector of the host's hard drive (or some combination of all of these).

Resident vs. Non-resident Viruses

A *memory-resident virus* (or simply "resident virus") installs itself as part of the operating system when executed, after which it remains in RAM from the time the computer is booted up to when it is shut down. Resident viruses overwrite interrupt handling code or other functions, and when the operating system attempts to access the target file or disk sector, the virus code intercepts the request and redirects the control flow to the replication module, infecting the target. In contrast, a *non-memory-resident virus* (or "non-resident virus"), when executed, scans the disk for targets, infects them, and then exits (i.e. it does not remain in memory after it is done executing).

Macro Viruses

Many common applications, such as Microsoft Outlook and Microsoft Word, allow macro programs to be embedded in documents or emails, so that the programs may be run automatically when the document is opened. A *macro virus* (or "document virus") is a virus that is written in a macro language, and embedded into these documents so that when users open the file, the virus code is executed, and can infect the user's computer. This is one of the reasons that it is dangerous to open unexpected or suspicious attachments in e-mails. While not opening attachments in e-mails from unknown persons or organizations can help to reduce the likelihood of contracting a virus, in some cases, the virus is designed so that the e-mail appears to be from a reputable organization (e.g., a major bank or credit card company).

Boot Sector Viruses

Boot sector viruses specifically target the boot sector and/or the Master Boot Record (MBR) of the host's hard disk drive, solid-state drive, or removable storage media (flash drives, floppy disks, etc.).

Email Virus

Email viruses are viruses that intentionally, rather than accidentally, uses the email system to spread. While virus infected files may be accidentally sent as email attachments, email viruses are aware of email system functions. They generally target a specific type of email system (Microsoft's Outlook is the most commonly used), harvest email addresses from various sources, and may append copies of themselves to all email sent, or may generate email messages containing copies of themselves as attachments.

Stealth Techniques

In order to avoid detection by users, some viruses employ different kinds of deception. Some old viruses, especially on the DOS platform, make sure that the "last modified" date of a host file stays the same when the file is infected by the virus. This approach does not fool antivirus software, however, especially those which maintain and date cyclic redundancy checks on file changes. Some viruses can infect files without increasing their sizes or damaging the files. They accomplish this by overwriting unused areas of executable files. These are called *cavity viruses*. For example, the CIH virus, or Chernobyl Virus, infects Portable Executable files. Because those files have many empty gaps, the virus, which was 1 KB in length, did not add to the size of the file. Some viruses try to avoid detection by killing the tasks associated with antivirus software before it can detect them (for example, Conficker). In the 2010s, as computers and operating systems grow larger and more complex, old hiding techniques need to be updated or replaced. Defending a computer against viruses may demand that a file system migrate towards detailed and explicit permission for every kind of file access.

Read Request Intercepts

While some kinds of antivirus software employ various techniques to counter stealth mechanisms, once the infection occurs any recourse to "clean" the system is unreliable. In Microsoft Windows operating systems, the NTFS file system is proprietary. This leaves antivirus software little alternative but to send a "read" request to Windows files that handle such requests. Some viruses trick antivirus software by intercepting its requests to the operating system. A virus can hide by intercepting the request to read the infected file, handling the request itself, and returning an un-infected version of the file to the antivirus software. The interception can occur by code injection of the actual operating system files that would handle the read request. Thus, an antivirus software attempting to detect the virus will either not be given permission to read the infected file, or, the "read" request will be served with the uninfected version of the same file.

The only reliable method to avoid "stealth" viruses is to "reboot" from a medium that is known to be "clear". Security software can then be used to check the dormant operating system files. Most security software relies on virus signatures, or they employ heuristics. Security software may also use a database of file "hashes" for Windows OS files, so the security software can identify altered files, and request Windows installation media to replace them with authentic versions. In older versions of Windows, file cryptographic hash functions of Windows OS files stored in Windows—to allow file integrity/authenticity to be checked—could be overwritten so that the System File Check-er would report that altered system files are authentic, so using file hashes to scan for altered files would not always guarantee finding an infection.

Self-modification

Most modern antivirus programs try to find virus-patterns inside ordinary programs by scanning them for so-called *virus signatures*. Unfortunately, the term is misleading, in that viruses do not possess unique signatures in the way that human beings do. Such a virus "signature" is merely a sequence of bytes that an antivirus program looks for because it is known to be part of the vi-rus. A better term would be "search strings". Different antivirus programs will employ different search strings, and indeed different search methods, when identifying viruses. If a virus scanner finds such a pattern in a file, it will perform other checks to make sure that it has found the virus, and not merely a coincidental sequence in an innocent file, before it notifies the user that the file is infected. The user can then delete, or (in some cases) "clean" or "heal" the infected file. Some viruses employ techniques that make detection by means of signatures difficult but probably not impossible. These viruses modify their code on each infection. That is, each infected file contains a different variant of the virus.

Encrypted Viruses

One method of evading signature detection is to use simple encryption to encipher (encode) the body of the virus, leaving only the encryption module and a static cryptographic key in cleartext which does not change from one infection to the next. In this case, the virus consists of a small decrypting module and an encrypted copy of the virus code. If the virus is encrypted with a dif-ferent key for each infected file, the only part of the virus that remains constant is the decrypting module, which would (for example) be appended to the end. In this case, a virus scanner cannot directly detect the virus using signatures, but it can still detect the decrypting module, which still makes indirect detection of the virus possible. Since these would be symmetric keys, stored on the infected host, it is entirely possible to decrypt the final virus, but this is probably not re-quired, since self-modifying code is such a rarity that it may be reason for virus scanners to at least "flag" the file as suspicious. An old but compact way will be the use of arithmetic operation like addition or subtraction and the use of logical conditions such as XORing, where each byte in a virus is with a constant, so that the exclusive-or operation had only to be repeated for decryption. It is suspicious for a code to modify itself, so the code to do the encryption/decryption may be part of the signature in many virus definitions. A simpler older approach did not use a key, where the encryption consisted only of operations with no parameters, like incrementing and decrementing, bitwise rotation, arithmetic negation, and logical NOT. Some viruses, called polymorphic viruses, will employ a means of encryption inside an executable in which the virus is encrypted under certain events, such as the virus scanner being disabled for updates or the computer being rebooted. This is called cryptovirology. At said times, the executable will decrypt the virus and execute its hidden runtimes, infecting the computer and sometimes disabling the antivirus software.

Polymorphic Code

Polymorphic code was the first technique that posed a serious threat to virus scanners. Just like regular encrypted viruses, a polymorphic virus infects files with an encrypted copy of itself, which is decoded by a decryption module. In the case of polymorphic viruses, however, this decryption module is also modified on each infection. A well-written polymorphic virus therefore has no parts which remain identical between infections, making it very difficult to detect directly using "signatures". Antivirus software can detect it by decrypting the viruses using an emulator, or by statistical pattern analysis of the encrypted virus body. To enable polymorphic code, the virus has to have a polymorphic engine (also called "mutating engine" or "mutation engine") somewhere in its encrypted body.

Some viruses employ polymorphic code in a way that constrains the mutation rate of the virus significantly. For example, a virus can be programmed to mutate only slightly over time, or it can be programmed to refrain from mutating when it infects a file on a computer that already contains copies of the virus. The advantage of using such slow polymorphic code is that it makes it more difficult for antivirus professionals and investigators to obtain representative samples of the virus, because "bait" files that are infected in one run will typically contain identical or similar samples of the virus. This will make it more likely that the detection by the virus scanner will be unreliable, and that some instances of the virus may be able to avoid detection.

Metamorphic Code

To avoid being detected by emulation, some viruses rewrite themselves completely each time they are to infect new executables. Viruses that utilize this technique are said to be in metamorphic code. To enable metamorphism, a "metamorphic engine" is needed. A metamorphic virus is usually very large and complex. For example, W32/Simile consisted of over 14,000 lines of assembly language code, 90% of which is part of the metamorphic engine.

Vulnerabilities and Infection Vectors

Software Bugs

As software is often designed with security features to prevent unauthorized use of system resources, many viruses must exploit and manipulate security bugs, which are security defects in a system or application software, to spread themselves and infect other computers. Software development strategies that produce large numbers of "bugs" will generally also produce potential exploitable "holes" or "entrances" for the virus.

Social Engineering and Poor Security Practices

In order to replicate itself, a virus must be permitted to execute code and write to memory. For this reason, many viruses attach themselves to executable files that may be part of legitimate programs. If a user attempts to launch an infected program, the virus' code may be executed simultaneously. In operating systems that use file extensions to determine program associations (such as Microsoft Windows), the extensions may be hidden from the user by default. This makes it possible to create a file that is of a different type than it appears to the user. For example, an executable may be created and named "picture.png.exe", in which the user sees only "picture.png" and therefore assumes that this file is a digital image and most likely is safe, yet when opened, it runs the executable on the client machine.

Vulnerability of Different Operating Systems

The vast majority of viruses target systems running Microsoft Windows. This is due to Microsoft's large market share of desktop computer users. The diversity of software systems on a network limits the destructive potential of viruses and malware. Open-source operating systems such as Linux allow users to choose from a variety of desktop environments, packaging tools, etc., which means that malicious code targeting any of these systems will only affect a subset of all users. Many Windows users are running the same set of applications, enabling viruses to rapidly spread among Microsoft Windows systems by targeting the same exploits on large numbers of hosts.

While Linux and Unix in general have always natively prevented normal users from making changes to the operating system environment without permission, Windows users are generally not prevented from making these changes, meaning that viruses can easily gain control of the entire system on Windows hosts. This difference has continued partly due to the widespread use of administrator accounts in contemporary versions like Windows XP. In 1997, researchers created and released a virus for Linux—known as "Bliss". Bliss, however, requires that the user run it explicitly, and it can only infect programs that the user has the access to modify. Unlike Windows users, most Unix users do not log in as an administrator, or "root user", except to install or configure software; as a result, even if a user ran the virus, it could not harm their operating system. The Bliss virus never became widespread, and remains chiefly a research curiosity. Its creator later posted the source code to Usenet, allowing researchers to see how it worked.

Counter Measures

Antivirus Software

Many users install antivirus software that can detect and eliminate known viruses when the computer attempts to download or run the executable file (which may be distributed as an email attachment, or on USB flash drives, for example). Some antivirus software blocks known malicious websites that attempt to install malware. Antivirus software does not change the underlying capability of hosts to transmit viruses. Users must update their software regularly to patch security vulnerabilities ("holes"). Antivirus software also needs to be regularly updated in order to recognize the latest threats. This is because malicious hackers and other individuals are always creating new viruses. The German AV-TEST Institute publishes evaluations of antivirus software for Windows and Android.

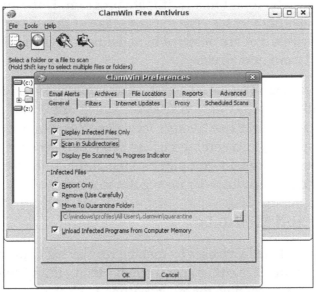

Screenshot of the open source ClamWin antivirus software
running in Wine on Ubuntu Linux.

Examples of Microsoft Windows anti virus and anti-malware software include the optional Microsoft Security Essentials (for Windows XP, Vista and Windows 7) for real-time protection, the Windows Malicious Software Removal Tool (now included with Windows (Security) Updates on "Patch Tuesday", the second Tuesday of each month), and Windows Defender (an optional download in the case of Windows XP). Additionally, several capable antivirus software programs are available for free download from the Internet (usually restricted to non-commercial use). Some such free programs are almost as good as commercial competitors. Common security vulnerabilities are assigned CVE IDs and listed in the US National Vulnerability Database. Secunia PSI is an example of software, free for personal use, that will check a PC for vulnerable out-of-date software, and attempt to update it. Ransomware and phishing scam alerts appear as press releases on the Internet Crime Complaint Center noticeboard. Ransomware is a virus that posts a message on the user's screen saying that the screen or system will remain locked or unusable until a ransom payment is made. Phishing is a deception in which the malicious individual pretends to be a friend, computer security expert, or other benevolent individual, with the goal of convincing the targeted individual to reveal passwords or other personal information.

Other commonly used preventative measures include timely operating system updates, software updates, careful Internet browsing (avoiding shady websites), and installation of only trusted software. Certain browsers flag sites that have been reported to Google and that have been confirmed as hosting malware by Google.

There are two common methods that an antivirus software application uses to detect viruses, as described in the antivirus software article. The first, and by far the most common method of virus detection is using a list of virus signature definitions. This works by examining the content of the computer's memory (its Random Access Memory (RAM), and boot sectors) and the files stored on fixed or removable drives (hard drives, floppy drives, or USB flash drives), and comparing those files against a database of known virus "signatures". Virus signatures are just strings of code that are used to identify individual viruses; for each virus, the antivirus designer tries to choose a unique signature string that will not be found in a legitimate program. Different antivirus programs use different "signatures" to identify viruses. The disadvantage of this detection method is that users are only protected from viruses that are detected by signatures in their most recent virus definition update, and not protected from new viruses.

A second method to find viruses is to use a heuristic algorithm based on common virus behaviors. This method has the ability to detect new viruses for which antivirus security firms have yet to define a "signature", but it also gives rise to more false positives than using signatures. False positives can be disruptive, especially in a commercial environment, because it may lead to a company instructing staff not to use the company computer system until IT services has checked the system for viruses. This can slow down productivity for regular workers.

Recovery Strategies and Methods

One may reduce the damage done by viruses by making regular backups of data (and the operating systems) on different media, that are either kept unconnected to the system (most of the time, as in a hard drive), read-only or not accessible for other reasons, such as using different file systems. This way, if data is lost through a virus, one can start again using the backup (which will hopefully be recent). If a backup session on optical media like CD and DVD is closed, it becomes read-only and can no longer be affected by a virus (so long as a virus or infected file was not copied onto the CD/DVD). Likewise, an operating system on a bootable CD can be used to start the computer if the installed operating systems become unusable. Backups on removable media must be carefully inspected before restoration. The Gammima virus, for example, propagates via removable flash drives.

Virus Removal

Many websites run by antivirus software companies provide free online virus scanning, with limited "cleaning" facilities (after all, the purpose of the websites is to sell antivirus products and services). Some websites—like Google subsidiary VirusTotal.com—allow users to upload one or more suspicious files to be scanned and checked by one or more antivirus programs in one operation. Additionally, several capable antivirus software programs are available for free download from the Internet (usually restricted to non-commercial use). Microsoft offers an optional free antivirus utility called Microsoft Security Essentials, a Windows Malicious Software Removal Tool that is updated as part of the regular Windows update regime, and an older optional anti-malware (malware removal) tool Windows Defender that has been upgraded to an antivirus product in Windows 8.

Some viruses disable System Restore and other important Windows tools such as Task Manager and CMD. An example of a virus that does this is CiaDoor. Many such viruses can be removed by rebooting the computer, entering Windows "safe mode" with networking, and then using system tools or Microsoft Safety Scanner. System Restore on Windows Me, Windows XP, Windows Vista and Windows 7 can restore the registry and critical system files to a previous checkpoint. Often a virus will cause a system to "hang" or "freeze", and a subsequent hard reboot will render a system restore point from the same day corrupted. Restore points from previous days should work, provided the virus is not designed to corrupt the restore files and does not exist in previous restore points.

Operating System Reinstallation

Microsoft's System File Checker (improved in Windows 7 and later) can be used to check for, and repair, corrupted system files. Restoring an earlier "clean" (virus-free) copy of the entire partition from a cloned disk, a disk image, or a backup copy is one solution—restoring an earlier backup disk "image" is relatively simple to do, usually removes any malware, and may be faster than "disinfecting" the computer—or reinstalling and reconfiguring the operating system and programs from scratch, as described below, then restoring user preferences. Reinstalling the operating system is another approach to virus removal. It may be possible to recover copies of essential user data by booting from a live CD, or connecting the hard drive to another computer and booting from the second computer's operating system, taking great care not to infect that computer by executing any infected programs on the original drive. The original hard drive can then be reformatted and the OS and all programs installed from original media. Once the system has been restored, precautions must be taken to avoid reinfection from any restored executable files.

Viruses and the Internet

Before computer networks became widespread, most viruses spread on removable media, particularly floppy disks. In the early days of the personal computer, many users regularly exchanged information and programs on floppies. Some viruses spread by infecting programs stored on these disks, while others installed themselves into the disk boot sector, ensuring that they would be run when the user booted the computer from the disk, usually inadvertently. Personal computers of the era would attempt to boot first from a floppy if one had been left in the drive. Until floppy disks fell out of use, this was the most successful infection strategy and boot sector viruses were the most common in the "wild" for many years. Traditional computer viruses emerged in the 1980s, driven by the spread of personal computers and the resultant increase in bulletin board system (BBS), modem use, and software sharing. Bulletin board–driven software sharing contributed directly to the spread of Trojan horse programs, and viruses were written to infect popularly traded software. Shareware and bootleg software were equally common vectors for viruses on BBSs. Viruses can increase their chances of spreading to other computers by infecting files on a network file system or a file system that is accessed by other computers.

Macro viruses have become common since the mid-1990s. Most of these viruses are written in the scripting languages for Microsoft programs such as Microsoft Word and Microsoft Excel and spread throughout Microsoft Office by infecting documents and spreadsheets. Since Word and Excel were also available for Mac OS, most could also spread to Macintosh computers. Although most of these viruses did not have the ability to send infected email messages, those viruses which did take advantage of the Microsoft Outlook Component Object Model (COM) interface. Some old versions of Microsoft Word allow macros to replicate themselves with additional blank lines. If two macro viruses simultaneously infect a document, the combination of the two, if also self-replicating, can appear as a "mating" of the two and would likely be detected as a virus unique from the "parents".

A virus may also send a web address link as an instant message to all the contacts (e.g., friends and colleagues' e-mail addresses) stored on an infected machine. If the recipient, thinking the link is from a friend (a trusted source) follows the link to the website, the virus hosted at the site may be able to infect this new computer and continue propagating. Viruses that spread using cross-site scripting were first reported in 2002, and were academically demonstrated in 2005. There have been multiple instances of the cross-site scripting viruses in the "wild", exploiting websites such as MySpace (with the Samy worm) and Yahoo!.

Computer Worm

```
0 00 00-6D 73 62 6C              msbl
0 6A 75-73 74 20 77  ast.exe I just w
9 20 4C-4F 56 45 20  ant to say LOVE
0 62 69-6C 6C 79 20  YOU SAN!! billy
0 64 6F-20 79 6F 75  gates why do you
3 20 70-6F 73 73 69   make this possi
0 20 6D-61 6B 69 6E  ble ? Stop makin
E 64 20-66 69 78 20  g money and fix
7 61 72-65 21 21 00  your software!!
0 00 00-7F 00 00 00
0 00 00-01 00 01 00
0 00 00-00 00 00 46
C C9 11-9F E8 08 00
0 00 03-10 00 00 00
3 00 00-01 00 04 00
```

Hex dump of the Blaster worm, showing a message left for Microsoft CEO Bill Gates by the worm programmer.

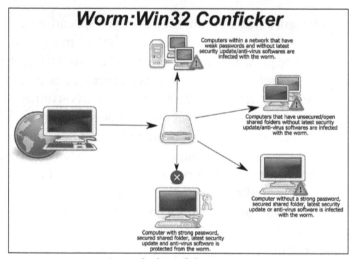

Spread of Conficker worm.

A computer worm is a standalone malware computer program that replicates itself in order to spread to other computers. Often, it uses a computer network to spread itself, relying on security failures on the target computer to access it. Worms almost always cause at least some harm to the network, even if only by consuming bandwidth, whereas viruses almost always corrupt or modify files on a targeted computer.

Many worms are designed only to spread, and do not attempt to change the systems they pass through. However, as the Morris worm and Mydoom showed, even these "payload-free" worms can cause major disruption by increasing network traffic and other unintended effects.

Harm

Any code designed to do more than spread the worm is typically referred to as the "payload". Typical malicious payloads might delete files on a host system (e.g., the ExploreZip worm), encrypt files in a ransomware attack, or exfiltrate data such as confidential documents or passwords.

Probably the most common payload for worms is to install a backdoor. This allows the computer to be remotely controlled by the worm author as a "zombie". Networks of such machines are often referred to as botnets and are very commonly used for a range of malicious purposes, including sending spam or performing DoS attacks.

Countermeasures

Worms spread by exploiting vulnerabilities in operating systems. Vendors with security problems supply regular security updates, and if these are installed to a machine then the majority of worms are unable to spread to it. If a vulnerability is disclosed before the security patch released by the vendor, a zero-day attack is possible.

Users need to be wary of opening unexpected email, and should not run attached files or programs, or visit web sites that are linked to such emails. However, as with the ILOVEYOU worm, and with the increased growth and efficiency of phishing attacks, it remains possible to trick the end-user into running malicious code.

Anti-virus and anti-spyware software are helpful, but must be kept up-to-date with new pattern files at least every few days. The use of a firewall is also recommended.

In the April–June 2008 issue of IEEE Transactions on Dependable and Secure Computing, computer scientists described a new and potentially effective way to combat internet worms. The researchers discovered how to contain worms that scanned the Internet randomly, looking for vulnerable hosts to infect. They found that the key was to use software to monitor the number of scans that machines on a network send out. When a machine started to send out too many scans, it was a sign that it has been infected, which allowed administrators to take it off line and check it for malware. In addition, machine learning techniques can be used to detect new worms, by analyzing the behavior of the suspected computer.

Users can minimize the threat posed by worms by keeping their computers' operating system and other software up to date, avoiding opening unrecognized or unexpected emails and running firewall and antivirus software.

Mitigation techniques include:

- ACLs in routers and switches,

- Packet-filters,

- TCP Wrapper/ACL enabled network service daemons,

- Nullroute.

Spyware

Spyware is software that aims to gather information about a person or organization, sometimes without their knowledge, that may send such information to another entity without the consumer's consent, that asserts control over a device without the consumer's knowledge, or it may send such information to another entity with the consumer's consent, through cookies.

Spyware" is mostly classified into four types: adware, system monitors, tracking cookies, and trojans; examples of other notorious types include digital rights management capabilities that "phone home", keyloggers, rootkits, and web beacons.

Spyware is mostly used for the stealing information and storing Internet users' movements on the Web and serving up pop-up ads to Internet users. Whenever spyware is used for malicious purposes, its presence is typically hidden from the user and can be difficult to detect. Some spyware, such as keyloggers, may be installed by the owner of a shared, corporate, or public computer intentionally in order to monitor users.

While the term *spyware* suggests software that monitors a user's computing, the functions of spyware can extend beyond simple monitoring. Spyware can collect almost any type of data, including personal information like internet surfing habits, user logins, and bank or credit account information. Spyware can also interfere with a user's control of a computer by installing additional software or redirecting web browsers. Some spyware can change computer settings, which can result in slow Internet connection speeds, un-authorized changes in browser settings, or changes to software settings.

Sometimes, spyware is included along with genuine software, and may come from a malicious website or may have been added to the intentional functionality of genuine software. In response to the emergence of spyware, a small industry has sprung up dealing in anti-spyware software. Running anti-spyware software has become a widely recognized element of computer security practices, especially for computers running Microsoft Windows. A number of jurisdictions have passed anti-spyware laws, which usually target any software that is surreptitiously installed to control a user's computer.

In German-speaking countries, spyware used or made by the government is called *govware* by computer experts Govware is typically a trojan horse software used to intercept communications from the target computer. Some countries, like Switzerland and Germany, have a legal framework governing the use of such software. In the US, the term "policeware" has been used for similar purposes.

Use of the term "spyware" has eventually declined as the practice of tracking users has been pushed ever further into the mainstream by major websites and data mining companies; these generally break no known laws and compel users to be tracked, not by fraudulent practices *per se*, but by the default settings created for users and the language of terms-of-service agreements. In one documented example, on CBS/CNet News reported, on March 7, 2011, on a *Wall Street Journal* analysis revealing the practice of Facebook and other websites of tracking users' browsing activity, linked to their identity, far beyond users' visits and activity within the Facebook site itself. The report stated: "Here's how it works. You go to Facebook, you log in, you spend some time there, and then you move on without logging out. Let's say the next site you go to is *New York Times*. Those buttons, without you clicking on them, have just reported back to Facebook and Twitter that you went there and also your identity within those accounts. Let's say you moved on to something like a site about depression. This one also has a tweet button, a Google widget, and those, too, can report back who you are and that you went there." The *WSJ* analysis was researched by Brian Kennish, founder of Disconnect, Inc.

Routes of Infection

Spyware does not necessarily spread in the same way as a virus or worm because infected systems generally do not attempt to transmit or copy the software to other computers. Instead, spyware installs itself on a system by deceiving the user or by exploiting software vulnerabilities.

Most spyware is installed without knowledge, or by using deceptive tactics. Spyware may try to deceive users by bundling itself with desirable software. Other common tactics are using a Trojan horse, spy gadgets that look like normal devices but turn out to be something else, such as a USB Keylogger. These devices actually are connected to the device as memory units but are capable of recording each stroke made on the keyboard. Some spyware authors infect a system through security holes in the Web browser or in other software. When the user navigates to a Web page controlled by the spyware author, the page contains code which attacks the browser and forces the download and installation of spyware.

The installation of spyware frequently involves Internet Explorer. Its popularity and history of security issues have made it a frequent target. Its deep integration with the Windows environment make it susceptible to attack into the Windows operating system. Internet Explorer also serves as a point of attachment for spyware in the form of Browser Helper Objects, which modify the browser's behavior.

Effects and Behaviors

A spyware rarely operates alone on a computer; an affected machine usually has multiple infections. Users frequently notice unwanted behavior and degradation of system performance. A spyware infestation can create significant unwanted CPU activity, disk usage, and network traffic. Stability issues, such as applications freezing, failure to boot, and system-wide crashes are also common. Spyware, which interferes with networking software commonly causes difficulty connecting to the Internet.

In some infections, the spyware is not even evident. Users assume in those situations that the performance issues relate to faulty hardware, Windows installation problems, or another malware infection. Some owners of badly infected systems resort to contacting technical support experts, or even buying a new computer because the existing system "has become too slow". Badly infected systems may require a clean reinstallation of all their software in order to return to full functionality.

Moreover, some types of spyware disable software firewalls and antivirus software, and/or reduce browser security settings, which opens the system to further opportunistic infections. Some spyware disables or even removes competing spyware programs, on the grounds that more spyware-related annoyances increase the likelihood that users will take action to remove the programs.

Keyloggers are sometimes part of malware packages downloaded onto computers without the owners' knowledge. Some keylogger software is freely available on the internet, while others are commercial or private applications. Most keyloggers allow not only keyboard keystrokes to be captured, they also are often capable of collecting screen captures from the computer.

A typical Windows user has administrative privileges, mostly for convenience. Because of this, any program the user runs has unrestricted access to the system. As with other operating systems, Windows users are able to follow the principle of least privilege and use non-administrator accounts. Alternatively, they can reduce the privileges of specific vulnerable Internet-facing processes, such as Internet Explorer.

Since Windows Vista is, by default, a computer administrator that runs everything under limited user privileges, when a program requires administrative privileges, a User Account Control pop-up will prompt the user to allow or deny the action. This improves on the design used by previous versions of Windows.

Remedies and Prevention

As the spyware threat has evolved, a number of techniques have emerged to counteract it. These include programs designed to remove or block spyware, as well as various user practices which reduce the chance of getting spyware on a system.

Nonetheless, spyware remains a costly problem. When a large number of pieces of spyware have infected a Windows computer, the only remedy may involve backing up user data, and fully re-installing the operating system. For instance, some spyware cannot be completely removed by Symantec, Microsoft, PC Tools.

Anti-spyware Programs

Many programmers and some commercial firms have released products dedicated to remove or block spyware. Programs such as PC Tools' Spyware Doctor, Lavasoft's Ad-Aware SE and Patrick Kolla's Spybot - Search & Destroy rapidly gained popularity as tools to remove, and in some cases intercept, spyware programs. On December 16, 2004, Microsoft acquired the GIANT AntiSpyware software, rebranding it as Windows AntiSpyware beta and releasing it as a free download for Genuine Windows XP and Windows 2003 users. (In 2006 it was renamed Windows Defender).

Major anti-virus firms such as Symantec, PC Tools, McAfee and Sophos have also added anti-spyware features to their existing anti-virus products. Early on, anti-virus firms expressed reluctance to add anti-spyware functions, citing lawsuits brought by spyware authors against the authors of web sites and programs which described their products as "spyware". However, recent versions of these major firms home and business anti-virus products do include anti-spyware functions, albeit treated differently from viruses. Symantec Anti-Virus, for instance, categorizes spyware programs as "extended threats" and now offers real-time protection against these threats.

How Anti-spyware Software Works?

Anti-spyware programs can combat spyware in two ways:

1. They can provide real-time protection in a manner similar to that of anti-virus protection: they scan all incoming network data for spyware and blocks any threats it detects.

2. Anti-spyware software programs can be used solely for detection and removal of spyware software that has already been installed into the computer. This kind of anti-spyware can often be set to scan on a regular schedule.

Such programs inspect the contents of the Windows registry, operating system files, and installed programs, and remove files and entries which match a list of known spyware. Real-time protection from spyware works identically to real-time anti-virus protection: the software scans disk files at download time, and blocks the activity of components known to represent spyware. In some cases, it may also intercept attempts to install start-up items or to modify browser settings. Earlier versions of anti-spyware programs focused chiefly on detection and removal. Javacool Software's SpywareBlaster, one of the first to offer real-time protection, blocked the installation of ActiveX-based spyware.

Like most anti-virus software, many anti-spyware/adware tools require a frequently updated database of threats. As new spyware programs are released, anti-spyware developers discover and evaluate them, adding to the list of known spyware, which allows the software to detect and remove new spyware. As a result, anti-spyware software is of limited usefulness without regular updates. Updates may be installed automatically or manually.

A popular generic spyware removal tool used by those that requires a certain degree of expertise is HijackThis, which scans certain areas of the Windows OS where spyware often resides and presents a list with items to delete manually. As most of the items are legitimate windows files/registry entries it is advised for those who are less knowledgeable on this subject to post a HijackThis log on the numerous antispyware sites and let the experts decide what to delete.

If a spyware program is not blocked and manages to get itself installed, it may resist attempts to terminate or uninstall it. Some programs work in pairs: when an anti-spyware scanner (or the user) terminates one running process, the other one respawns the killed program. Likewise, some spyware will detect attempts to remove registry keys and immediately add them again. Usually, booting the infected computer in safe mode allows an anti-spyware program a better chance of removing persistent spyware. Killing the process tree may also work.

Security Practices

To detect spyware, computer users have found several practices useful in addition to installing anti-spyware programs. Many users have installed a web browser other than Internet Explorer, such as Mozilla Firefox or Google Chrome. Though no browser is completely safe, Internet Explorer was once at a greater risk for spyware infection due to its large user base as well as vulnerabilities such as ActiveX but these three major browsers are now close to equivalent when it comes to security.

Some ISPs—particularly colleges and universities—have taken a different approach to blocking spyware: they use their network firewalls and web proxies to block access to Web sites known to install spyware. On March 31, 2005, Cornell University's Information Technology department released a report detailing the behavior of one particular piece of proxy-based spyware, *Marketscore*, and the steps the university took to intercept it. Many other educational institutions have taken similar steps.

Individual users can also install firewalls from a variety of companies. These monitor the flow of information going to and from a networked computer and provide protection against spyware and malware. Some users install a large hosts file which prevents the user's computer from connecting to known spyware-related web addresses. Spyware may get installed via certain shareware programs offered for download. Downloading programs only from reputable sources can provide some protection from this source of attack.

Individual users can use cellphone / computer with physical (electric) switch, or isolated electronic switch that disconnects microphone, camera without bypass and keep it in disconnected position where not in use, that limits information that spyware can collect.

Applications

"Stealware" and Affiliate Fraud

A few spyware vendors, notably 180 Solutions, have written what the *New York Times* has dubbed "stealware", and what spyware researcher Ben Edelman terms *affiliate fraud*, a form of click fraud. Stealware diverts the payment of affiliate marketing revenues from the legitimate affiliate to the spyware vendor.

Spyware which attacks affiliate networks places the spyware operator's affiliate tag on the user's activity – replacing any other tag, if there is one. The spyware operator is the only party that gains from this. The user has their choices thwarted, a legitimate affiliate loses revenue, networks' reputations are injured, and vendors are harmed by having to pay out affiliate revenues to an "affiliate" who is not party to a contract. Affiliate fraud is a violation of the terms of service of most affiliate marketing networks. As a result, spyware operators such as 180 Solutions have been terminated from affiliate networks including LinkShare and ShareSale. Mobile devices can also be vulnerable to chargeware, which manipulates users into illegitimate mobile charges.

Identity Theft and Fraud

In one case, spyware has been closely associated with identity theft. In August 2005, researchers from security software firm Sunbelt Software suspected the creators of the common CoolWebSearch spyware had used it to transmit "chat sessions, user names, passwords, bank information, etc."; however it turned out that "it actually (was) its own sophisticated criminal little trojan that's independent of CWS." This case is currently under investigation by the FBI.

The Federal Trade Commission estimates that 27.3 million Americans have been victims of identity theft, and that financial losses from identity theft totaled nearly $48 billion for businesses and financial institutions and at least $5 billion in out-of-pocket expenses for individuals.

Digital Rights Management

Some copy-protection technologies have borrowed from spyware. In 2005, Sony BMG Music Entertainment was found to be using rootkits in its XCP digital rights management technology Like spyware, not only was it difficult to detect and uninstall, it was so poorly written that most efforts to remove it could have rendered computers unable to function. Texas Attorney General Greg Abbott filed suit, and three separate class-action suits were filed. Sony BMG later provided a workaround on its website to help users remove it.

Beginning on April 25, 2006, Microsoft's Windows Genuine Advantage Notifications application was installed on most Windows PCs as a "critical security update". While the main purpose of this deliberately uninstallable application is to ensure the copy of Windows on the machine was lawfully purchased and installed, it also installs software that has been accused of "phoning home" on a daily basis, like spyware. It can be removed with the RemoveWGA tool.

Personal Relationships

Spyware has been used to monitor electronic activities of partners in intimate relationships. At least one software package, Loverspy, was specifically marketed for this purpose. Depending on local laws regarding communal/marital property, observing a partner's online activity without their consent may be illegal; the author of Loverspy and several users of the product were indicted in California in 2005 on charges of wiretapping and various computer crimes.

Browser Cookies

Anti-spyware programs often report Web advertisers' HTTP cookies, the small text files that track browsing activity, as spyware. While they are not always inherently malicious, many users object to third parties using space on their personal computers for their business purposes, and many anti-spyware programs offer to remove them.

Examples:

These common spyware programs illustrate the diversity of behaviors found in these attacks. Note that as with computer viruses, researchers give names to spyware programs which may not be used by their creators. Programs may be grouped into "families" based not on shared program code, but on common behaviors, or by "following the money" of apparent financial or business connections. For instance, a number of the spyware programs distributed by Claria are collectively known as "Gator". Likewise, programs that are frequently installed together may be described as parts of the same spyware package, even if they function separately.

- CoolWebSearch, a group of programs, takes advantage of Internet Explorer vulnerabilities. The package directs traffic to advertisements on Web sites including *coolwebsearch.com*. It displays pop-up ads, rewrites search engine results, and alters the infected computer's hosts file to direct DNS lookups to these sites.

- FinFisher, sometimes called FinSpy is a high-end surveillance suite sold to law enforcement and intelligence agencies. Support services such as training and technology updates are part of the package.

- GO Keyboard virtual Android keyboard apps (GO Keyboard - Emoji keyboard and GO Keyboard - Emoticon keyboard) transmit personal information to its remote servers without explicit users' consent. This information includes user's Google account email, language, IMSI, location, network type, Android version and build, and device's model and screen size. The apps also download and execute a code from a remote server, breaching the Malicious Behavior section of the Google Play privacy policies. Some of these plugins are detected as Adware or PUP by many Anti-Virus engines, while the developer, a Chinese company GOMO Dev Team, claims in the apps' description that they will never collect personal data including credit card information. The apps with about 2 million users in total were caught spying in September 2017 by security researchers from AdGuard who then reported their findings to Google.

- HuntBar, aka WinTools or Adware.Websearch, was installed by an ActiveX drive-by download at affiliate Web sites, or by advertisements displayed by other spyware programs—an example of how spyware can install more spyware. These programs add toolbars to IE, track aggregate browsing behavior, redirect affiliate references, and display advertisements.

- Internet Optimizer, also known as DyFuCa, redirects Internet Explorer error pages to advertising. When users follow a broken link or enter an erroneous URL, they see a page of advertisements. However, because password-protected Web sites (HTTP Basic authentication) use the same mechanism as HTTP errors, Internet Optimizer makes it impossible for the user to access password-protected sites.

- Spyware such as Look2Me hides inside system-critical processes and start up even in safe mode. With no process to terminate they are harder to detect and remove, which is a combination of both spyware and a rootkit. Rootkit technology is also seeing increasing use, as newer spyware programs also have specific countermeasures against well known anti-malware products and may prevent them from running or being installed, or even uninstall them.

- Movieland, also known as Moviepass.tv and Popcorn.net, is a movie download service that has been the subject of thousands of complaints to the Federal Trade Commission (FTC), the Washington State Attorney General's Office, the Better Business Bureau, and other agencies. Consumers complained they were held hostage by a cycle of oversized pop-up windows demanding payment of at least $29.95, claiming that they had signed up for a three-day free trial but had not cancelled before the trial period was over, and were thus obligated to pay. The FTC filed a complaint, since settled, against Movieland and eleven other defendants charging them with having "engaged in a nationwide scheme to use deception and coercion to extract payments from consumers."

- Onavo Protect is used by Facebook to monetize usage habits within a privacy-focused environment, and was criticized because the app listing did not contain a prominent disclosure of Facebook's ownership. The app was removed from the Apple iOS App Store Apple deemed it a violation of guidelines barring apps from harvesting data from other apps on a user's device.

- Zango (formerly 180 Solutions) transmits detailed information to advertisers about the Web sites which users visit. It also alters HTTP requests for affiliate advertisements linked from a Web site, so that the advertisements make unearned profit for the 180 Solutions company. It opens pop-up ads that cover over the Web sites of competing companies (as seen in their [Zango End User License Agreement]).

- Zlob trojan, or just Zlob, downloads itself to a computer via an ActiveX codec and reports information back to Control Server. Some information can be the search-history, the Websites visited, and even keystrokes. More recently, Zlob has been known to hijack routers set to defaults.

- Zwangi redirects URLs typed into the browser's address bar to a search page at www.abc. com, and may also take screenshots without permission.

Programs Distributed with Spyware

- Kazaa,

- Morpheus,

- WeatherBug,

- WildTangent.

Programs Formerly Distributed with Spyware

- AOL Instant Messenger (AOL Instant Messenger still packages Viewpoint Media Player, and WildTangent),

- DivX,

- FlashGet,

- magicJack.

Rogue Anti-spyware Programs

Malicious programmers have released a large number of rogue (fake) anti-spyware programs, and widely distributed Web banner ads can warn users that their computers have been infected with spyware, directing them to purchase programs which do not actually remove spyware—or else, may add more spyware of their own.

The recent proliferation of fake or spoofed antivirus products that bill themselves as antispyware can be troublesome. Users may receive popups prompting them to install them to protect their computer, when it will in fact add spyware. This software is called rogue software. It is recommended that users do not install any freeware claiming to be anti-spyware unless it is verified to be legitimate. Some known offenders include:

- AntiVirus 360,

- Antivirus 2009,

- AntiVirus Gold,

- ContraVirus,

- MacSweeper,

- Pest Trap,

- PSGuard,

- Spy Wiper,

- Spydawn,
- Spylocked,
- Spysheriff,
- SpyShredder,
- Spyware Quake,
- SpywareStrike,
- UltimateCleaner,
- WinAntiVirus Pro 2006,
- Windows Police Pro,
- WinFixer,
- WorldAntiSpy.

Fake antivirus products constitute 15 percent of all malware.

On January 26, 2006, Microsoft and the Washington state attorney general filed suit against Secure Computer for its Spyware Cleaner product.

Rootkit

A rootkit is a collection of computer software, typically malicious, designed to enable access to a computer or an area of its software that is not otherwise allowed (for example, to an unauthorized user) and often masks its existence or the existence of other software. The term *rootkit* is a concatenation of "root" (the traditional name of the privileged account on Unix-like operating systems) and the word "kit" (which refers to the software components that implement the tool). The term "rootkit" has negative connotations through its association with malware.

Rootkit installation can be automated, or an attacker can install it after having obtained root or Administrator access. Obtaining this access is a result of direct attack on a system, i.e. exploiting a known vulnerability (such as privilege escalation) or a password (obtained by cracking or social engineering tactics like "phishing"). Once installed, it becomes possible to hide the intrusion as well as to maintain privileged access. The key is the root or administrator access. Full control over a system means that existing software can be modified, including software that might otherwise be used to detect or circumvent it.

Rootkit detection is difficult because a rootkit may be able to subvert the software that is intended to find it. Detection methods include using an alternative and trusted operating system, behavioral-based methods, signature scanning, difference scanning, and memory dump analysis. Removal can be complicated or practically impossible, especially in cases where the rootkit resides in the kernel; reinstallation of the operating system may be the only available solution to the problem. When dealing with firmware rootkits, removal may require hardware replacement, or specialized equipment.

Uses

Modern rootkits do not elevate access, but rather are used to make another software payload undetectable by adding stealth capabilities. Most rootkits are classified as malware, because the payloads they are bundled with are malicious. For example, a payload might covertly steal user passwords, credit card information, computing resources, or conduct other unauthorized activities. A small number of rootkits may be considered utility applications by their users: for example, a rootkit might cloak a CD-ROM-emulation driver, allowing video game users to defeat anti-piracy measures that require insertion of the original installation media into a physical optical drive to verify that the software was legitimately purchased.

Rootkits and their payloads have many uses:

- Provide an attacker with full access via a backdoor, permitting unauthorized access to, for example, steal or falsify documents. One of the ways to carry this out is to subvert the login mechanism, such as the /bin/login program on Unix-like systems or GINA on Windows. The replacement appears to function normally, but also accepts a secret login combination that allows an attacker direct access to the system with administrative privileges, bypassing standard authentication and authorization mechanisms.

- Conceal other malware, notably password-stealing key loggers and computer viruses.

- Appropriate the compromised machine as a zombie computer for attacks on other computers. (The attack originates from the compromised system or network, instead of the attacker's system.) "Zombie" computers are typically members of large botnets that can launch denial-of-service attacks, distribute e-mail spam, conduct click fraud, etc.

- Enforcement of digital rights management (DRM).

In some instances, rootkits provide desired functionality, and may be installed intentionally on behalf of the computer user:

- Conceal cheating in online games from software like Warden.

- Detect attacks, for example, in a honeypot.

- Enhance emulation software and security software. Alcohol 120% and Daemon Tools are commercial examples of non-hostile rootkits used to defeat copy-protection mechanisms such as SafeDisc and SecuROM. Kaspersky antivirus software also uses techniques resembling rootkits to protect itself from malicious actions. It loads its own drivers to intercept system activity, and then prevents other processes from doing harm to itself. Its processes are not hidden, but cannot be terminated by standard methods.

- Anti-theft protection: Laptops may have BIOS-based rootkit software that will periodically report to a central authority, allowing the laptop to be monitored, disabled or wiped of information in the event that it is stolen.

- Bypassing Microsoft Product Activation.

Types

There are at least five types of rootkit, ranging from those at the lowest level in firmware (with the highest privileges), through to the least privileged user-based variants that operate in Ring 3. Hybrid combinations of these may occur spanning, for example, user mode and kernel mode.

User Mode

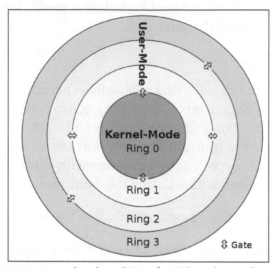

Computer security rings (Note that Ring 1 is not shown).

User-mode rootkits run in Ring 3, along with other applications as user, rather than low-level system processes. They have a number of possible installation vectors to intercept and modify the standard behavior of application programming interfaces (APIs). Some inject a dynamically linked library (such as a .DLL file on Windows, or a .dylib file on Mac OS X) into other processes, and are thereby able to execute inside any target process to spoof it; others with sufficient privileges simply overwrite the memory of a target application. Injection mechanisms include:

- Use of vendor-supplied application extensions. For example, Windows Explorer has public interfaces that allow third parties to extend its functionality.

- Interception of messages.

- Debuggers.

- Exploitation of security vulnerabilities.

- Function hooking or patching of commonly used APIs, for example, to hide a running process or file that resides on a filesystem.

  "Since user mode applications all run in their own memory space, the rootkit needs to perform this patching in the memory space of every running application. In addition, the rootkit needs to monitor the system for any new applications that execute and patch those programs' memory space before they fully execute".

  —Windows Rootkit Overview, Symantec

Kernel Mode

Kernel-mode rootkits run with the highest operating system privileges (Ring 0) by adding code or replacing portions of the core operating system, including both the kernel and associated device drivers. Most operating systems support kernel-mode device drivers, which execute with the same privileges as the operating system itself. As such, many kernel-mode rootkits are developed as device drivers or loadable modules, such as loadable kernel modules in Linux or device drivers in Microsoft Windows. This class of rootkit has unrestricted security access, but is more difficult to write. The complexity makes bugs common, and any bugs in code operating at the kernel level may seriously impact system stability, leading to discovery of the rootkit. One of the first widely known kernel rootkits was developed for Windows NT 4.0 and released in Phrack magazine in 1999 by Greg Hoglund. Kernel rootkits can be especially difficult to detect and remove because they operate at the same security level as the operating system itself, and are thus able to intercept or subvert the most trusted operating system operations. Any software, such as antivirus software, running on the compromised system is equally vulnerable. In this situation, no part of the system can be trusted.

A rootkit can modify data structures in the Windows kernel using a method known as *direct kernel object manipulation* (DKOM). This method can be used to hide processes. A kernel mode rootkit can also hook the System Service Descriptor Table (SSDT), or modify the gates between user mode and kernel mode, in order to cloak itself. Similarly for the Linux operating system, a rootkit can modify the *system call table* to subvert kernel functionality. It is common that a rootkit creates a hidden, encrypted filesystem in which it can hide other malware or original copies of files it has infected. Operating systems are evolving to counter the threat of kernel-mode rootkits. For example, 64-bit editions of Microsoft Windows now implement mandatory signing of all kernel-level drivers in order to make it more difficult for untrusted code to execute with the highest privileges in a system.

Bootkits

A kernel-mode rootkit variant called a bootkit can infect startup code like the Master Boot Record (MBR), Volume Boot Record (VBR), or boot sector, and in this way can be used to attack full disk encryption systems.

An example of such an attack on disk encryption is the "evil maid attack", in which an attacker installs a bootkit on an unattended computer. The envisioned scenario is a maid sneaking into the hotel room where the victims left their hardware. The bootkit replaces the legitimate boot loader with one under their control. Typically the malware loader persists through the transition to protected mode when the kernel has loaded, and is thus able to subvert the kernel. For example, the "Stoned Bootkit" subverts the system by using a compromised boot loader to intercept encryption keys and passwords. More recently, the Alureon rootkit has successfully subverted the requirement for 64-bit kernel-mode driver signing in Windows 7, by modifying the master boot record. Although not malware in the sense of doing something the user doesn't want, certain "Vista Loader" or "Windows Loader" software work in a similar way by injecting an ACPI SLIC (System Licensed Internal Code) table in the RAM-cached version of the BIOS during boot, in order to defeat the Windows Vista and Windows 7 activation process. This vector of attack was rendered useless in the (non-server) versions of Windows 8, which use a unique, machine-specific key for each system, that can only be used by that one machine. Many antivirus companies provide free utilities and programs to remove bootkits.

Hypervisor Level

Rootkits have been created as Type II Hypervisors in academia as proofs of concept. By exploiting hardware virtualization features such as Intel VT or AMD-V, this type of rootkit runs in Ring -1 and hosts the target operating system as a virtual machine, thereby enabling the rootkit to intercept hardware calls made by the original operating system. Unlike normal hypervisors, they do not have to load before the operating system, but can load into an operating system before promoting it into a virtual machine. A hypervisor rootkit does not have to make any modifications to the kernel of the target to subvert it; however, that does not mean that it cannot be detected by the guest operating system. For example, timing differences may be detectable in CPU instructions. The "SubVirt" laboratory rootkit, developed jointly by Microsoft and University of Michigan researchers, is an academic example of a virtual machine–based rootkit (VMBR), while Blue Pill software is another. In 2009, researchers from Microsoft and North Carolina State University demonstrated a hypervisor-layer anti-rootkit called Hooksafe, which provides generic protection against kernel-mode rootkits. Windows 10 introduced a new feature called "Device Guard", that takes advantage of virtualization to provide independent external protection of an operating system against rootkit-type malware.

Firmware and Hardware

A firmware rootkit uses device or platform firmware to create a persistent malware image in hardware, such as a router, network card, hard drive, or the system BIOS. The rootkit hides in firmware, because firmware is not usually inspected for code integrity. John Heasman demonstrated the viability of firmware rootkits in both ACPI firmware routines and in a PCI expansion card ROM. In October 2008, criminals tampered with European credit card-reading machines before they were installed. The devices intercepted and transmitted credit card details via a mobile phone network. In March 2009, researchers Alfredo Ortega and Anibal Sacco published details of a BIOS-level Windows rootkit that was able to survive disk replacement and operating system re-installation. A few months later they learned that some laptops are sold with a legitimate rootkit, known as Absolute CompuTrace or Absolute LoJack for Laptops, preinstalled in many BIOS images. This is an anti-theft technology system that researchers showed can be turned to malicious purposes.

Intel Active Management Technology, part of Intel vPro, implements out-of-band management, giving administrators remote administration, remote management, and remote control of PCs with no involvement of the host processor or BIOS, even when the system is powered off. Remote administration includes remote power-up and power-down, remote reset, redirected boot, console redirection, pre-boot access to BIOS settings, programmable filtering for inbound and outbound network traffic, agent presence checking, out-of-band policy-based alerting, access to system information, such as hardware asset information, persistent event logs, and other information that is stored in dedicated memory (not on the hard drive) where it is accessible even if the OS is down or the PC is powered off. Some of these functions require the deepest level of rootkit, a second non-removable spy computer built around the main computer. Sandy Bridge and future chipsets have "the ability to remotely kill and restore a lost or stolen PC via 3G". Hardware rootkits built into the chipset can help recover stolen computers, remove data, or render them useless, but they also present privacy and security concerns of undetectable spying and redirection by management or hackers who might gain control.

Installation and Cloaking

Rootkits employ a variety of techniques to gain control of a system; the type of rootkit influences the choice of attack vector. The most common technique leverages security vulnerabilities to achieve surreptitious privilege escalation. Another approach is to use a Trojan horse, deceiving a computer user into trusting the rootkit's installation program as benign—in this case, social engineering convinces a user that the rootkit is beneficial. The installation task is made easier if the principle of least privilege is not applied, since the rootkit then does not have to explicitly request elevated (administrator-level) privileges. Other classes of rootkits can be installed only by someone with physical access to the target system. Some rootkits may also be installed intentionally by the owner of the system or somebody authorized by the owner, e.g. for the purpose of employee monitoring, rendering such subversive techniques unnecessary. Some malicious rootkit installations are commercially driven, with a pay-per-install (PPI) compensation method typical for distribution.

Once installed, a rootkit takes active measures to obscure its presence within the host system through subversion or evasion of standard operating system security tools and application programming interface (APIs) used for diagnosis, scanning, and monitoring. Rootkits achieve this by modifying the behavior of core parts of an operating system through loading code into other processes, the installation or modification of drivers, or kernel modules. Obfuscation techniques include concealing running processes from system-monitoring mechanisms and hiding system files and other configuration data. It is not uncommon for a rootkit to disable the event logging capacity of an operating system, in an attempt to hide evidence of an attack. Rootkits can, in theory, subvert *any* operating system activities. The "perfect rootkit" can be thought of as similar to a "perfect crime": one that nobody realizes has taken place. Rootkits also take a number of measures to ensure their survival against detection and "cleaning" by antivirus software in addition to commonly installing into Ring 0 (kernel-mode), where they have complete access to a system. These include polymorphism (changing so their "signature" is hard to detect), stealth techniques, regeneration, disabling or turning off anti-malware software, and not installing on virtual machines where it may be easier for researchers to discover and analyze them.

Detection

The fundamental problem with rootkit detection is that if the operating system has been subverted, particularly by a kernel-level rootkit, it cannot be trusted to find unauthorized modifications to itself or its components. Actions such as requesting a list of running processes, or a list of files in a directory, cannot be trusted to behave as expected. In other words, rootkit detectors that work while running on infected systems are only effective against rootkits that have some defect in their camouflage, or that run with lower user-mode privileges than the detection software in the kernel. As with computer viruses, the detection and elimination of rootkits is an ongoing struggle between both sides of this conflict. Detection can take a number of different approaches, including looking for virus "signatures" (e.g. antivirus software), integrity checking (e.g. digital signatures), difference-based detection (comparison of expected vs. actual results), and behavioral detection (e.g. monitoring CPU usage or network traffic).

For kernel-mode rootkits, detection is considerably more complex, requiring careful scrutiny of the System Call Table to look for hooked functions where the malware may be subverting system behavior, as well as forensic scanning of memory for patterns that indicate hidden processes. Unix rootkit detection offerings include Zeppoo, chkrootkit, rkhunter and OSSEC. For Windows, detection tools include Microsoft Sysinternals RootkitRevealer, Avast Antivirus, Sophos Anti-Rootkit, F-Secure, Radix, GMER, and WindowsSCOPE. Any rootkit detectors that prove effective ultimately contribute to their own ineffectiveness, as malware authors adapt and test their code to escape detection by well-used tools. Detection by examining storage while the suspect operating system is not operational can miss rootkits not recognised by the checking software, as the rootkit is not active and suspicious behavior is suppressed; conventional anti-malware software running with the rootkit operational may fail if the rootkit hides itself effectively.

Alternative Trusted Medium

The best and most reliable method for operating-system-level rootkit detection is to shut down the computer suspected of infection, and then to check its storage by booting from an alternative trusted medium (e.g. a "rescue" CD-ROM or USB flash drive). The technique is effective because a rootkit cannot actively hide its presence if it is not running.

Behavioral-based

The behavioral-based approach to detecting rootkits attempts to infer the presence of a rootkit by looking for rootkit-like behavior. For example, by profiling a system, differences in the timing and frequency of API calls or in overall CPU utilization can be attributed to a rootkit. The method is complex and is hampered by a high incidence of false positives. Defective rootkits can sometimes introduce very obvious changes to a system: the Alureon rootkit crashed Windows systems after a security update exposed a design flaw in its code. Logs from a packet analyzer, firewall, or intrusion prevention system may present evidence of rootkit behaviour in a networked environment.

Signature-based

Antivirus products rarely catch all viruses in public tests (depending on what is used and to what extent), even though security software vendors incorporate rootkit detection into their products. Should a rootkit attempt to hide during an antivirus scan, a stealth detector may notice; if the rootkit attempts to temporarily unload itself from the system, signature detection (or "fingerprinting") can still find it. This combined approach forces attackers to implement counterattack mechanisms, or "retro" routines, that attempt to terminate antivirus programs. Signature-based detection methods can be effective against well-published rootkits, but less so against specially crafted, custom-root rootkits.

Difference-based

Another method that can detect rootkits compares "trusted" raw data with "tainted" content returned by an API. For example, binaries present on disk can be compared with their copies within operating memory (in some operating systems, the in-memory image should be identical to the on-disk image), or the results returned from file system or Windows Registry APIs can be checked against raw structures on the underlying physical disks—however, in the case of the former, some valid differences can be introduced by operating system mechanisms like memory relocation or shimming. A rootkit may detect the presence of such a difference-based scanner or virtual machine (the latter being commonly used to perform forensic analysis), and adjust its behaviour so that no differences can be detected. Difference-based detection was used by Russinovich's *RootkitRevealer* tool to find the Sony DRM rootkit.

Integrity Checking

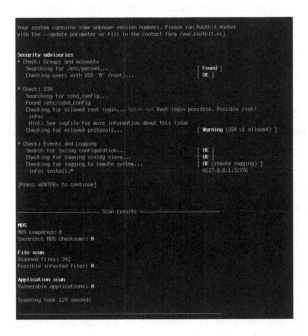

Code signing uses public-key infrastructure to check if a file has been modified since being digitally signed by its publisher. Alternatively, a system owner or administrator can use a cryptographic hash function to compute a "fingerprint" at installation time that can help to detect subsequent unauthorized changes to on-disk code libraries. However, unsophisticated schemes check only whether the code has been modified since installation time; subversion prior to that time is not detectable. The fingerprint must be re-established each time changes are made to the system: for example, after installing security updates or a service pack. The hash function creates a *message digest*, a relatively short code calculated from each bit in the file using an algorithm that creates large changes in the message digest with even smaller changes to the original file. By recalculating and comparing the message digest of the installed files at regular intervals against a trusted list of message digests, changes in the system can be detected and monitored—as long as the original baseline was created before the malware was added.

More-sophisticated rootkits are able to subvert the verification process by presenting an unmodi-fied copy of the file for inspection, or by making code modifications only in memory, reconfigura-tion registers, which are later compared to a white list of expected values. The code that performs hash, compare, or extend operations must also be protected—in this context, the notion of an *immutable root-of-trust* holds that the very first code to measure security properties of a system must itself be trusted to ensure that a rootkit or bootkit does not compromise the system at its most fundamental level.

Memory Dumps

Forcing a complete dump of virtual memory will capture an active rootkit (or a kernel dump in the case of a kernel-mode rootkit), allowing offline forensic analysis to be performed with a debugger against the resulting dump file, without the rootkit being able to take any measures to cloak itself. This technique is highly specialized, and may require access to non-public source code or debugging symbols. Memory dumps initiated by the operating system cannot always be used to detect a hypervisor-based rootkit, which is able to intercept and subvert the lowest-level attempts to read memory—a hardware device, such as one that implements a non-maskable interrupt, may be required to dump memory in this scenario. Virtual machines also make it easier to analyze the memory of a compromised machine from the underlying hypervisor, so some rootkits will avoid infecting virtual machines for this reason.

Removal

Manual removal of a rootkit is often too difficult for a typical computer user, but a number of security-software vendors offer tools to automatically detect and remove some rootkits, typically as part of an antivirus suite. As of 2005, Microsoft's monthly Windows Malicious Software Removal Tool is able to detect and remove some classes of rootkits. Also, Windows Defender Offline can remove rootkits, as it runs from a trusted environment before the operating system starts. Some antivirus scanners can bypass file system APIs, which are vulnerable to manipulation by a rootkit. Instead, they access raw file system structures directly, and use this information to validate the results from the system APIs to identify any differences that may be caused by a rootkit. There are experts who believe that the only reliable way to remove them is to re-install the operating system from trusted media. This is because antivirus and malware removal tools running on an untrusted system may be ineffective against well-written kernel-mode rootkits. Booting an alternative operating system from trusted media can allow an infected system volume to be mounted and potentially safely cleaned and critical data to be copied off—or, alternatively, a forensic examination performed. Lightweight operating systems such as Windows PE, Windows Recovery Console, Windows Recovery Environment, BartPE, or Live Distros can be used for this purpose, allowing the system to be "cleaned". Even if the type and nature of a rootkit is known, manual repair may be impractical, while re-installing the operating system and applications is safer, simpler and quicker.

Public Availability

Like much malware used by attackers, many rootkit implementations are shared and are easily available on the Internet. It is not uncommon to see a compromised system in which a sophisticated, publicly available rootkit hides the presence of unsophisticated worms or attack tools apparently written by inexperienced programmers. Most of the rootkits available on the Internet originated as exploits or as academic "proofs of concept" to demonstrate varying methods of hiding things within a computer system and of taking unauthorized control of it. Often not fully optimized for stealth, such rootkits sometimes leave unintended evidence of their presence. Even so, when such rootkits are used in an attack, they are often effective. Other rootkits with keylogging features such as GameGuard are installed as part of online commercial games.

Defenses

System hardening represents one of the first layers of defence against a rootkit, to prevent it from being able to install. Applying security patches, implementing the principle of least privilege, reducing the attack surface and installing antivirus software are some standard security best practices that are effective against all classes of malware. New secure boot specifications like Unified Extensible Firmware Interface have been designed to address the threat of bootkits, but even these are vulnerable if the security features they offer are not utilized. For server systems, remote server attestation using technologies such as Intel Trusted Execution Technology (TXT) provide a way of verifying that servers remain in a known good state. For example, Microsoft Bitlocker's encryption of data-at-rest verifies that servers are in a known "good state" on bootup. PrivateCore vCage is a software offering that secures data-in-use (memory) to avoid bootkits and rootkits by verifying servers are in a known "good" state on bootup. The PrivateCore implementation works in concert with Intel TXT and locks down server system interfaces to avoid potential bootkits and rootkits.

Keystroke Logging

Keystroke logging, often referred to as keylogging or keyboard capturing, is the action of recording (logging) the keys struck on a keyboard, typically covertly, so that person using the keyboard is unaware that their actions are being monitored. Data can then be retrieved by the person operating the logging program. A keylogger can be either software or hardware.

While the programs themselves are legal, with many of them being designed to allow employers to oversee the use of their computers, keyloggers are most often used for the purpose of stealing passwords and other confidential information.

Keylogging can also be used to study human–computer interaction. Numerous keylogging methods exist: they range from hardware and software-based approaches to acoustic analysis.

Application

Software-based Keyloggers

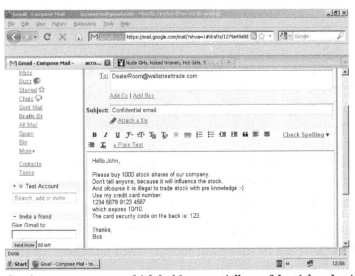

A keylogger example of a screencapture, which holds potentially confidential and private information.

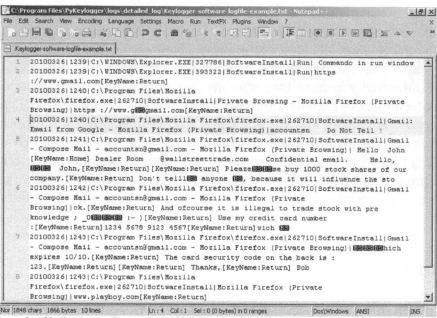

A logfile from a software-based keylogger, based on the screencapture above.

Software-based keyloggers are computer programs designed to work on the target computer's software. Keyloggers are used in IT organizations to troubleshoot technical problems with computers and business networks. Families and business people use keyloggers legally to monitor network usage without their users' direct knowledge. Even Microsoft publicly admitted that Windows 10 operation system has a built-in keylogger in its final version "to improve typing and writing services". However, malicious individuals can use keyloggers on public computers to steal passwords or credit card information. Most keyloggers are not stopped by HTTPS encryption because that only protects data in transit between computers, thus the threat being from the user's computer.

From a technical perspective there are several categories:

- Hypervisor-based: The keylogger can theoretically reside in a malware hypervisor running underneath the operating system, which thus remains untouched. It effectively becomes a virtual machine. Blue Pill is a conceptual example.

- Kernel-based: A program on the machine obtains root access to hide itself in the OS and intercepts keystrokes that pass through the kernel. This method is difficult both to write and to combat. Such keyloggers reside at the kernel level, which makes them difficult to detect, especially for user-mode applications that don't have root access. They are frequently implemented as rootkits that subvert the operating system kernel to gain unauthorized access to the hardware. This makes them very powerful. A keylogger using this method can act as a keyboard device driver, for example, and thus gain access to any information typed on the keyboard as it goes to the operating system.

- API-based: These keyloggers hook keyboard APIs inside a running application. The keylogger registers keystroke events, as if it was a normal piece of the application instead of malware. The keylogger receives an event each time the user presses or releases a key. The keylogger simply records it.

- Windows APIs such as GetAsyncKeyState(), GetForegroundWindow(), etc. are used to poll the state of the keyboard or to subscribe to keyboard events. A more recent example simply polls the BIOS for pre-boot authentication PINs that have not been cleared from memory.

- **Form grabbing based:** Form grabbing-based keyloggers log web form submissions by recording the web browsing on submit events. This happens when the user completes a form and submits it, usually by clicking a button or hitting enter. This type of keylogger records form data before it is passed over the Internet.

- **Javascript-based:** A malicious script tag is injected into a targeted web page, and listens for key events such as onKeyUp(). Scripts can be injected via a variety of methods, including cross-site scripting, man-in-the-browser, man-in-the-middle, or a compromise of the remote web site.

- **Memory-injection-based:** Memory Injection (MitB)-based keyloggers perform their logging function by altering the memory tables associated with the browser and other system functions. By patching the memory tables or injecting directly into memory, this technique can be used by malware authors to bypass Windows UAC (User Account Control). The Zeus and SpyEye trojans use this method exclusively. Non-Windows systems have protection mechanisms that allow access to locally recorded data from a remote location. Remote communication may be achieved when one of these methods is used:

  - Data is uploaded to a website, database or an FTP server.

  - Data is periodically emailed to a pre-defined email address.

  - Data is wirelessly transmitted by means of an attached hardware system.

  - The software enables a remote login to the local machine from the Internet or the local network, for data logs stored on the target machine.

Keystroke Logging in Writing Process Research

Keystroke logging is now an established research method for the study of writing processes. Different programs have been developed to collect online process data of writing activities, including Inputlog, Scriptlog, and Translog.

Keystroke logging is legitimately used as a suitable research instrument in a number of writing contexts. These include studies on cognitive writing processes, which include:

- Descriptions of writing strategies; the writing development of children (with and without writing difficulties),

- Spelling,

- First and second language writing, and

- Specialist skill areas such as translation and subtitling.

Keystroke logging can be used to research writing, specifically. It can also be integrated in educational domains for second language learning, programming skills, and typing skills.

Related Features

Software keyloggers may be augmented with features that capture user information without relying on keyboard key presses as the sole input. Some of these features include:

- Clipboard logging: Anything that has been copied to the clipboard can be captured by the program.

- Screen logging: Screenshots are taken to capture graphics-based information. Applications with screen logging abilities may take screenshots of the whole screen, of just one application, or even just around the mouse cursor. They may take these screenshots periodically or in response to user behaviours (for example, when a user clicks the mouse). A practical application that is used by some keyloggers with this screen logging ability, is to take small screenshots around where a mouse has just clicked; thus defeating web-based keyboards (for example, the web-based screen keyboards that are often used by banks), and any web-based on-screen keyboard without screenshot protection.

- Programmatically capturing the text in a control: The Microsoft Windows API allows programs to request the text 'value' in some controls. This means that some passwords may be captured, even if they are hidden behind password masks (usually asterisks).

- The recording of every program/folder/window opened including a screenshot of each and every website visited.

- The recording of search engines queries, instant messenger conversations, FTP downloads and other Internet-based activities (including the bandwidth used).

Hardware-based Keyloggers

A hardware-based keylogger.

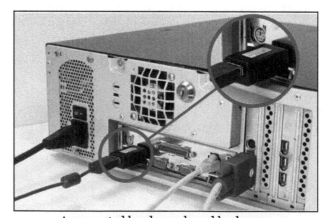

A connected hardware-based keylogger.

Hardware-based keyloggers do not depend upon any software being installed as they exist at a hardware level in a computer system.

- Firmware-based: BIOS-level firmware that handles keyboard events can be modified to record these events as they are processed. Physical and/or root-level access is required to the machine, and the software loaded into the BIOS needs to be created for the specific hardware that it will be running on.

- Keyboard hardware: Hardware keyloggers are used for keystroke logging by means of a hardware circuit that is attached somewhere in between the computer keyboard and the computer, typically inline with the keyboard's cable connector. There are also USB connectors based Hardware keyloggers as well as ones for Laptop computers (the Mini-PCI card plugs into the expansion slot of a laptop). More stealthy implementations can be installed or built into standard keyboards, so that no device is visible on the external cable. Both types log all keyboard activity to their internal memory, which can be subsequently accessed, for example, by typing in a secret key sequence. A hardware keylogger has an advantage over a software solution: it is not dependent on being installed on the target computer's operating system and therefore will not interfere with any program running on the target machine or be detected by any software. However its physical presence may be detected if, for example, it is installed outside the case as an inline device between the computer and the keyboard. Some of these implementations have the ability to be controlled and monitored remotely by means of a wireless communication standard.

- Wireless keyboard and mouse sniffers: These passive sniffers collect packets of data being transferred from a wireless keyboard and its receiver. As encryption may be used to secure the wireless communications between the two devices, this may need to be cracked beforehand if the transmissions are to be read. In some cases this enables an attacker to type arbitrary commands into a victim's computer.

- Keyboard overlays: Criminals have been known to use keyboard overlays on ATMs to capture people's PINs. Each keypress is registered by the keyboard of the ATM as well as the criminal's keypad that is placed over it. The device is designed to look like an integrated part of the machine so that bank customers are unaware of its presence.

- Acoustic keyloggers: Acoustic cryptanalysis can be used to monitor the sound created by someone typing on a computer. Each key on the keyboard makes a subtly different acoustic signature when struck. It is then possible to identify which keystroke signature relates to which keyboard character via statistical methods such as frequency analysis. The repetition frequency of similar acoustic keystroke signatures, the timings between different keyboard strokes and other context information such as the probable language in which the user is writing are used in this analysis to map sounds to letters. A fairly long recording (1000 or more keystrokes) is required so that a big enough sample is collected.

- Electromagnetic emissions: It is possible to capture the electromagnetic emissions of a wired keyboard from up to 20 metres (66 ft) away, without being physically wired to it. In 2009, Swiss researchers tested 11 different USB, PS/2 and laptop keyboards in a semi-anechoic chamber and found them all vulnerable, primarily because of the prohibitive cost of adding shielding during manufacture. The researchers used a wideband receiver to tune into the specific frequency of the emissions radiated from the keyboards.

- Optical surveillance: Optical surveillance, while not a keylogger in the classical sense, is nonetheless an approach that can be used to capture passwords or PINs. A strategically placed camera, such as a hidden surveillance camera at an ATM, can allow a criminal to watch a PIN or password being entered.

- Physical evidence: For a keypad that is used only to enter a security code, the keys which are in actual use will have evidence of use from many fingerprints. A passcode of four digits, if the four digits in question are known, is reduced from 10,000 possibilities to just 24 possibilities (10^4 versus 4! (factorial of 4)). These could then be used on separate occasions for a manual "brute force attack".

- Smartphone sensors: Researchers have demonstrated that it is possible to capture the keystrokes of nearby computer keyboards using only the commodity accelerometer found in smartphones. The attack is made possible by placing a smartphone near a keyboard on the same desk. The smartphone's accelerometer can then detect the vibrations created by typing on the keyboard, and then translate this raw accelerometer signal into readable sentences with as much as 80 percent accuracy. The technique involves working through probability by detecting pairs of keystrokes, rather than individual keys. It models "keyboard events" in pairs and then works out whether the pair of keys pressed is on the left or the right side of the keyboard and whether they are close together or far apart on the QWERTY keyboard. Once it has worked this out, it compares the results to a preloaded dictionary where each word has been broken down in the same way. Similar techniques have also been shown to be effective at capturing keystrokes on touchscreen keyboards while in some cases, in combination with gyroscope or with the ambient-light sensor.

Cracking

Writing simple software applications for keylogging can be trivial, and like any nefarious computer program, can be distributed as a trojan horse or as part of a virus. What is not trivial for an attacker, however, is installing a covert keystroke logger without getting caught and downloading data that has been logged without being traced. An attacker that manually connects to a host machine to download logged keystrokes risks being traced. A trojan that sends keylogged data to a fixed e-mail address or IP address risks exposing the attacker.

Trojans

Researchers devised several methods for solving this problem. They presented a deniable password snatching attack in which the keystroke logging trojan is installed using a virus or worm. An attacker who is caught with the virus or worm can claim to be a victim. The cryptotrojan asymmetrically encrypts the pilfered login/password pairs using the public key of the trojan author and covertly broadcasts the resulting ciphertext. They mentioned that the ciphertext can be steganographically encoded and posted to a public bulletin board such as Usenet.

Use by Police

In 2000, the FBI used FlashCrest iSpy to obtain the PGP passphrase of Nicodemo Scarfo, Jr., son of mob boss Nicodemo Scarfo. Also in 2000, the FBI lured two suspected Russian cyber criminals to the US in an elaborate ruse, and captured their usernames and passwords with a keylogger that was covertly installed on a machine that they used to access their computers in Russia. The FBI then used these credentials to hack into the suspects' computers in Russia in order to obtain evidence to prosecute them.

Countermeasures

The effectiveness of countermeasures varies, because keyloggers use a variety of techniques to capture data and the countermeasure needs to be effective against the particular data capture technique. In the case of Windows 10 keylogging from Microsoft it is enough to change some privacy settings on your computer. For example, an on-screen keyboard will be effective against hardware keyloggers, transparency will defeat some—but not all—screenloggers and an anti-spyware application that can only disable hook-based keyloggers will be ineffective against kernel-based keyloggers.

Also, keylogger program authors may be able to update the code to adapt to countermeasures that may have proven to be effective against them.

Anti-keyloggers

An anti-keylogger is a piece of software specifically designed to detect keyloggers on a computer, typically comparing all files in the computer against a database of keyloggers looking for similarities which might signal the presence of a hidden keylogger. As anti-keyloggers have been designed specifically to detect keyloggers, they have the potential to be more effective than conventional antivirus software; some antivirus software do not consider a keylogger to be a virus, as under some circumstances a keylogger can be considered a legitimate piece of software.

Live CD/USB

Rebooting the computer using a Live CD or write-protected Live USB is a possible countermeasure against software keyloggers if the CD is clean of malware and the operating system contained on it is secured and fully patched so that it cannot be infected as soon as it is started. Booting a different operating system does not impact the use of a hardware or BIOS based keylogger.

Anti-spyware / Anti-virus programs

Many anti-spyware applications are able to detect some software based keyloggers and quarantine, disable or cleanse them. However, because many keylogging programs are legitimate pieces of software under some circumstances, anti spyware often neglects to label keylogging programs as spyware or a virus. These applications are able to detect software-based keyloggers based on patterns in executable code, heuristics and keylogger behaviours (such as the use of hooks and certain APIs).

No software-based anti-spyware application can be 100% effective against all keyloggers. Also, software-based anti-spyware cannot defeat non-software keyloggers (for example, hardware keyloggers attached to keyboards will always receive keystrokes before any software-based anti-spyware application).

However, the particular technique that the anti-spyware application uses will influence its potential effectiveness against software keyloggers. As a general rule, anti-spyware applications with higher privileges will defeat keyloggers with lower privileges. For example, a hook-based anti-spyware application cannot defeat a kernel-based keylogger (as the keylogger will receive the keystroke messages before the anti-spyware application), but it could potentially defeat hook- and API-based keyloggers.

Network Monitors

Network monitors (also known as reverse-firewalls) can be used to alert the user whenever an application attempts to make a network connection. This gives the user the chance to prevent the keylogger from "phoning home" with his or her typed information.

Automatic Form Filler Programs

Automatic form-filling programs may prevent keylogging by removing the requirement for a user to type personal details and passwords using the keyboard. Form fillers are primarily designed for web browsers to fill in checkout pages and log users into their accounts. Once the user's account and credit card information has been entered into the program, it will be automatically entered into forms without ever using the keyboard or clipboard, thereby reducing the possibility that private data is being recorded. However someone with physical access to the machine may still be able to install software that is able to intercept this information elsewhere in the operating system or while in transit on the network. (Transport Layer Security (TLS) reduces the risk that data in transit may be intercepted by network sniffers and proxy tools.)

One-time Passwords (OTP)

Using one-time passwords may be keylogger-safe, as each password is invalidated as soon as it is used. This solution may be useful for someone using a public computer. However, an attacker who has remote control over such a computer can simply wait for the victim to enter his/her credentials before performing unauthorised transactions on their behalf while their session is active.

Security Tokens

Use of smart cards or other security tokens may improve security against replay attacks in the face of a successful keylogging attack, as accessing protected information would require both the (hardware) security token *as well as* the appropriate password/passphrase. Knowing the keystrokes, mouse actions, display, clipboard etc. used on one computer will not subsequently help an attacker gain access to the protected resource. Some security tokens work as a type of hardware-assisted one-time password system, and others implement a cryptographic challenge-response authentication, which can improve security in a manner conceptually similar to one time passwords. Smart-card readers and their associated keypads for PIN entry may be vulnerable to keystroke logging through a so-called supply chain attack where an attacker substitutes the card reader/PIN entry hardware for one which records the user's PIN.

On-screen Keyboards

Most on-screen keyboards (such as the on-screen keyboard that comes with Windows XP) send normal keyboard event messages to the external target program to type text. Software key loggers can log these typed characters sent from one program to another. Additionally, keylogging software can take screenshots of what is displayed on the screen (periodically, and/or upon each mouse click), which means that although certainly a useful security measure, an on-screen keyboard will not protect from all keyloggers.

Keystroke Interference Software

Keystroke interference software is also available. These programs attempt to trick keyloggers by introducing random keystrokes, although this simply results in the keylogger recording more information than it needs to. An attacker has the task of extracting the keystrokes of interest—the security of this mechanism, specifically how well it stands up to cryptanalysis, is unclear.

Speech Recognition

Similar to on-screen keyboards, speech-to-text conversion software can also be used against keyloggers, since there are no typing or mouse movements involved. The weakest point of using voice-recognition software may be how the software sends the recognized text to target software after the recognition took place.

Handwriting Recognition and Mouse Gestures

Also, many PDAs and lately tablet PCs can already convert pen (also called stylus) movements on their touchscreens to computer understandable text successfully. Mouse gestures use this principle by using mouse movements instead of a stylus. Mouse gesture programs convert these strokes to user-definable actions, such as typing text. Similarly, graphics tablets and light pens can be used to input these gestures, however these are less common everyday.

The same potential weakness of speech recognition applies to this technique as well.

Macro Expanders/Recorders

With the help of many programs, a seemingly meaningless text can be expanded to a meaningful text and most of the time context-sensitively, e.g. "en.wikipedia.org" can be expanded when a web browser window has the focus. The biggest weakness of this technique is that these programs send their keystrokes directly to the target program. However, this can be overcome by using the 'alternating' technique described below, i.e. sending mouse clicks to non-responsive areas of the target program, sending meaningless keys, sending another mouse click to target area (e.g. password field) and switching back-and-forth.

Deceptive Typing

Alternating between typing the login credentials and typing characters somewhere else in the focus window can cause a keylogger to record more information than they need to, although this could easily be filtered out by an attacker. Similarly, a user can move their cursor using the mouse during typing, causing the logged keystrokes to be in the wrong order e.g., by typing a password beginning with the last letter and then using the mouse to move the cursor for each subsequent letter.

Lastly, someone can also use context menus to remove, cut, copy, and paste parts of the typed text without using the keyboard. An attacker who is able to capture only parts of a password will have a larger key space to attack if he chose to execute a brute-force attack.

Another very similar technique uses the fact that any selected text portion is replaced by the next key typed. e.g., if the password is "secret", one could type "s", then some dummy keys "asdfsd". Then, these dummies could be selected with the mouse, and the next character from the password "e" is typed, which replaces the dummies "asdf".

These techniques assume incorrectly that keystroke logging software cannot directly monitor the clipboard, the selected text in a form, or take a screenshot every time a keystroke or mouse click occurs. They may however be effective against some hardware keyloggers.

Web Shell

A web shell is a web security threat that is a web-based implementation of the shell concept. A web shell is able to be uploaded to a web server to allow remote access to the web server, such as the web server's file system. A web shell is unique in that it enables users to access a web server by way of a web browser that acts like a command-line interface. A user can access a remote computer via the World Wide Web using a web browser on any type of system, whether it's a desktop computer or a mobile phone with a web browser, and perform tasks on the remote system. No command-line environment is required on either the host or the client. A web shell is often considered a remote access trojan.

A web shell could be programmed in any language that the target server supports. Web shells are most commonly written in PHP, Active Server Pages, or ASP.NET, but Python, Perl, Ruby and Unix shell scripts are also used, although not as common because it is not very common for web servers to support these languages.

Using network monitoring tools such as Wireshark, an attacker can find vulnerabilities which are exploited resulting in a web shell installation. These vulnerabilities may be present in content management system applications (abbreviated CMS) or the web server's software.

An attacker can use a web shell to issue commands, perform privilege escalation on the web server, and the ability to upload, delete, download and run scripts and files on the web server.

Web shells are used in attacks mostly because they are multi-purpose and are difficult to detect.

Web shells are commonly used for:

- Data theft,

- Infecting website visitors (watering hole attacks),

- Website defacement by modifying files with a malicious intent,

- Launch distributed denial of service (DDoS) attacks,

- To relay commands inside the network which is inaccessible over the Internet,

- To use as command and control base, for example as a bot in a botnet system or in way to compromise the security of additional external networks.

Delivery of Web Shells

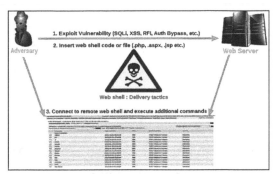

Graphical representation of how web shells are delivered.

Web shells are installed through vulnerabilities in web application or weak server security configuration including the following:

- SQL injection;

- Vulnerabilities in applications and services (e.g. web server software such as NGINX or content management system applications such as WordPress);

- File processing and uploading vulnerabilities, which can be mitigated by e.g. limiting the file types that can be uploaded;

- Remote file inclusion (RFI) and local file inclusion (LFI) vulnerabilities;

- Remote code execution;

- Exposed administration interfaces;

- Cross-site scripting.

An attacker may also modify (spoof) the Content-Type header to be sent by the attacker in a file upload to bypass improper file validation (validation using MIME type sent by the client) and upload the attacker's shell.

Examples of Web Shells

```
root@kali:~# cd /usr/share/webshells/php
root@kali:/usr/share/webshells/php# ls -al
total 44
drwxr-xr-x 3 root root  4096 Jul 23 15:25 .
drwxr-xr-x 8 root root  4096 Jul 23 15:26 ..
drwxr-xr-x 2 root root  4096 Jul 23 15:25 findsocket
-rw-r--r-- 1 root root  2800 Jul 17 11:45 php-backdoor.php
-rwxr-xr-x 1 root root  5491 Jul 17 11:45 php-reverse-shell.php
-rw-r--r-- 1 root root 13585 Jul 17 11:45 qsd-php-backdoor.php
-rw-r--r-- 1 root root   328 Jul 17 11:45 simple-backdoor.php
root@kali:/usr/share/webshells/php#
```

Shell running on a Linux server.

An example of what a fake error page might look like in a WSO web shell:

- b374k – A web shell written in PHP with abilities such as monitoring processes & command execution. The latest version of the b374k shell is 3.2.3.

- C99 – A web shell capable of showing the web server's security standards and has a self-destruction option. The original version of C99Shell does not work in PHP 7 due to removed functions.

- China Chopper – A web shell which is only 4 kilobytes in size, which was first discovered in 2012. This web shell is commonly used by malicious Chinese actors, including advanced persistent threat (APT) groups, to remotely access web servers. This web shell has two parts, the client interface (an executable file) and the receiver host file on the compromised web server. Has many commands and control features such as a password brute-force attack option.

- R57 – The R57 web shell has tools to scan the infected web server for other web shell installations, with the option to remove or overwrite them.

- WSO (web shell by orb) – Has the ability to be password protected with a login form, some variants can disguise as a fake HTTP error page.

Web shells can be as short as just one line of code. The following example PHP script is 15 bytes in size:

```
<?=`$_GET[x]`?>
```

If an attacker inserts this line of code into a malicious file with a PHP filename extension (such as .php) on a web server that is running PHP, the attacker can issue commands, for example reading the /etc/passwd file, through a web browser using the following Uniform Resource Locator if the web shell was located at uploads/webshell.php (regardless if the page is encrypted with TLS or SSL):

```
http://example.com/uploads/webshell.php?x=cat%20%2Fetc%2Fpasswd
```

The above request will take the value of the x URL parameter, decode the URL and send the following Bash command:

```
cat /etc/passwd
```

If the permissions of the /etc/passwd file allow viewing the file, the web server will send the contents of /etc/passwd to the web browser and the browser will then display the contents of the /etc/passwd file or any other file the attacker wishes to view.

This attack could have been prevented if the file permissions did not allow viewing the file or if the shell functions of PHP were disabled so that arbitrary shell commands cannot be executed from PHP.

Other malicious actions are able to be executed by attackers with that web shell, such as replacing the contents of a file on the web server. For example, consider the following Bash command:

```
echo Hijacked page contents > index.php
```

The above command could be used to replace the contents of the index.php file with the text "Hijacked page contents", which is one way a web page could be defaced, or create the index.php file with the contents if the file does not exist. Attackers can also use the Bash command rm to delete files on the web server and mv to move files.

Prevention and Mitigation

A web shell is usually installed by taking advantage of vulnerabilities present in the web server's software. That is why removal of these vulnerabilities are important to avoid the potential risk of a compromised web server.

The following are security measures for preventing the installation of a web shell:

- Regularly update the applications and the host server's operating system to ensure immunity from known bugs.
- Deploy a demilitarized zone (DMZ) between the web facing servers and the internal networks.
- Secure configuration of the web server.
- Ports and services which are not used should be closed or blocked.
- Using user input data validation to limit local and remote file inclusion vulnerabilities.
- Use a reverse proxy service to restrict the administrative URL's to known legitimate ones.
- Frequent vulnerability scan to detect areas of risk and conduct regular scans using web security software (this does not prevent zero day attacks).
- Deploy a firewall.
- Disable directory browsing.
- Not using default passwords.

Detection

Web shells can be easily modified, so it's not easy to detect web shells and antivirus software are often not able to detect these web shells.

The following are common indicators that a web shell is present on a web server:

- Abnormal high web server usage (due to heavy downloading and uploading by the attacker);

- Files with an abnormal timestamp (e.g. newer than the last modification date);

- Unknown files in server;

- Files having dubious references, for example, cmd.exe or eval;

- Unknown connections in the logs of web server.

For example, a file generating suspicious traffic (e.g. a PNG file requesting with POST parameters); Dubious logins from DMZ servers to internal sub-nets and vice versa.

Web shells may also contain a login form, which can be hidden in fake error pages.

Using web shells, adversaries can modify the .htaccess file (on servers running the Apache HTTP Server software) on web servers to redirect search engine requests to the web page with malware or spam. Often web shells detect the user-agent and the content presented to the search engine spider is different from that presented to the user's browser. To find a web shell a user-agent change of the crawler bot is usually required. Once the web shell is identified, it can be deleted easily.

Analyzing the web server's log could specify the exact location of the web shell. Legitimate users/ visitor usually have different user-agents and referers (referrers), on the other hand, a web shell is usually only visited by the attacker, therefore have very few variants of user-agent strings.

Phishing

Phishing is a form of fraud in which an attacker masquerades as a reputable entity or person in email or other communication channels. The attacker uses phishing emails to distribute malicious links or attachments that can perform a variety of functions, including the extraction of login credentials or account information from victims.

Phishing is popular with cybercriminals, as it is far easier to trick someone into clicking a malicious link in a seemingly legitimate phishing email than trying to break through a computer's defenses.

Phishing attacks typically rely on social networking techniques applied to email or other electronic communication methods, including direct messages sent over social networks, SMS text messages and other instant messaging modes.

Phishers may use social engineering and other public sources of information, including social networks like LinkedIn, Facebook and Twitter, to gather background information about the victim's personal and work history, his interests, and his activities.

Pre-phishing attack reconnaissance can uncover names, job titles and email addresses of potential victims, as well as information about their colleagues and the names of key employees in their organizations. This information can then be used to craft a believable email. Targeted attacks, including those carried out by advanced persistent threat (APT) groups, typically begin with a phishing email containing a malicious link or attachment.

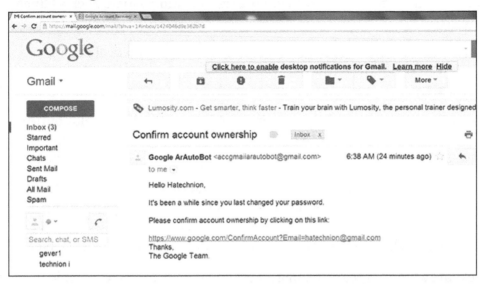

Although many phishing emails are poorly written and clearly fake, cybercriminal groups increasingly use the same techniques professional marketers use to identify the most effective types of messages, the phishing hooks that get the highest open or click-through rate and the Facebook posts that generate the most likes. Phishing campaigns are often built around major events, holidays and anniversaries, or take advantage of breaking news stories, both true and fictitious.

Typically, a victim receives a message that appears to have been sent by a known contact or organization. The attack is carried out either through a malicious file attachment that contains phishing software, or through links connecting to malicious websites. In either case, the objective is to install malware on the user's device or direct the victim to a malicious website set up to trick them into divulging personal and financial information, such as passwords, account IDs or credit card details.

Recognizing a Phishing E-mail

Successful phishing messages, usually represented as being from a well-known company, are difficult to distinguish from authentic messages: a phishing email can include corporate logos and other identifying graphics and data collected from the company being misrepresented. Malicious links within phishing messages are usually also designed to make it appear as though they go to the spoofed organization.

However, there are several clues that can indicate that a message is a phishing attempt. These include:

- The use of subdomains, misspelled URLs (typosquatting) or otherwise suspicious URLs.

- The recipient uses a Gmail or other public email address rather than a corporate email address.

- The message is written to invoke fear or a sense of urgency.

- The message includes a request to verify personal information, such as financial details or a password.

- The message is poorly written and has spelling and grammatical errors.

Types of Phishing

As defenders continue to educate their users in phishing defense and deploy anti-phishing strategies, cybercriminals continue to hone their skills at existing phishing attacks and roll out new types of phishing scams. Some of the more common types of phishing attacks include the following:

Spear phishing attacks are directed at specific individuals or companies, usually using information specific to the victim that has been gathered to more successfully represent the message as being authentic. Spear phishing emails might include references to coworkers or executives at the victim's organization, as well as the use of the victim's name, location or other personal information.

Whaling attacks are a type of spear phishing attack that specifically targets senior executives within an organization, often with the objective of stealing large sums. Those preparing a spear phishing campaign research their victims in detail to create a more genuine message, as using information relevant or specific to a target increases the chances of the attack being successful.

A typical whaling attack targets an employee with the ability to authorize payments, with the phishing message appearing to be a command from an executive to authorize a large payment to a vendor when, in fact, the payment would be made to the attackers.

Pharming is a type of phishing that depends on DNS cache poisoning to redirect users from a legitimate site to a fraudulent one, and tricking users into using their login credentials to attempt to log in to the fraudulent site.

Clone phishing attacks use previously delivered, but legitimate emails that contain either a link or an attachment. Attackers make a copy or clone of the legitimate email, replacing one or more links or attached files with malicious links or malware attachments. Because the message appears to be a duplicate of the original, legitimate email, victims can often be tricked into clicking the malicious link or opening the malicious attachment.

This technique is often used by attackers who have taken control of another victim's system. In this case, the attackers leverage their control of one system to pivot within an organization using email messages from a trusted sender known to the victims.

Phishers sometimes use the evil twin Wi-Fi attack by standing up a Wi-Fi access point and advertising it with a deceptive name that is similar to a legitimate access point. When victims connect to the evil twin Wi-Fi network, the attackers gain access to all the transmissions sent to or from victim devices, including user IDs and passwords. Attackers can also use this vector to target victim devices with their own fraudulent prompts for system credentials that appear to originate from legitimate systems.

Voice phishing, also known as vishing, is a form of phishing that occurs over voice communications media, including voice over IP (VoIP) or POTS (plain old telephone service). A typical vishing scam uses speech synthesis software to leave voicemails purporting to notify the victim of suspicious activity in a bank or credit account, and solicits the victim to respond to a malicious phone number to verify his identity thus compromising the victim's account credentials.

Another mobile device-oriented phishing attack, SMS phishing also sometimes called SMishing or SMShing uses text messaging to convince victims to disclose account credentials or to install malware.

Phishing Techniques

Phishing attacks depend on more than simply sending an email to victims and hoping that they click on a malicious link or open a malicious attachment. Attackers use a number of techniques to entrap their victims:

- JavaScript can be used to place a picture of a legitimate URL over a browser's address bar. The URL revealed by hovering over an embedded link can also be changed by using JavaScript.

- A variety of link manipulation techniques to trick victims into clicking on the link. Link manipulation is also often referred to as URL hiding and is present in many common types of phishing, and used in different ways depending on the attacker and the target. The simplest approach to link manipulation is to create a malicious URL that is displayed as if it were linking to a legitimate site or webpage, but to have the actual link point to a malicious web resource.

- Link shortening services like Bitly may be used to hide the link destination. Victims have no way of knowing whether the shortened URLs point to legitimate web resources or to malicious resources.

- Homograph spoofing depends on URLs that were created using different logical characters to read exactly like a trusted domain. For example, attackers may register domains that use different character sets that display close enough to established, well-known domains. Early examples of homograph spoofing include the use of the numerals 0 or 1 to replace the letters O or l. For example, attackers might attempt to spoof the microsoft.com domain with m!crosoft.com, replacing the letter i with an exclamation mark. Malicious domains may also replace Latin characters with Cyrillic, Greek or other character sets that display similarly.

- Rendering all or part of a message as a graphical image sometimes enables attackers to bypass phishing defenses that scan emails for particular phrases or terms common in phishing emails.

- Another phishing tactic relies on a covert redirect, where an open redirect vulnerability fails to check that a redirected URL is pointing to a trusted resource. In that case, the redirected URL is an intermediate, malicious page which solicits authentication information from the victim before forwarding the victim's browser to the legitimate site.

Preventing Phishing

Phishing defense begins with security awareness training. Security awareness training should be regularly updated to reflect new phishing techniques and teach users:

- How to identify phishing attacks.

- To be cautious of pop-ups on websites.

- To think twice before clicking on links sent via email or other messages. Users knowledge-able enough to hover over the link to see where it goes can avoid accessing malicious pages.

- To verify a website's security by ensuring that the URL begins with "https" and that there's a closed lock icon near the address bar.

To help prevent phishing messages from reaching end users, experts recommend layering security controls, including:

- Antivirus software.

- Both desktop and network firewalls.

- Antispyware software.

- Anti-phishing toolbar (installed in web browsers).

- Gateway email filter.

- Web security gateway.

In addition, enterprise mail servers should make use of at least one email authentication standard to verify that inbound email is verified. These include the Sender Policy Framework (SPF) proto-col, which can help reduce unsolicited email (spam); the DomainKeys Identified Mail (DKIM) pro-tocol, which enables users to block all messages except for those that have been cryptographically signed; and the Domain-based Message Authentication, Reporting and Conformance (DMARC) protocol, which specifies that both SPF and DKIM be in use for inbound email, and which also provides a framework for using those protocols to block unsolicited email including phishing email more effectively.

There are several resources on the internet that provide help in combating phishing. The An-ti-Phishing Working Group Inc. and the federal government's OnGuardOnline.gov website both provide advice on how to spot, avoid and report phishing attacks. Interactive security awareness training aids, such as Wombat Security Technologies' Anti-Phishing Training Suite or PhishMe, can help teach employees how to avoid phishing traps, while sites like Fraud-Watch International and MillerSmiles publish the latest phishing email subject lines that are circulating the internet.

Phishing Examples

Phishing scams come in all shapes and sizes. Users can stay safe, alert and prepared by knowing about some of the more recent ways that scammers have been phishing. A few examples of more modern phishing attacks include:

Digital Payment-based Scams

These happen when major payment applications and websites are used as a ruse to gain sensitive information from phishing victims. In this scam, a phisher masquerades as an online payment service (such as PayPal, Venmo, or Transferwise).

Generally, these attacks are performed through email, where a fake version of a trusted payment service asks a user to verify their log-in details and other identifying information. Usually, they claim that this is necessary in order to resolve an issue with the user's account. Often, these phishing attempts include a link to a fraudulent "spoof" page.

PayPal is aware of these threats, and have released informational materials for their customers to reference in order to stay prepared against phishing attacks. They recommend that anyone who receives a suspicious email from an account claiming to be PayPal should not click any links, but instead, use the hovering technique outlined above to see if the link address matches PayPal's actual domain.

It is also advised to then separately log into their account to make sure everything looks like it should. It is important to keep in mind that a fake email from a major brand like PayPal will likely have graphics and other elements that make it look legitimate.

If a user is unsure of how to spot a fraudulent online-payment phishing email, there are a few examples of how these phishing scams often look. Generally, a phishing email from PayPal has been known to include:

- Dodgy greetings that do not include the victim's name. Official emails from PayPal will always address users by their actual name or business title. Phishing attempts in this sector tend to begin with "Dear user," or use an email address instead.

- Alarming urgency works by whipping a potential victim up into a frenzy and scaring them into giving their information away. In the case of PayPal and other online payment services, this can come about in a few ways. Some of these scams "alert" their potential victims to the fact that their account will soon be suspended. Others claim that users were accidentally "overpaid" and now need to send money back to a fake account.

- Downloadable attachments are not something that PayPal sends to their users. If a person receives an email from PayPal or another similar service that includes an attachment, they should definitely not download it.

If a person receives one of these emails, they should open their payment page on a separate browser tab or window, and see if their account has any alerts. If a user has been overpaid or are facing suspension, it will say so there. Additionally, PayPal urges users to report any suspicious activity to them, so they can continue to monitor these attempts and prevent their users from getting scammed.

Finance-based Phishing Attacks

These are a common form of scamming, and they operate on the assumption that victims will panic into giving them personal information. Usually, in these cases, the attacker poses as a bank or other financial institution. In an email or phone call, the attacker informs their potential victim that their security has been compromised. Often, the scammer actually uses the threat of identity theft to successfully do just that.

A few examples of this tricky scam include:

- Suspicious emails about money transfers that will confuse the victim. In these phishing attempts, the potential victim receives an email that contains a receipt or rejection email regarding an AHC transfer. Often, the victim who sees this email will instantly assume fraudulent charges have been made in their account and clicks a bad link in the message, leaving their personal data vulnerable to being mined.

- Direct deposit scams are often used on new employees of a company or business. In these scams, the victims receive notice that their login information is not working. Anxious about not getting paid, the victims click a "phishy" link in the email, which leads them to a spoof website that installs malware to their system. From there, their banking information is vulnerable to harvesting, leading to fraudulent charges.

Work-related Phishing Scams

These are especially alarming, as this type of scam can be very personalized and hard to spot. In these cases, an attacker purporting to be the recipient's boss, CEO or CFO contacts the victim, and requests a wire transfer or other fraudulent purchase.

One work-related scam that has been popping up around businesses in the last couple of years is a ploy to harvest passwords. This scam often targets executive-level employees, who likely are not considering that an email from their boss could be a scam. The fraudulent email often works because, instead of being alarmist, it simply talks about regular workplace subjects. Usually, it informs the victim that a scheduled meeting needs to be changed.

From there, the employee is asked to fill out a poll about when a good time to reschedule would be via a link. That link will then bring the victim to a spoof login page for Office 365 or Microsoft Outlook. Once they have entered your login information, the scammers steal their password.

References

- Cyber-risk-appetite, white-paper, en, dam, content, rsa.com, Retrieved 5 June, 2019

- "Do you know who is sucking data from your computer?". Archived from the original on August 19, 2007. Retrieved 15 February 2015

- Internetsecurity-privacy-security-breach: norton.com, Retrieved 6 February, 2019

- Xing, Liudong; Levitin, Gregory (November 2017). "Balancing theft and corruption threats by data partition in cloud system with independent server protection". Reliability Engineering & System Safety. 167: 248–254. Doi:10.1016/j.ress.2017.06.006

- Constantine., Photopoulos, (2008). Managing catastrophic loss of sensitive data : a guide for IT and security professionals. Rockland, Mass.: Syngress. ISBN 9781597492393. OCLC 228148168

- Hanspach, Michael; Goetz, Michael (November 2013). "On Covert Acoustical Mesh Networks in Air". Journal of Communications. 8 (11): 758–767. Arxiv:1406.1213. Doi:10.12720/jcm.8.11.758-767

- Vincentas (July 11, 2013). "Trojan Horse in spywareloop.com". Spyware Loop. Retrieved July 28, 2013

- Dressler, J. (2007). "United States v. Morris". Cases and Materials on Criminal Law. St. Paul, MN: Thomson/West. ISBN 978-0-314-17719-3

- Virvilis, Nikos; Mylonas, Alexios; Tsalis, Nikolaos; Gritzalis, Dimitris (2015). "Security Busters: Web Browser security vs. Rogue sites". Computers & Security. 52: 90–105. Doi:10.1016/j.cose.2015.04.009

- Cooley, Brian (March 7, 2011). "'Like,' 'tweet' buttons divulge sites you visit: CNET News Video". Cnet News. Retrieved March 7, 2011

- Andrew Hay; Daniel Cid; Rory Bray (2008). OSSEC Host-Based Intrusion Detection Guide. Syngress. P. 276. ISBN 978-1-59749-240-9

- "Stuxnet Introduces the First Known Rootkit for Industrial Control Systems". Symantec. 2010-08-06. Retrieved 2010-12-04

- Phishing, definition: techtarget.com, Retrieved 16 July, 2019

- V. W. Berninger (Ed., 2012), Past, present, and future contributions of cognitive writing research to cognitive psychology. New York/Sussex: Taylor & Francis. ISBN 9781848729636

- Spreitzer, Raphael (2014). PIN Skimming: Exploiting the Ambient-Light Sensor in Mobile Devices. Proceedings of the 4th ACM Workshop on Security and Privacy in Smartphones & Mobile Devices. ACM. Pp. 51–62. Arxiv:1405.3760. Doi:10.1145/2666620.2666622

4

Information Security Management

Information security management refers to the controls implemented by organizations to ensure that they are protecting the integrity and confidentiality of assets from threats and vulnerabilities. It involves the use of antivirus software and disk encryption. This chapter closely examines the key concepts of information security management.

ISM describes the controls which are necessary to be implemented by an organization to make sure that is sensibly managing the risks.

The main purpose of Information Security Management is to align IT security with business security and make sure that it matches the required needs of the business.

Objective of Information Security Management

The objectives of Information Security Management are to ensure that:

- Information is available and ready to use whenever it is required.

- The systems which provide information can resist attacks adequately and recover from failures/prevent them.

- The information is visible or disclosed to only those people who have the necessary clearance and have the right to know.

- The information is complete, accurate and has complete protection against modification by unauthorized personnel.

- The business transactions and exchange of information between enterprises or partners are trustworthy.

Scope of Information Security Management

Things such as data stores, databases, metadata and all the channels used to exchange that information. Information Security Management raises awareness all across the organization regarding the need to keep all the information assets safe. Information Security Management should understand the following:

- The plans and policies of business security.

- The present operations the business and security requirements.

- The plans and requirements of the business for the future.

- The legislative requirements.

- The responsibilities and obligations regarding the security contained in the service level agreements.

- The risks in business and IT and their management.

Value of Information Security Management

Implementing Information Security Management in an organization imparts a lot of benefits such as:

- It ensures that the information security policy is maintained and enforced properly such that the needs of the business security policy and corporate governance are fulfilled.

- It helps to protect all forms of information such as the ones which are digitally stored on devices and the cloud, paper-based, company secrets and intellectual property.

- It increases the resistance to cyber-attacks and malware by if implemented properly.

- It provides a framework for keeping all the information safe which is managed from one place.

- It adapts to constant changes in the threat environment and reduces the security threats which are constantly evolving.

- It helps to reduce the costs which are associated with information security by adding only the protection layers which are necessary and removing the redundant ones.

Basic Concepts of Information Security Management

The following basic concepts are necessary to understand Information Security Management.

Information Security Policy

The information security policy needs to have complete support and commitment from the senior level IT and business management in the organization. It should have under its purview all the areas of information security and the appropriate measures to meet the objectives of Information security management.

Risk Assessment and Management

It is vital to have a formal risk assessment and management policy which is related to information security and processing. Information security management often collaborates with the business, It service continuity management and availability management in order to perform risk assessments.

Information Security Management System

The Information Security Management System forms the basis for developing a cost-effective program for information security which supports the objectives of the business. It focuses on the five key elements which are control, plan, implement, evaluate and maintain. Organizations can seek independent certification of their Information Security Management against the ISO/IEC 27001 standard.

Framework of Information Security Management

There are five key elements which are addressed in an Information Security Management system framework. They are:

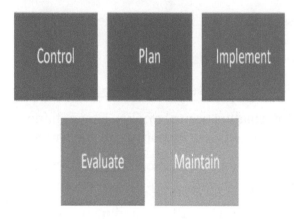

1. Control

A management framework should be established to manage information security, to prepare and implement an information security policy, to allocate responsibilities, to establish and control the documentation.

2. Plan

This phase of the framework involves the collection of information and understanding the security requirements of the organization. Afterward, the appropriate solutions should be recommended keeping in mind the budget and corporate culture.

3. Implement

In the implementation phase, the plan will be put into action. While doing so, it is important to ensure that the adequate safeguards are in place to enact and enforce the information security policy.

4. Evaluate

After the security policies and plans have been implemented, it is necessary to monitor them and make sure that the systems are completely secure and operating in accordance with the policies, security requirements and service level agreements of the organization.

5. Maintain

For an information management system to be effective, it needs to be improved on a continuous basis. This involves revising the service level agreements, security policies and the techniques used to monitor and control.

Process Activities of Information Security Management

The main activities of Information Security Management are:

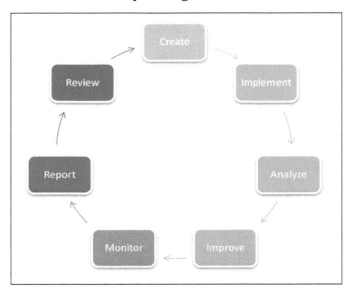

- Create, review and revise the information security policy as per the requirements.

- Communicate, implement and enforce the security policies adequately.

- Analyze and classify all the information and documentation in possession.

- Implement a set of security controls and risk responses and improve them.

- Constantly monitor and manage all breaches of security and any major security incidents.

- Analyze, report on and take the necessary actions in order to decrease the volume and effect of security incidents.

- Schedule and perform security reviews, audits, and penetration tests.

Challenges of Information Security Management

The challenges faced by information security management are:

- It has to ensure that there is adequate support for the information security policy from the business. This is because information security objects cannot be fulfilled with adequate support and endorsement from the top level management.

- A constantly evolving threat scenario where newer and stronger threats keep popping up.

Risks of Information Security Management

The risks which are encountered by information security management are:

- A lack of commitment from the business to the information security management process.

- A lack of resources or budget for the information security management process.

- Risk assessment being conducted in an isolated manner without combining with availability management and IT Service Continuity Management.

Through proper implementation, Information Security Management ensures that information is available and ready to use whenever it is required, and the systems which provide information can resist attacks adequately and recover from failures or prevent them.

Network Security

Network security consists of the policies and practices adopted to prevent and monitor unauthorized access, misuse, modification, or denial of a computer network and network-accessible resources. Network security involves the authorization of access to data in a network, which is controlled by the network administrator. Users choose or are assigned an ID and password or other authenticating information that allows them access to information and programs within their authority. Network security covers a variety of computer networks, both public and private, that are used in everyday jobs; conducting transactions and communications among businesses, government agencies and individuals. Networks can be private, such as within a company, and others which might be open to public access. Network security is involved in organizations, enterprises, and other types of institutions. It does as its title explains: It secures the network, as well as protecting and overseeing operations being done. The most common and simple way of protecting a network resource is by assigning it a unique name and a corresponding password.

Network Security Concept

Network security starts with authentication, commonly with a username and a password. Since this requires just one detail authenticating the user name—i.e., the password—this is sometimes termed one-factor authentication. With two-factor authentication, something the user 'has' is also used (e.g., a security token or 'dongle', an ATM card, or a mobile phone); and with three-factor authentication, something the user 'is' is also used (e.g., a fingerprint or retinal scan).

Once authenticated, a firewall enforces access policies such as what services are allowed to be accessed by the network users. Though effective to prevent unauthorized access, this component may fail to check potentially harmful content such as computer worms or Trojans being transmitted over the network. Anti-virus software or an intrusion prevention system (IPS) help detect and inhibit the action of such malware. An anomaly-based intrusion detection system may also monitor the network like wireshark traffic and may be logged for audit purposes and for later high-level analysis. Newer systems combining unsupervised machine learning with full network traffic analysis can detect active network attackers from malicious insiders or targeted external attackers that have compromised a user machine or account.

Communication between two hosts using a network may be encrypted to maintain privacy.

Honeypots, essentially decoy network-accessible resources, may be deployed in a network as surveillance and early-warning tools, as the honeypots are not normally accessed for legitimate purposes. Techniques used by the attackers that attempt to compromise these decoy resources are studied during and after an attack to keep an eye on new exploitation techniques. Such analysis may be used to further tighten security of the actual network being protected by the honeypot. A honeypot can also direct an attacker's attention away from legitimate servers. A honeypot encourages attackers to spend their time and energy on the decoy server while distracting their attention from the data on the real server. Similar to a honeypot, a honeynet is a network set up with intentional vulnerabilities. Its purpose is also to invite attacks so that the attacker's methods can be studied and that information can be used to increase network security. A honeynet typically contains one or more honeypots.

Security Management

Security management for networks is different for all kinds of situations. A home or small office may only require basic security while large businesses may require high-maintenance and advanced software and hardware to prevent malicious attacks from hacking and spamming. In order to minimize susceptibility to malicious attacks from external threats to the network, corporations often employ tools which carry out network security verifications.

Types of Attacks

Networks are subject to attacks from malicious sources. Attacks can be from two categories: "Passive" when a network intruder intercepts data traveling through the network, and "Active" in which an intruder initiates commands to disrupt the network's normal operation or to conduct reconnaissance and lateral movement to find and gain access to assets available via the network.

Types of attacks include:

- Passive

  ○ Network

- Wiretapping

- Port scanner

- Idle scan

- Encryption

- Traffic analysis

- Active

- Virus

- Eavesdropping

- Data modification

- Denial-of-service attack

- DNS spoofing

- Man in the middle

- ARP poisoning

- VLAN hopping

- Smurf attack

- Buffer overflow

- Heap overflow

- Format string attack

- SQL injection

- Phishing

- Cross-site scripting

- CSRF

- Cyber-attack

Firewall (Computing)

In computing, a firewall is a network security system that monitors and controls incoming and outgoing network traffic based on predetermined security rules. A firewall typically establishes a barrier between a trusted internal network and untrusted external network, such as the Internet.

Firewalls are often categorized as either network firewalls or host-based firewalls. Network firewalls filter traffic between two or more networks and run on network hardware. Host-based firewalls run on host computers and control network traffic in and out of those machines.

The term *firewall* originally referred to a wall intended to confine a fire within a building. Later uses refer to similar structures, such as the metal sheet separating the engine compartment of a vehicle or aircraft from the passenger compartment. The term was applied in the late 1980s to network technology that emerged when the Internet was fairly new in terms of its global use and connectivity. The predecessors to firewalls for network security were the routers used in the late 1980s, because they separated networks from one another, thus halting the spread of problems from one network to another.

First Generation: Packet Filters

Screenshot of Gufw: The firewall shows its settings for incoming and outgoing traffic.

The first reported type of network firewall is called a packet filter. Packet filters act by inspecting packets transferred between computers. When a packet does not match the packet filter's set of filtering rules, the packet filter either drops (silently discards) the packet, or rejects the packet (discards it and generates an Internet Control Message Protocol notification for the sender) else it is allowed to pass. Packets may be filtered by source and destination network addresses, protocol, source and destination port numbers. The bulk of Internet communication in 20th and early 21st century used either Transmission Control Protocol (TCP) or User Datagram Protocol (UDP) in conjunction with well-known ports, enabling firewalls of that era to distinguish between, and thus control, specific types of traffic (such as web browsing, remote printing, email transmission, file transfer), unless the machines on each side of the packet filter used the same non-standard ports.

The first paper published on firewall technology was in 1988, when engineers from Digital Equipment Corporation (DEC) developed filter systems known as packet filter firewalls. At AT&T Bell Labs, Bill Cheswick and Steve Bellovin continued their research in packet filtering and developed a working model for their own company based on their original first generation architecture.

Second Generation: Stateful Filters

From 1989–1990, three colleagues from AT&T Bell Laboratories, Dave Presotto, Janardan Sharma, and Kshitij Nigam, developed the second generation of firewalls, calling them circuit-level gateways.

Second-generation firewalls perform the work of their first-generation predecessors but also maintain knowledge of specific conversations between endpoints by remembering which port number the two IP addresses are using at layer 4 (transport layer) of the OSI model for their conversation, allowing examination of the overall exchange between the nodes.

This type of firewall is potentially vulnerable to denial-of-service attacks that bombard the firewall with fake connections in an attempt to overwhelm the firewall by filling its connection state memory.

Third Generation: Application Layer

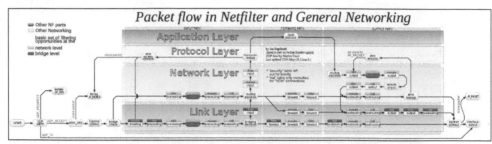

Flow of network packets through Netfilter, a Linux kernel module

Marcus Ranum, Wei Xu, and Peter Churchyard released an application firewall known as Firewall Toolkit (FWTK) in October 1993. This became the basis for Gauntlet firewall at Trusted Information Systems.

The key benefit of application layer filtering is that it can understand certain applications and protocols (such as File Transfer Protocol (FTP), Domain Name System (DNS), or Hypertext Transfer Protocol (HTTP)). This is useful as it is able to detect if an unwanted application or service is attempting to bypass the firewall using a disallowed protocol on an allowed port, or detect if a protocol is being abused in any harmful way.

As of 2012, the so-called next-generation firewall (NGFW) is a wider or deeper inspection at the application layer. For example, the existing deep packet inspection functionality of modern firewalls can be extended to include:

- Intrusion prevention systems (IPS).

- User identity management integration (by binding user IDs to IP or MAC addresses for "reputation").

- Web application firewall (WAF). WAF attacks may be implemented in the tool "WAF Fingerprinting utilizing timing side channels" (WAFFle).

Types

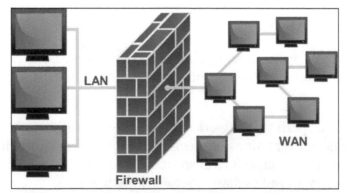

An illustration of where a firewall would be located in a network

Firewalls are generally categorized as network-based or host-based. Network-based firewalls are positioned on the gateway computers of LANs, WANs and intranets. They are either software appliances running on general-purpose hardware, or hardware-based firewall computer appliances. Firewall appliances may also offer other functionality to the internal network they protect, such as acting as a DHCP or VPN server for that network. Host-based firewalls are positioned on the host itself and control network traffic in and out of those machines. The host-based firewall may be a daemon or service as a part of the operating system or an agent application such as endpoint security or protection. Each has advantages and disadvantages. However, each has a role in layered security.

Firewalls also vary in type depending on where communication originates, where it is intercepted, and the state of communication being traced.

Network Layer or Packet Filters

Network layer firewalls, also called packet filters, operate at a relatively low level of the TCP/IP protocol stack, not allowing packets to pass through the firewall unless they match the established rule set. The firewall administrator may define the rules; or default rules may apply. The term "packet filter" originated in the context of BSD operating systems.

Network layer firewalls generally fall into two sub-categories, stateful and stateless.

Commonly used packet filters on various versions of Unix are *ipfw* (FreeBSD, Mac OS X (< 10.7)), *NPF* (NetBSD), *PF* (Mac OS X (> 10.4), OpenBSD, and some other BSDs), *iptables/ipchains* (Linux) and *IPFilter*.

Application-layer

Application-layer firewalls work on the application level of the TCP/IP stack (i.e., all browser traffic, or all telnet or FTP traffic), and may intercept all packets traveling to or from an application.

Application firewalls function by determining whether a process should accept any given connection. Application firewalls accomplish their function by hooking into socket calls to filter the connections between the application layer and the lower layers of the OSI model. Application firewalls that hook into socket calls are also referred to as socket filters. Application firewalls work much like a packet filter but application filters apply filtering rules (allow/block) on a per process basis instead of filtering connections on a per port basis. Generally, prompts are used to define rules for processes that have not yet received a connection. It is rare to find application firewalls not combined or used in conjunction with a packet filter.

Also, application firewalls further filter connections by examining the process ID of data packets against a rule set for the local process involved in the data transmission. The extent of the filtering that occurs is defined by the provided rule set. Given the variety of software that exists, application firewalls only have more complex rule sets for the standard services, such as sharing services. These per-process rule sets have limited efficacy in filtering every possible association that may occur with other processes. Also, these per-process rule sets cannot defend against modification of the process via exploitation, such as memory corruption exploits. Because of these limitations, application firewalls are beginning to be supplanted by a new generation of application firewalls that rely on mandatory access control (MAC), also referred to as sandboxing, to protect vulnerable services.

Proxies

A proxy server (running either on dedicated hardware or as software on a general-purpose machine) may act as a firewall by responding to input packets (connection requests, for example) in the manner of an application, while blocking other packets. A proxy server is a gateway from one network to another for a specific network application, in the sense that it functions as a proxy on behalf of the network user.

Proxies make tampering with an internal system from the external network more difficult, so that misuse of one internal system would not necessarily cause a security breach exploitable from outside the firewall (as long as the application proxy remains intact and properly configured). Conversely, intruders may hijack a publicly reachable system and use it as a proxy for their own purposes; the proxy then masquerades as that system to other internal machines. While use of internal address spaces enhances security, crackers may still employ methods such as IP spoofing to attempt to pass packets to a target network.

Network Address Translation

Firewalls often have network address translation (NAT) functionality, and the hosts protected behind a firewall commonly have addresses in the "private address range", as defined in RFC 1918. Firewalls often have such functionality to hide the true address of computer which is connected to the network. Originally, the NAT function was developed to address the limited number of IPv4 routable addresses that could be used or assigned to companies or individuals as well as reduce both the amount and therefore cost of obtaining enough public addresses for every computer in an organization. Although NAT on its own is not considered a security feature, hiding the addresses of protected devices has become an often used defense against network reconnaissance.

Intrusion Detection System

An intrusion detection system (IDS) is a device or software application that monitors a network or systems for malicious activity or policy violations. Any malicious activity or violation is typically reported either to an administrator or collected centrally using a security information and event management (SIEM) system. A SIEM system combines outputs from multiple sources, and uses alarm filtering techniques to distinguish malicious activity from false alarms.

IDS types range in scope from single computers to large networks. The most common classifications are network intrusion detection systems (NIDS) and host-based intrusion detection systems (HIDS). A system that monitors important operating system files is an example of an HIDS, while a system that analyzes incoming network traffic is an example of an NIDS. It is also possible to classify IDS by detection approach: the most well-known variants are signature-based detection (recognizing bad patterns, such as malware); and anomaly-based detection (detecting deviations from a model of "good" traffic, which often relies on machine learning), another is reputation-based detection (recognizing the potential threat according to the reputation scores). Some IDS products have the ability to respond to detected intrusions. Systems with response capabilities are typically referred to as an intrusion prevention system. Intrusion detection systems can also serve specific purposes by augmenting them with custom tools, such as using a honeypot to attract and characterize malicious traffic.

Comparison with Firewalls

Although they both relate to network security, an IDS differs from a firewall in that a firewall looks outwardly for intrusions in order to stop them from happening. Firewalls limit access between networks to prevent intrusion and do not signal an attack from inside the network. An IDS describes a suspected intrusion once it has taken place and signals an alarm. An IDS also watches for attacks that originate from within a system. This is traditionally achieved by examining network communications, identifying heuristics and patterns (often known as signatures) of common computer attacks, and taking action to alert operators. A system that terminates connections is called an intrusion prevention system, and performs access control like an application layer firewall.

Intrusion Detection Category

IDS can be classified by where detection takes place (network or host) or the detection method that is employed (signature or anomaly-based).

Analyzed Activity

Network Intrusion Detection Systems

Network intrusion detection systems (NIDS) are placed at a strategic point or points within the network to monitor traffic to and from all devices on the network. It performs an analysis of passing traffic on the entire subnet, and matches the traffic that is passed on the subnets to the library of known attacks. Once an attack is identified, or abnormal behavior is sensed, the alert can be sent to the administrator. An example of an NIDS would be installing it on the subnet where firewalls are located in order to see if someone is trying to break into the firewall. Ideally one would scan all inbound and outbound traffic, however doing so might create a bottleneck that would impair the overall speed of the network. OPNET and NetSim are commonly used tools for simulating network intrusion detection systems. NID Systems are also capable of comparing signatures for similar packets to link and drop harmful detected packets which have a signature matching the records in the NIDS. When we classify the design of the NIDS according to the system interactivity property, there are two types: on-line and off-line NIDS, often referred to as inline and tap mode, respectively. On-line NIDS deals with the network in real time. It analyses the Ethernet packets and applies some rules, to decide if it is an attack or not. Off-line NIDS deals with stored data and passes it through some processes to decide if it is an attack or not.

NIDS can be also combined with other technologies to increase detection and prediction rates. Artificial Neural Network based IDS are capable of analyzing huge volumes of data, in a smart way, due to the self-organizing structure that allows INS IDS to more efficiently recognize intrusion patterns. Neural networks assist IDS in predicting attacks by learning from mistakes; INN IDS help develop an early warning system, based on two layers. The first layer accepts single values, while the second layer takes the first's layers output as input; the cycle repeats and allows the system to automatically recognize new unforeseen patterns in the network. This system can average 99.9% detection and classification rate, based on research results of 24 network attacks, divided in four categories: DOS, Probe, Remote-to-Local, and user-to-root.

Host Intrusion Detection Systems

Host intrusion detection systems (HIDS) run on individual hosts or devices on the network. A HIDS monitors the inbound and outbound packets from the device only and will alert the user or administrator if suspicious activity is detected. It takes a snapshot of existing system files and matches it to the previous snapshot. If the critical system files were modified or deleted, an alert is sent to the administrator to investigate. An example of HIDS usage can be seen on mission critical machines, which are not expected to change their configurations.

Detection Method

Signature-based

Signature-based IDS refers to the detection of attacks by looking for specific patterns, such as byte sequences in network traffic, or known malicious instruction sequences used by malware. This terminology originates from anti-virus software, which refers to these detected patterns as signatures. Although signature-based IDS can easily detect known attacks, it is difficult to detect new attacks, for which no pattern is available.

In Signature-based IDS, the signatures are released by a vendor for its all products. On-time updating of the IDS with the signature is a key aspect.

Anomaly-based

Anomaly-based intrusion detection systems were primarily introduced to detect unknown attacks, in part due to the rapid development of malware. The basic approach is to use machine learning to create a model of trustworthy activity, and then compare new behavior against this model. Since these models can be trained according to the applications and hardware configurations, machine learning based method has a better generalized property in comparison to traditional signature-based IDS. Although this approach enables the detection of previously unknown attacks, it may suffer from false positives: previously unknown legitimate activity may also be classified as malicious. Most of the existing IDSs suffer from the time-consuming during detection process that degrades the performance of IDSs. Efficient feature selection algorithm makes the classification process used in detection more reliable.

New types of what could be called anomaly-based intrusion detection systems are being viewed by Gartner as User and Entity Behavior Analytics (UEBA) (an evolution of the user behavior analytics category) and network traffic analysis (NTA). In particular, NTA deals with malicious insiders as well as targeted external attacks that have compromised a user machine or account. Gartner has noted that some organizations have opted for NTA over more traditional IDS.

Intrusion Prevention

Some systems may attempt to stop an intrusion attempt but this is neither required nor expected of a monitoring system. Intrusion detection and prevention systems (IDPS) are primarily focused on identifying possible incidents, logging information about them, and reporting attempts. In addition, organizations use IDPS for other purposes, such as identifying problems with security policies, documenting existing threats and deterring individuals from violating security policies. IDPS have become a necessary addition to the security infrastructure of nearly every organization.

IDPS typically record information related to observed events, notify security administrators of important observed events and produce reports. Many IDPS can also respond to a detected threat by attempting to prevent it from succeeding. They use several response techniques, which involve the IDPS stopping the attack itself, changing the security environment (e.g. reconfiguring a firewall) or changing the attack's content.

Intrusion prevention systems (IPS), also known as intrusion detection and prevention systems (IDPS), are network security appliances that monitor network or system activities for malicious activity. The main functions of intrusion prevention systems are to identify malicious activity, log information about this activity, report it and attempt to block or stop it.

Intrusion prevention systems are considered extensions of intrusion detection systems because they both monitor network traffic and/or system activities for malicious activity. The main differences are, unlike intrusion detection systems, intrusion prevention systems are placed in-line and are able to actively prevent or block intrusions that are detected. IPS can take such actions as sending an alarm, dropping detected malicious packets, resetting a connection or blocking traffic from the offending IP address. An IPS also can correct cyclic redundancy check (CRC) errors, defragment packet streams, mitigate TCP sequencing issues, and clean up unwanted transport and network layer options.

Classification

Intrusion prevention systems can be classified into four different types:

- Network-based intrusion prevention system (NIPS): Monitors the entire network for suspicious traffic by analyzing protocol activity.

- Wireless intrusion prevention system (WIPS): Monitor a wireless network for suspicious traffic by analyzing wireless networking protocols.

- Network behavior analysis (NBA): Examines network traffic to identify threats that generate unusual traffic flows, such as distributed denial of service (DDoS) attacks, certain forms of malware and policy violations.

- Host-based intrusion prevention system (HIPS): An installed software package which monitors a single host for suspicious activity by analyzing events occurring within that host.

Detection Methods

The majority of intrusion prevention systems utilize one of three detection methods: signature-based, statistical anomaly-based, and stateful protocol analysis.

- Signature-based detection: Signature-based IDS monitors packets in the Network and compares with pre-configured and pre-determined attack patterns known as signatures.

- Statistical anomaly-based detection: An IDS which is anomaly-based will monitor network traffic and compare it against an established baseline. The baseline will identify what is "normal" for that network – what sort of bandwidth is generally used and what protocols are used. It may however, raise a False Positive alarm for legitimate use of bandwidth if the baselines are not intelligently configured.

- Stateful protocol analysis detection: This method identifies deviations of protocol states by comparing observed events with "pre-determined profiles of generally accepted definitions of benign activity".

Limitations

- Noise can severely limit an intrusion detection system's effectiveness. Bad packets generated from software bugs, corrupt DNS data, and local packets that escaped can create a significantly high false-alarm rate.

- It is not uncommon for the number of real attacks to be far below the number of false-alarms. Number of real attacks is often so far below the number of false-alarms that the real attacks are often missed and ignored.

- Many attacks are geared for specific versions of software that are usually outdated. A constantly changing library of signatures is needed to mitigate threats. Outdated signature databases can leave the IDS vulnerable to newer strategies.

- For signature-based IDS, there will be lag between a new threat discovery and its signature being applied to the IDS. During this lag time, the IDS will be unable to identify the threat.

- It cannot compensate for weak identification and authentication mechanisms or for weaknesses in network protocols. When an attacker gains access due to weak authentication mechanisms then IDS cannot prevent the adversary from any malpractice.

- Encrypted packets are not processed by most intrusion detection devices. Therefore, the encrypted packet can allow an intrusion to the network that is undiscovered until more significant network intrusions have occurred.

- Intrusion detection software provides information based on the network address that is associated with the IP packet that is sent into the network. This is beneficial if the network address contained in the IP packet is accurate. However, the address that is contained in the IP packet could be faked or scrambled.

- Due to the nature of NIDS systems, and the need for them to analyse protocols as they are captured, NIDS systems can be susceptible to the same protocol-based attacks to which network hosts may be vulnerable. Invalid data and TCP/IP stack attacks may cause an NIDS to crash.

Evasion Techniques

There are a number of techniques which attackers are using, the following are considered 'simple' measures which can be taken to evade IDS:

- Fragmentation: by sending fragmented packets, the attacker will be under the radar and can easily bypass the detection system's ability to detect the attack signature.

- Avoiding defaults: The TCP port utilised by a protocol does not always provide an indication to the protocol which is being transported. For example, an IDS may expect to detect a trojan on port 12345. If an attacker had reconfigured it to use a different port, the IDS may not be able to detect the presence of the trojan.

- Coordinated, low-bandwidth attacks: Coordinating a scan among numerous attackers (or agents) and allocating different ports or hosts to different attackers makes it difficult for the IDS to correlate the captured packets and deduce that a network scan is in progress.

- Address spoofing/proxying: attackers Can increase the difficulty of the Security Administrators ability to determine the source of the attack by using poorly secured or incorrectly configured proxy servers to bounce an attack. If the source is spoofed and bounced by a server, it makes it very difficult for IDS to detect the origin of the attack.

- Pattern change evasion: IDS generally rely on 'pattern matching' to detect an attack. By changing the data used in the attack slightly, it may be possible to evade detection. For example, an Internet Message Access Protocol (IMAP) server may be vulnerable to a buffer overflow, and an IDS is able to detect the attack signature of 10 common attack tools. By modifying the payload sent by the tool, so that it does not resemble the data that the IDS expects, it may be possible to evade detection.

Computer Access Control

In computer security, general access control includes identification, authorization, authentication, access approval, and audit. A more narrow definition of access control would cover only access approval, whereby the system makes a decision to grant or reject an access request from an already authenticated subject, based on what the subject is authorized to access. Authentication and access control are often combined into a single operation, so that access is approved based on successful authentication, or based on an anonymous access token. Authentication methods and tokens include passwords, biometric scans, physical keys, electronic keys and devices, hidden paths, social barriers, and monitoring by humans and automated systems.

The two possibilities for imposing computer access control are those based on capabilities and those based on access control lists (ACLs):

- In a capability-based model, holding an unforge-able reference or *capability* to an object provides access to the object (roughly analogous to how possession of one's house key grants one access to one's house); access is conveyed to another party by transmitting such a capability over a secure channel.

- In an ACL-based model, a subject's access to an object depends on whether its identity appears on a list associated with the object (roughly analogous to how a bouncer at a private party would check an ID to see if a name appears on the guest list); access is conveyed by editing the list. (Different ACL systems have a variety of different conventions regarding who or what is responsible for editing the list and how it is edited.)

Both capability-based and ACL-based models have mechanisms to allow access rights to be granted to all members of a *group* of subjects (often the group is itself modeled as a subject).

Services

Access control systems provide the essential services of authorization, identification and authentication (I&A), access approval, and accountability where:

- Authorization specifies what a subject can do.

- Identification and authentication ensure that only legitimate subjects can log on to a system.

- Access approval grants access during operations, by association of users with the resources that they are allowed to access, based on the authorization policy.

- Accountability identifies what a subject (or all subjects associated with a user) did.

Authorization

Authorization involves the act of defining access-rights for subjects. An authorization policy specifies the operations that subjects are allowed to execute within a system.

Most modern operating systems implement authorization policies as formal sets of permissions that are variations or extensions of three basic types of access:

- Read (R): The subject can:

  ○ Read file contents

  ○ List directory contents

- Write (W): The subject can change the contents of a file or directory with the following tasks:

  ○ Add

  ○ Update

  ○ Delete

  ○ Rename

- Execute (X): If the file is a program, the subject can cause the program to be run. (In Unix-style systems, the "execute" permission doubles as a "traverse directory" permission when granted for a directory.)

These rights and permissions are implemented differently in systems based on discretionary access control (DAC) and mandatory access control (MAC).

Identification and Authentication (I&A)

Identification and Authentication (I&A) is the process of verifying that an identity is bound to the entity that makes an assertion or claim of identity. The I&A process assumes that there was an initial validation of the identity, commonly called identity proofing. Various methods of identity proofing are available, ranging from in-person validation using government issued identification, to anonymous methods that allow the claimant to remain anonymous, but known to the system if they return. The method used for identity proofing and validation should provide an assurance level commensurate with the intended use of the identity within the system. Subsequently, the entity asserts an identity together with an authenticator as a means for validation. The only requirements for the identifier is that it must be unique within its security domain.

Authenticators are commonly based on at least one of the following four factors:

- Something you know, such as a password or a personal identification number (PIN). This assumes that only the owner of the account knows the password or PIN needed to access the account.

- Something you have, such as a smart card or security token. This assumes that only the owner of the account has the necessary smart card or token needed to unlock the account.

- Something you are, such as fingerprint, voice, retina, or iris characteristics.

- Where you are, for example inside or outside a company firewall, or proximity of login location to a personal GPS device.

Access Approval

Access approval is the function that actually grants or rejects access during operations.

During access approval, the system compares the formal representation of the authorization policy with the access request, to determine whether the request shall be granted or rejected. Moreover, the access evaluation can be done online/ongoing.

Accountability

Accountability uses such system components as audit trails (records) and logs, to associate a subject with its actions. The information recorded should be sufficient to map the subject to a controlling user. Audit trails and logs are important for

- Detecting security violations.

- Re-creating security incidents.

If no one is regularly reviewing your logs and they are not maintained in a secure and consistent manner, they may not be admissible as evidence.

Many systems can generate automated reports, based on certain predefined criteria or thresholds, known as clipping levels. For example, a clipping level may be set to generate a report for the following:

- More than three failed logon attempts in a given period.

- Any attempt to use a disabled user account.

These reports help a system administrator or security administrator to more easily identify possible break-in attempts.

Definition of clipping level: a disk's ability to maintain its magnetic properties and hold its content. A high-quality level range is 65–70%; low quality is below 55%.

Access Control Models

Access control models are sometimes categorized as either discretionary or non-discretionary. The three most widely recognized models are Discretionary Access Control (DAC), Mandatory Access Control (MAC), and Role Based Access Control (RBAC). MAC is non-discretionary.

Discretionary Access Control

Discretionary access control (DAC) is a policy determined by the owner of an object. The owner decides who is allowed to access the object, and what privileges they have.

Two important concepts in DAC are:

- File and data ownership: Every object in the system has an *owner*. In most DAC systems, each object's initial owner is the subject that caused it to be created. The access policy for an object is determined by its owner.

- Access rights and permissions: These are the controls that an owner can assign to other subjects for specific resources.

Access controls may be discretionary in ACL-based or capability-based access control systems. (In capability-based systems, there is usually no explicit concept of 'owner', but the creator of an object has a similar degree of control over its access policy.)

Mandatory Access Control

Mandatory access control refers to allowing access to a resource if and only if rules exist that allow a given user to access the resource. It is difficult to manage, but its use is usually justified when used to protect highly sensitive information. Examples include certain government and military information. Management is often simplified (over what can be required) if the information can be protected using hierarchical access control, or by implementing sensitivity labels. What makes the method "mandatory" is the use of either rules or sensitivity labels.

- Sensitivity labels: In such a system subjects and objects must have labels assigned to them. A subject's sensitivity label specifies its level of trust. An object's sensitivity label specifies the level of trust required for access. In order to access a given object, the subject must have a sensitivity level equal to or higher than the requested object.

- Data import and export: Controlling the import of information from other systems and export to other systems (including printers) is a critical function of these systems, which must ensure that sensitivity labels are properly maintained and implemented so that sensitive information is appropriately protected at all times.

Two methods are commonly used for applying mandatory access control:

- Rule-based (or label-based) access control: This type of control further defines specific conditions for access to a requested object. A Mandatory Access Control system implements a simple form of rule-based access control to determine whether access should be granted or denied by matching:

- ◦ An object's sensitivity label.

- ◦ A subject's sensitivity label.

- Lattice-based access control: These can be used for complex access control decisions involving multiple objects and/or subjects. A lattice model is a mathematical structure that defines greatest lower-bound and least upper-bound values for a pair of elements, such as a subject and an object.

Few systems implement MAC; XTS-400 and SELinux are examples of systems that do.

Role-based Access Control

Role-based access control (RBAC) is an access policy determined by the system, not by the owner. RBAC is used in commercial applications and also in military systems, where multi-level security requirements may also exist. RBAC differs from DAC in that DAC allows users to control access to their resources, while in RBAC, access is controlled at the system level, outside of the user's control. Although RBAC is non-discretionary, it can be distinguished from MAC primarily in the way permissions are handled. MAC controls read and write permissions based on a user's clearance level and additional labels. RBAC controls collections of permissions that may include complex operations such as an e-commerce transaction, or may be as simple as read or write. A role in RBAC can be viewed as a set of permissions.

Three primary rules are defined for RBAC:

- Role assignment: A subject can execute a transaction only if the subject has selected or been assigned a suitable role.

- Role authorization: A subject's active role must be authorized for the subject. With rule 1 above, this rule ensures that users can take on only roles for which they are authorized.

- Transaction authorization: A subject can execute a transaction only if the transaction is authorized for the subject's active role. With rules 1 and 2, this rule ensures that users can execute only transactions for which they are authorized.

Additional constraints may be applied as well, and roles can be combined in a hierarchy where higher-level roles subsume permissions owned by lower-level sub-roles.

Most IT vendors offer RBAC in one or more products.

Attribute-based Access Control

In attribute-based access control (ABAC), access is granted not based on the rights of the subject associated with a user after authentication, but based on attributes of the user. The user has to prove so-called claims about his attributes to the access control engine. An attribute-based access control policy specifies which claims need to be satisfied in order to grant access to an object. For instance the claim could be "older than 18". Any user that can prove this claim is granted access. Users can be anonymous when authentication and identification are not strictly required. One does, however, require means for proving claims anonymously. This can for instance be achieved using anonymous credentials. XACML (extensible access control markup language) is a standard for attribute-based access control, XACML 3.0 was standardized in January 2013.

Break-glass Access Control Models

Traditionally, access has the purpose of restricting access, thus most access control models follow the "default deny principle", i.e. if a specific access request is not explicitly allowed, it will be denied. This behavior might conflict with the regular operations of a system. In certain situations, humans are willing to take the risk that might be involved in violating an access control policy, if the potential benefit that can be achieved outweighs this risk. This need is especially visible in the health-care domain, where a denied access to patient records can cause the death of a patient. Break-Glass (also called break-the-glass) try to mitigate this by allowing users to override access control decision. Break-Glass can either be implemented in an access control specific manner (e.g. into RBAC), or generic (i.e., independent from the underlying access control model).

Access Control based on the Responsibility

In Aligning Access Rights to Governance Needs with the Responsibility MetaModel (ReMMo) in the Frame of Enterprise Architecture an expressive Responsibility metamodel has been defined and allows representing the existing responsibilities at the business layer and, thereby, allows engineering the access rights required to perform these responsibilities, at the application layer. A method has been proposed to define the access rights more accurately, considering the alignment of the responsibility and RBAC.

Authorization

Authorization is the function of specifying access rights/privileges to resources, which is related to information security and computer security in general and to access control in particular. More formally, "to authorize" is to define an access policy. For example, human resources staff are normally authorized to access employee records and this policy is usually formalized as access control rules in a computer system. During operation, the system uses the access control rules to decide whether access requests from (authenticated) consumers shall be approved (granted) or disapproved (rejected). Resources include individual files or an item's data, computer programs, computer devices and functionality provided by computer applications. Examples of consumers are computer users, computer Software and other Hardware on the computer.

Access control in computer systems and networks rely on access policies. The access control process can be divided into the following phases: policy definition phase where access is authorized, and policy enforcement phase where access requests are approved or disapproved. Authorization is the function of the policy definition phase which precedes the policy enforcement phase where access requests are approved or disapproved based on the previously defined authorizations.

Most modern, multi-user operating systems include access control and thereby rely on authorization. Access control also uses authentication to verify the identity of consumers. When a consumer tries to access a resource, the access control process checks that the consumer has been authorized to use that resource. Authorization is the responsibility of an authority, such as a department manager, within the application domain, but is often delegated to a custodian such as a system administrator. Authorizations are expressed as access policies in some types of "policy definition application", e.g. in the form of an access control list or a capability, or a policy administration point e.g. XACML. On the basis of the "principle of least privilege": consumers should only be authorized to access whatever they need to do their jobs. Older and single user operating systems often had weak or non-existent authentication and access control systems.

"Anonymous consumers" or "guests", are consumers that have not been required to authenticate. They often have limited authorization. On a distributed system, it is often desirable to grant access without requiring a unique identity. Familiar examples of access tokens include keys, certificates and tickets: they grant access without proving identity.

Trusted consumers are often authorized for unrestricted access to resources on a system, but must be verified so that the access control system can make the access approval decision. "Partially trusted" and guests will often have restricted authorization in order to protect resources against improper access and usage. The access policy in some operating systems, by default, grant all consumers full access to all resources. Others do the opposite, insisting that the administrator explicitly authorizes a consumer to use each resource.

Even when access is controlled through a combination of authentication and access control lists, the problems of maintaining the authorization data is not trivial, and often represents as much administrative burden as managing authentication credentials. It is often necessary to change or remove a user's authorization: this is done by changing or deleting the corresponding access rules on the system. Using atomic authorization is an alternative to per-system authorization management, where a trusted third party securely distributes authorization information.

Antivirus Software

Antivirus software, or anti-virus software (abbreviated to AV software), also known as anti-malware, is a computer program used to prevent, detect, and remove malware.

Antivirus software was originally developed to detect and remove computer viruses, hence the name. However, with the proliferation of other kinds of malware, antivirus software started to provide protection from other computer threats. In particular, modern antivirus software can protect users from: malicious browser helper objects (BHOs), browser hijackers, ransomware, keyloggers, backdoors, rootkits, trojan horses, worms, malicious LSPs, dialers, fraudtools, adware and spyware. Some products also include protection from other computer threats, such as infected and malicious URLs, spam, scam and phishing attacks, online identity (privacy), online banking attacks, social engineering techniques, advanced persistent threat (APT) and botnet DDoS attacks.

Identification Methods

One of the few solid theoretical results in the study of computer viruses is Frederick B. Cohen's 1987 demonstration that there is no algorithm that can perfectly detect all possible viruses. However, using different layers of defense, a good detection rate may be achieved.

There are several methods which antivirus engine can use to identify malware:

- Sandbox detection: A particular behavioural-based detection technique that, instead of detecting the behavioural fingerprint at run time, it executes the programs in a virtual environment, logging what actions the program performs. Depending on the actions logged, the antivirus engine can determine if the program is malicious or not. If not, then, the program is executed in the real environment. Albeit this technique has shown to be quite effective, given its heaviness and slowness, it is rarely used in end-user antivirus solutions.

- Data mining techniques: One of the latest approaches applied in malware detection. Data mining and machine learning algorithms are used to try to classify the behaviour of a file (as either malicious or benign) given a series of file features, that are extracted from the file itself.

Signature-based Detection

Traditional antivirus software relies heavily upon signatures to identify malware.

Substantially, when a malware arrives in the hands of an antivirus firm, it is analysed by malware researchers or by dynamic analysis systems. Then, once it is determined to be a malware, a proper signature of the file is extracted and added to the signatures database of the antivirus software.

Although the signature-based approach can effectively contain malware outbreaks, malware authors have tried to stay a step ahead of such software by writing "oligomorphic", "polymorphic" and, more recently, "metamorphic" viruses, which encrypt parts of themselves or otherwise modify themselves as a method of disguise, so as to not match virus signatures in the dictionary.

Heuristics

Many viruses start as a single infection and through either mutation or refinements by other attackers, can grow into dozens of slightly different strains, called variants. Generic detection refers to the detection and removal of multiple threats using a single virus definition.

For example, the Vundo trojan has several family members, depending on the antivirus vendor's classification. Symantec classifies members of the Vundo family into two distinct categories, Trojan.Vundo and Trojan.Vundo.B.

While it may be advantageous to identify a specific virus, it can be quicker to detect a virus family through a generic signature or through an inexact match to an existing signature. Virus researchers find common areas that all viruses in a family share uniquely and can thus create a single generic signature. These signatures often contain non-contiguous code, using wildcard characters where differences lie. These wildcards allow the scanner to detect viruses even if they are padded with extra, meaningless code. A detection that uses this method is said to be "heuristic detection."

Rootkit Detection

Anti-virus software can attempt to scan for rootkits. A rootkit is a type of malware designed to gain administrative-level control over a computer system without being detected. Rootkits can change how the operating system functions and in some cases can tamper with the anti-virus program and render it ineffective. Rootkits are also difficult to remove, in some cases requiring a complete re-installation of the operating system.

Real-time Protection

Real-time protection, on-access scanning, background guard, resident shield, autoprotect, and other synonyms refer to the automatic protection provided by most antivirus, anti-spyware, and other anti-malware programs. This monitors computer systems for suspicious activity such as computer viruses, spyware, adware, and other malicious objects in 'real-time', in other words while data loaded into the computer's active memory: when inserting a CD, opening an email, or browsing the web, or when a file already on the computer is opened or executed.

Issues of Concern

Unexpected Renewal Costs

Some commercial antivirus software end-user license agreements include a clause that the subscription will be automatically renewed, and the purchaser's credit card automatically billed, at the renewal time without explicit approval. For example, McAfee requires users to unsubscribe at least 60 days before the expiration of the present subscription while BitDefender sends notifications to unsubscribe 30 days before the renewal. Norton AntiVirus also renews subscriptions automatically by default.

Rogue Security Applications

Some apparent antivirus programs are actually malware masquerading as legitimate software, such as WinFixer, MS Antivirus, and Mac Defender.

Problems Caused by False Positives

A "false positive" or "false alarm" is when antivirus software identifies a non-malicious file as malware. When this happens, it can cause serious problems. For example, if an antivirus program is configured to immediately delete or quarantine infected files, as is common on Microsoft Windows antivirus applications, a false positive in an essential file can render the Windows operating system or some applications unusable. Recovering from such damage to critical software infrastructure incurs technical support costs and businesses can be forced to close whilst remedial action is undertaken.

Examples of serious false-positives:

- May 2007: A faulty virus signature issued by Symantec mistakenly removed essential operating system files, leaving thousands of PCs unable to boot.

- May 2007: The executable file required by Pegasus Mail on Windows was falsely detected by Norton AntiVirus as being a Trojan and it was automatically removed, preventing Pegasus Mail from running. Norton AntiVirus had falsely identified three releases of Pegasus Mail as malware, and would delete the Pegasus Mail installer file when that happened.

- April 2010: McAfee VirusScan detected svchost.exe, a normal Windows binary, as a virus on machines running Windows XP with Service Pack 3, causing a reboot loop and loss of all network access.

- December 2010: A faulty update on the AVG anti-virus suite damaged 64-bit versions of Windows 7, rendering it unable to boot, due to an endless boot loop created.

- October 2011: Microsoft Security Essentials (MSE) removed the Google Chrome web browser, rival to Microsoft's own Internet Explorer. MSE flagged Chrome as a Zbot banking trojan.

- September 2012: Sophos' anti-virus suite identified various update-mechanisms, including its own, as malware. If it was configured to automatically delete detected files, Sophos Antivirus could render itself unable to update, required manual intervention to fix the problem.

- September 2017: the Google Play Protect anti-virus started identifying Motorola's Moto G4 Bluetooth application as malware, causing Bluetooth functionality to become disabled.

System and Interoperability Related Issues

Running (the real-time protection of) multiple antivirus programs concurrently can degrade performance and create conflicts. However, using a concept called multiscanning, several companies (including G Data Software and Microsoft) have created applications which can run multiple engines concurrently.

It is sometimes necessary to temporarily disable virus protection when installing major updates such as Windows Service Packs or updating graphics card drivers. Active antivirus protection may partially or completely prevent the installation of a major update. Anti-virus software can cause problems during the installation of an operating system upgrade, e.g. when upgrading to a newer version of Windows "in place" — without erasing the previous version of Windows. Microsoft recommends that anti-virus software be disabled to avoid conflicts with the upgrade installation process. Active anti-virus software can also interfere with a firmware update process.

The functionality of a few computer programs can be hampered by active anti-virus software. For example, TrueCrypt, a disk encryption program, states on its troubleshooting page that anti-virus programs can conflict with TrueCrypt and cause it to malfunction or operate very slowly. Anti-virus software can impair the performance and stability of games running in the Steam platform.

Support issues also exist around antivirus application interoperability with common solutions like SSL VPN remote access and network access control products. These technology solutions often have policy assessment applications that require an up-to-date antivirus to be installed and running. If the antivirus application is not recognized by the policy assessment, whether because the antivirus application has been updated or because it is not part of the policy assessment library, the user will be unable to connect.

Effectiveness

Studies in December 2007 showed that the effectiveness of antivirus software had decreased in the previous year, particularly against unknown or zero day attacks. The computer magazine *c't* found that detection rates for these threats had dropped from 40–50% in 2006 to 20–30% in 2007. At that time, the only exception was the NOD32 antivirus, which managed a detection rate of 68%. According to the *ZeuS tracker* website the average detection rate for all variants of the well-known ZeuS trojan is as low as 40%.

The problem is magnified by the changing intent of virus authors. Some years ago it was obvious when a virus infection was present. At the time, viruses were written by amateurs and exhibited destructive behavior or pop-ups. Modern viruses are often written by professionals, financed by criminal organizations.

In 2008, Eva Chen, CEO of Trend Micro, stated that the anti-virus industry has over-hyped how effective its products are — and so has been misleading customers — for years.

Independent testing on all the major virus scanners consistently shows that none provides 100% virus detection. The best ones provided as high as 99.9% detection for simulated real-world situations, while the lowest provided 91.1% in tests conducted in August 2013. Many virus scanners produce false positive results as well, identifying benign files as malware.

Although methods may differ, some notable independent quality testing agencies include AV-Comparatives, ICSA Labs, West Coast Labs, Virus Bulletin, AV-TEST and other members of the Anti-Malware Testing Standards Organization.

New Viruses

Anti-virus programs are not always effective against new viruses, even those that use non-signature-based methods that should detect new viruses. The reason for this is that the virus designers test their new viruses on the major anti-virus applications to make sure that they are not detected before releasing them into the wild.

Some new viruses, particularly ransomware, use polymorphic code to avoid detection by virus scanners.

A proof of concept virus has used the Graphics Processing Unit (GPU) to avoid detection from anti-virus software. The potential success of this involves bypassing the CPU in order to make it much harder for security researchers to analyse the inner workings of such malware.

Rootkits

Detecting rootkits is a major challenge for anti-virus programs. Rootkits have full administrative access to the computer and are invisible to users and hidden from the list of running processes in the task manager. Rootkits can modify the inner workings of the operating system and tamper with antivirus programs.

Damaged Files

If a file has been infected by a computer virus, anti-virus software will attempt to remove the virus code from the file during disinfection, but it is not always able to restore the file to its undamaged state. In such circumstances, damaged files can only be restored from existing backups or shadow copies (this is also true for ransomware); installed software that is damaged requires re-installation.

Firmware Infections

Any writeable firmware in the computer can be infected by malicious code. This is a major concern, as an infected BIOS could require the actual BIOS chip to be replaced to ensure the malicious code is completely removed. Anti-virus software is not effective at protecting firmware and the motherboard BIOS from infection. In 2014, security researchers discovered that USB devices contain writeable firmware which can be modified with malicious code (dubbed "BadUSB"), which anti-virus software cannot detect or prevent. The malicious code can run undetected on the computer and could even infect the operating system prior to it booting up.

Performance and other Drawbacks

Antivirus software has some drawbacks, first of which that it can impact a computer's performance.

Furthermore, inexperienced users can be lulled into a false sense of security when using the computer, considering their computers to be invulnerable, and may have problems understanding the prompts and decisions that antivirus software presents them with. An incorrect decision may lead to a security breach. If the antivirus software employs heuristic detection, it must be fine-tuned to minimize misidentifying harmless software as malicious (false positive).

Antivirus software itself usually runs at the highly trusted kernel level of the operating system to allow it access to all the potential malicious process and files, creating a potential avenue of attack. The US National Security Agency (NSA) and the UK Government Communications Headquarters (GCHQ) intelligence agencies, respectively, have been exploiting anti-virus software to spy on users. Anti-virus software has highly privileged and trusted access to the underlying operating system, which makes it a much more appealing target for remote attacks. Additionally anti-virus software is "years behind security-conscious client-side applications like browsers or document readers. It means that Acrobat Reader, Microsoft Word or Google Chrome are harder to exploit than 90 percent of the anti-virus products out there", according to Joxean Koret, a researcher with Coseinc, a Singapore-based information security consultancy.

Alternative Solutions

Antivirus software running on individual computers is the most common method employed of guarding against malware, but it is not the only solution. Other solutions can also be employed by users, including Unified Threat Management (UTM), hardware and network firewalls, Cloud-based antivirus and online scanners.

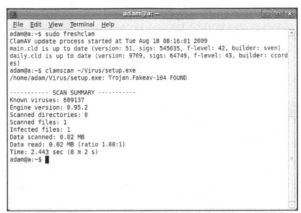

The command-line virus scanner of Clam AV 0.95.2 running a virus signature definition update, scanning a file, and identifying a Trojan.

Hardware and Network Firewall

Network firewalls prevent unknown programs and processes from accessing the system. However, they are not antivirus systems and make no attempt to identify or remove anything. They may protect against infection from outside the protected computer or network, and limit the activity of any malicious software which is present by blocking incoming or outgoing requests on certain TCP/IP ports. A firewall is designed to deal with broader system threats that come from network connections into the system and is not an alternative to a virus protection system.

Cloud Antivirus

Cloud antivirus is a technology that uses lightweight agent software on the protected computer, while offloading the majority of data analysis to the provider's infrastructure.

One approach to implementing cloud antivirus involves scanning suspicious files using multiple antivirus engines. This approach was proposed by an early implementation of the cloud antivirus concept called CloudAV. CloudAV was designed to send programs or documents to a network cloud where multiple antivirus and behavioral detection programs are used simultaneously in order to improve detection rates. Parallel scanning of files using potentially incompatible antivirus scanners is achieved by spawning a virtual machine per detection engine and therefore eliminating any possible issues. CloudAV can also perform "retrospective detection," whereby the cloud detection engine rescans all files in its file access history when a new threat is identified thus improving new threat detection speed. Finally, CloudAV is a solution for effective virus scanning on devices that lack the computing power to perform the scans themselves.

Some examples of cloud anti-virus products are Panda Cloud Antivirus, Crowdstrike, Cb Defense and Immunet. Comodo group has also produced cloud-based anti-virus.

Online Scanning

Some antivirus vendors maintain websites with free online scanning capability of the entire computer, critical areas only, local disks, folders or files. Periodic online scanning is a good idea for those that run antivirus applications on their computers because those applications are frequently slow to catch threats. One of the first things that malicious software does in an attack is disable any existing antivirus software and sometimes the only way to know of an attack is by turning to an online resource that is not installed on the infected computer.

Specialized Tools

The command-line rkhunter scanner, an engine to scan for Linux rootkits running on Ubuntu.

Virus removal tools are available to help remove stubborn infections or certain types of infection. Examples include Avast Free Anti- Malware, AVG Free Malware Removal Tools, and Avira AntiVir Removal Tool. It is also worth noting that sometimes antivirus software can produce a false positive result, indicating an infection where there is none.

A rescue disk that is bootable, such as a CD or USB storage device, can be used to run antivirus software outside of the installed operating system, in order to remove infections while they are dormant. A bootable antivirus disk can be useful when, for example, the installed operating system is no longer bootable or has malware that is resisting all attempts to be removed by the installed antivirus software. Examples of some of these bootable disks include the Bitdefender Rescue CD, Kaspersky Rescue Disk 2018, and Windows Defender Offline (integrated into Windows 10 since the Anniversary Update). Most of the Rescue CD software can also be installed onto a USB storage device, that is bootable on newer computers.

Secure Coding

Secure coding is the practice of developing computer software in a way that guards against the accidental introduction of security vulnerabilities. Defects, bugs and logic flaws are consistently the primary cause of commonly exploited software vulnerabilities. Through the analysis of thousands of reported vulnerabilities, security professionals have discovered that most vulnerabilities stem from a relatively small number of common software programming errors. By identifying the insecure coding practices that lead to these errors and educating developers on secure alternatives, organizations can take proactive steps to help significantly reduce or eliminate vulnerabilities in software before deployment.

Buffer-overflow Prevention

Buffer overflows, a common software security vulnerability, happen when a process tries to store data beyond a fixed-length buffer. For example, if there are 8 slots to store items in, there will be a problem if there is an attempt to store 9 items. In computer memory the overflowed data may overwrite data in the next location which can result in a security vulnerability (stack smashing) or program termination (segmentation fault).

An example of a C program prone to a buffer overflow is:

```
int vulnerable_function(char * large_user_input) {

        char dst[SMALL];

        strcpy(dst, large_user_input);

}
```

If the user input is larger than the destination buffer, a buffer overflow will occur. To fix this unsafe program, use strncpy to prevent a possible buffer overflow.

```
int secure_function(char * user_input) {

        char dst[BUF_SIZE];

    //copy a maximum of BUF_SIZE bytes

        strncpy(dst, user_input,BUF_SIZE);

}
```

Another secure alternative is to dynamically allocate memory on the heap using malloc.

```
char * secure_copy(char * src) {

        size_t len = strlen(src);

        char * dst = (char *) malloc(len + 1);

        if(dst != NULL){

                strncpy(dst, src, len);

                //append null terminator

            dst[len] = '\0';

        }

        return dst;

}
```

In the above code snippet, the program attempts to copy the contents of src into dst, while also checking the return value of malloc to ensure that enough memory was able to be allocated for the destination buffer.

Format-string Attack Prevention

A Format String Attack is when a malicious user supplies specific inputs that will eventually be entered as an argument to a function that performs formatting, such as printf(). The attack involves the adversary reading from or writing to the stack.

The C printf function writes output to stdout. If the parameter of the printf function is not properly formatted, several security bugs can be introduced. Below is a program that is vulnerable to a format string attack.

```
int vulnerable_print(char * malicious_input) {

        printf(malicious_input);

}
```

A malicious argument passed to the program could be "%s%s%s%s%s%s%s", which can crash the program from improper memory reads.

Integer-overflow Prevention

Integer overflow occurs when an arithmetic operation results in an integer too large to be represented within the available space. A program which does not properly check for integer overflow introduces potential software bugs and exploits.

Below is a function in C++ which attempts to confirm that the sum of x and y is less than or equal to a defined value MAX:

```
bool sumIsValid_flawed(unsigned int x, unsigned int y) {

        unsigned int sum = x + y;

        return sum <= MAX;

}
```

The problem with the code is it does not check for integer overflow on the addition operation. If the sum of x and y is greater than the maximum possible value of an unsigned int, the addition operation will overflow and perhaps result in a value less than or equal to MAX, even though the sum of x and y is greater than MAX.

Below is a function which checks for overflow by confirming the sum is greater than or equal to both x and y. If the sum did overflow, the sum would be less than x or less than y.

```
bool sumIsValid_secure(unsigned int x, unsigned int y) {

        unsigned int sum = x + y;

        return sum >= x && sum >= y && sum <= MAX;

}
```

Disk Encryption

Disk encryption is a technology which protects information by converting it into unreadable code that cannot be deciphered easily by unauthorized people. Disk encryption uses disk encryption software or hardware to encrypt every bit of data that goes on a disk or disk volume. It is used to prevent unauthorized access to data storage.

Expressions *full disk encryption (FDE)* or *whole disk encryption* signify that everything on disk is encrypted, but the master boot record (MBR), or similar area of a bootable disk, with code that starts the operating system loading sequence, is not encrypted. Some hardware-based full disk encryption systems can truly encrypt an entire boot disk, including the MBR.

Transparent Encryption

Transparent encryption, also known as real-time encryption and on-the-fly encryption (OTFE), is a method used by some disk encryption software. "Transparent" refers to the fact that data is automatically encrypted or decrypted as it is loaded or saved.

With transparent encryption, the files are accessible immediately after the key is provided, and the entire volume is typically mounted as if it were a physical drive, making the files just as accessible as any unencrypted ones. No data stored on an encrypted volume can be read (decrypted) without using the correct password/keyfile(s) or correct encryption keys. The entire file system within the volume is encrypted (including file names, folder names, file contents, and other meta-data).

To be transparent to the end user, transparent encryption usually requires the use of device drivers to enable the encryption process. Although administrator access rights are normally required to install such drivers, encrypted volumes can typically be used by normal users without these rights.

In general, every method in which data is seamlessly encrypted on write and decrypted on read, in such a way that the user and/or application software remains unaware of the process, can be called transparent encryption.

Disk Encryption vs. Filesystem-level Encryption

Disk encryption does not replace file encryption in all situations. Disk encryption is sometimes used in conjunction with filesystem-level encryption with the intention of providing a more secure implementation. Since disk encryption generally uses the same key for encrypting the whole drive, all data is decryptable when the system runs. However, some disk encryption solutions use multiple keys for encrypting different volumes. If an attacker gains access to the computer at run-time, the attacker has access to all files. Conventional file and folder encryption instead allows different keys for different portions of the disk. Thus an attacker cannot extract information from still-encrypted files and folders.

Unlike disk encryption, filesystem-level encryption does not typically encrypt filesystem metadata, such as the directory structure, file names, modification timestamps or sizes.

Disk Encryption and Trusted Platform Module

Trusted Platform Module (TPM) is a secure cryptoprocessor embedded in the motherboard that can be used to authenticate a hardware device. Since each TPM chip is unique to a particular device, it is capable of performing platform authentication. It can be used to verify that the system seeking the access is the expected system.

A limited number of disk encryption solutions have support for TPM. These implementations can wrap the decryption key using the TPM, thus tying the hard disk drive (HDD) to a particular device. If the HDD is removed from that particular device and placed in another, the decryption process will fail. Recovery is possible with the decryption password or token.

Although this has the advantage that the disk cannot be removed from the device, it might create a single point of failure in the encryption. For example, if something happens to the TPM or the motherboard, a user would not be able to access the data by connecting the hard drive to another computer, unless that user has a separate recovery key.

Implementations

There are multiple tools available in the market that allow for disk encryption. However, they vary greatly in features and security. They are divided into three main categories: software-based, hardware-based within the storage device, and hardware-based elsewhere (such as CPU or host bus adaptor). Hardware-based full disk encryption within the storage device are called self-encrypting drives and have no impact on performance whatsoever. Furthermore, the media-encryption key never leaves the device itself and is therefore not available to any virus in the operating system.

The Trusted Computing Group Opal Storage Specification provides industry accepted standardization for self-encrypting drives. External hardware is considerably faster than the software-based solutions although CPU versions may still have a performance impact, and the media encryption keys are not as well protected.

All solutions for the boot drive require a pre-boot authentication component which is available for all types of solutions from a number of vendors. It is important in all cases that the authentication credentials are usually a major potential weakness since the symmetric cryptography is usually strong.

Password/data Recovery Mechanism

Secure and safe recovery mechanisms are essential to the large-scale deployment of any disk encryption solutions in an enterprise. The solution must provide an easy but secure way to recover passwords (most importantly data) in case the user leaves the company without notice or forgets the password.

Challenge–response Password Recovery Mechanism

Challenge–response password recovery mechanism allows the password to be recovered in a secure manner. It is offered by a limited number of disk encryption solutions.

Some benefits of challenge–response password recovery:

- No need for the user to carry a disc with recovery encryption key.

- No secret data is exchanged during the recovery process.

- No information can be sniffed.

- Does not require a network connection, i.e. it works for users that are at a remote location.

Emergency Recovery Information (ERI)-file Password Recovery Mechanism

An emergency recovery information (ERI) file provides an alternative for recovery if a challenge–response mechanism is unfeasible due to the cost of helpdesk operatives for small companies or implementation challenges.

Some benefits of ERI-file recovery:

- Small companies can use it without implementation difficulties.

- No secret data is exchanged during the recovery process.

- No information can be sniffed.

- Does not require a network connection, i.e. it works for users that are at a remote location.

Security Concerns

Most full disk encryption schemes are vulnerable to a cold boot attack, whereby encryption keys can be stolen by cold-booting a machine already running an operating system, then dumping the contents of memory before the data disappears. The attack relies on the data remanence property of computer memory, whereby data bits can take up to several minutes to degrade after power has been removed. Even a Trusted Platform Module (TPM) is not effective against the attack, as the operating system needs to hold the decryption keys in memory in order to access the disk.

Full disk encryption is also vulnerable when a computer is stolen when suspended. As wake-up does not involve a BIOS boot sequence, it typically does not ask for the FDE password. Hibernation, in contrast goes via a BIOS boot sequence, and is safe.

All software-based encryption systems are vulnerable to various side channel attacks such as acoustic cryptanalysis and hardware keyloggers. In contrast, self-encrypting drives are not vulnerable to these attacks since the hardware encryption key never leaves the disk controller.

Also, most of full disk encryption schemes don't protect from data tampering (or silent data corruption, i.e. bitrot). That means they only provide privacy, but not integrity. Block cipher-based encryption modes used for full disk encryption are not authenticated encryption themselves because of concerns of the storage overhead needed for authentication tags. Thus, if tampering would be done to data on the disk, the data would be decrypted to garbled random data when read and hopefully errors may be indicated depending on which data is tampered with (for the case of OS metadata – by the file system; and for the case of file data – by the corresponding program that would process the file). One of the ways to mitigate these concerns, is to use file systems with full data integrity checks via checksums (like Btrfs or ZFS) on top of full disk encryption. However, cryptsetup started experimentally to support authenticated encryption.

Full Disk Encryption

Benefits

Full disk encryption has several benefits compared to regular file or folder encryption, or encrypted vaults. The following are some benefits of disk encryption:

- Nearly everything including the swap space and the temporary files is encrypted. Encrypting these files is important, as they can reveal important confidential data. With a software implementation, the bootstrapping code cannot be encrypted however. For example, Bit-Locker Drive Encryption leaves an unencrypted volume to boot from, while the volume containing the operating system is fully encrypted.

- With full disk encryption, the decision of which individual files to encrypt is not left up to users' discretion. This is important for situations in which users might not want or might forget to encrypt sensitive files.

- Immediate data destruction, such as simply destroying the cryptographic keys (crypto-shredding), renders the contained data useless. However, if security towards future attacks is a concern, purging or physical destruction is advised.

The boot Key Problem

One issue to address in full disk encryption is that the blocks where the operating system is stored must be decrypted before the OS can boot, meaning that the key has to be available before there is a user interface to ask for a password. Most Full Disk Encryption solutions utilize Pre-Boot Authentication by loading a small, highly secure operating system which is strictly locked down and hashed versus system variables to check for the integrity of the Pre-Boot kernel. Some implementations such as BitLocker Drive Encryption can make use of hardware such as a Trusted Platform Module to ensure the integrity of the boot environment, and thereby frustrate attacks that target the boot loader by replacing it with a modified version. This ensures that authentication can take place in a controlled environment without the possibility of a bootkit being used to subvert the pre-boot decryption.

With a pre-boot authentication environment, the key used to encrypt the data is not decrypted until an external key is input into the system.

Solutions for storing the external key include:

- Username / password.

- Using a smartcard in combination with a PIN.

- Using a biometric authentication method such as a fingerprint.

- Using a dongle to store the key, assuming that the user will not allow the dongle to be stolen with the laptop or that the dongle is encrypted as well.

- Using a boot-time driver that can ask for a password from the user.

- Using a network interchange to recover the key, for instance as part of a PXE boot.

- Using a TPM to store the decryption key, preventing unauthorized access of the decryption key or subversion of the boot loader.

- Using a combination.

All these possibilities have varying degrees of security; however, most are better than an unencrypted disk.

Data Security

Data security means protecting digital data, such as those in a database, from destructive forces and from the unwanted actions of unauthorized users, such as a cyberattack or a data breach.

Technologies

Disk Encryption

Disk encryption refers to encryption technology that encrypts data on a hard disk drive. Disk encryption typically takes form in either software or hardware Disk encryption is often referred to as on-the-fly encryption (OTFE) or transparent encryption.

Software versus Hardware-based Mechanisms for Protecting Data

Software-based security solutions encrypt the data to protect it from theft. However, a malicious program or a hacker could corrupt the data in order to make it unrecoverable, making the system unusable. Hardware-based security solutions can prevent read and write access to data and hence offer very strong protection against tampering and unauthorized access.

Hardware based security or assisted computer security offers an alternative to software-only computer security. Security tokens such as those using PKCS#11 may be more secure due to the physical access required in order to be compromised. Access is enabled only when the token is connected and correct PIN is entered. However, dongles can be used by anyone who can gain physical access to it. Newer technologies in hardware-based security solves this problem offering full proof security for data.

Working of hardware-based security: A hardware device allows a user to log in, log out and set different privilege levels by doing manual actions. The device uses biometric technology to prevent malicious users from logging in, logging out, and changing privilege levels. The current state of a user of the device is read by controllers in peripheral devices such as hard disks. Illegal access by a malicious user or a malicious program is interrupted based on the current state of a user by hard disk and DVD controllers making illegal access to data impossible. Hardware-based access control is more secure than protection provided by the operating systems as operating systems are vulnerable to malicious attacks by viruses and hackers. The data on hard disks can be corrupted after a malicious access is obtained. With hardware-based protection, software cannot manipulate the user privilege levels. It is impossible for a hacker or a malicious program to gain access to secure data protected by hardware or perform unauthorized privileged operations. This assumption is broken only if the hardware itself is malicious or contains a backdoor. The hardware protects the operating system image and file system privileges from being tampered. Therefore, a completely secure system can be created using a combination of hardware-based security and secure system administration policies.

Backups

Backups are used to ensure data which is lost can be recovered from another source. It is considered essential to keep a backup of any data in most industries and the process is recommended for any files of importance to a user.

Data Masking

Data masking of structured data is the process of obscuring (masking) specific data within a database table or cell to ensure that data security is maintained and sensitive information is not exposed to unauthorized personnel. This may include masking the data from users (for example so banking customer representatives can only see the last 4 digits of a customers national identity number), developers (who need real production data to test new software releases but should not be able to see sensitive financial data), outsourcing vendors, etc.

Data Erasure

Data erasure is a method of software based overwriting that completely destroys all electronic data residing on a hard drive or other digital media to ensure that no sensitive data is lost when an asset is retired or reused.

Data Encryption

In computing, encryption is the method by which plaintext or any other type of data is converted from a readable form to an encoded version that can only be decoded by another entity if they have access to a decryption key. Encryption is one of the most important methods for providing data security, especially for end-to-end protection of data transmitted across networks.

Encryption is widely used on the internet to protect user information being sent between a browser and a server, including passwords, payment information and other personal information that should be considered private. Organizations and individuals also commonly use encryption to protect sensitive data stored on computers, servers and mobile devices like phones or tablets.

Unencrypted data, often referred to as plaintext, is encrypted using an encryption algorithm and an encryption key. This process generates ciphertextthat can only be viewed in its original form if decrypted with the correct key. Decryption is simply the inverse of encryption, following the same steps but reversing the order in which the keys are applied. Today's most widely used encryption algorithms fall into two categories: symmetric and asymmetric.

Symmetric-key ciphers, also referred to as "secret key," use a single key, sometimes referred to as a shared secret because the system doing the encryption must share it with any entity it intends to be able to decrypt the encrypted data. The most widely used symmetric-key cipher is the Advanced Encryption Standard (AES), which was designed to protect government classified information.

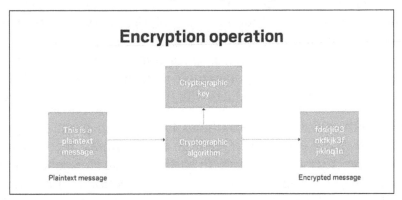

Symmetric-key encryption is usually much faster than asymmetric encryption, but the sender must exchange the key used to encrypt the data with the recipient before the recipient can perform decryption on the ciphertext. The need to securely distribute and manage large numbers of keys means most cryptographic processes use a symmetric algorithm to efficiently encrypt data, but they use an asymmetric algorithm to securely exchange the secret key.

Asymmetric cryptography, also known as public key cryptography, uses two different but mathematically linked keys, one public and one private. The public key can be shared with everyone, whereas the private key must be kept secret. The RSA encryption algorithm is the most widely used public key algorithm, partly because both the public and the private keys can encrypt a message; the opposite key from the one used to encrypt a message is used to decrypt it. This attribute provides a method of assuring not only confidentiality, but also the integrity, authenticity and nonreputability of electronic communications and data at rest through the use of digital signatures.

Benefits of Encryption

The primary purpose of encryption is to protect the confidentiality of digital data stored on computer systems or transmitted via the internet or any other computer network. A number of organizations and standards bodies either recommend or require sensitive data to be encrypted in order to prevent unauthorized third parties or threat actors from accessing the data. For example, the Payment Card Industry Data Security Standard (PCI DSS) requires merchants to encrypt customers' payment card data when it is both stored at rest and transmitted across public networks.

Modern encryption algorithms also play a vital role in the security assurance of IT systems and communications as they can provide not only confidentiality, but also the following key elements of security:

- Authentication: the origin of a message can be verified.

- Integrity: proof that the contents of a message have not been changed since it was sent.

- Nonrepudiation: the sender of a message cannot deny sending the message.

Types of Encryption

Traditional public key cryptography depends on the properties of large prime numbers and the computational difficulty of factoring those primes. Elliptical curve cryptography (ECC) enables another kind of public key cryptography that depends on the properties of the elliptic curve equation; the resulting cryptographic algorithms can be faster and more efficient and can produce comparable levels of security with shorter cryptographic keys. As a result, ECC algorithms are often implemented in IoT devices and other products with limited computing resources.

As development of quantum computing continues to approach practical application, quantum cryptography will become more important. Quantum cryptography depends on the quantum mechanical properties of particles to protect data. In particular, the Heisenberg uncertainty principle posits that the two identifying properties of a particle its location and its momentum cannot be measured without changing the values of those properties. As a result, quantum encoded data cannot be copied because any attempt to access the encoded data will change the data. Likewise, any attempt to copy or access the data will cause a change in the data, thus notifying the authorized parties to the encryption that an attack has occurred.

Encryption is used to protect data stored on a system (encryption in place or encryption at rest); many internet protocols define mechanisms for encrypting data moving from one system to another (data in transit).

Some applications tout the use of end-to-end encryption (E2EE) to guarantee data being sent between two parties cannot be viewed by an attacker that intercepts the communication channel. Use of an encrypted communication circuit, as provided by Transport Layer Security (TLS) between web client and web server software, is not always enough to insure E2EE; typically, the actual content being transmitted is encrypted by client software before being passed to a web client and decrypted only by the recipient.

Messaging apps that provide E2EE include Facebook's WhatsApp and Open Whisper Systems' Signal. Facebook Messenger users may also get E2EE messaging with the "Secret Conversations" option.

Uses of Encryption

Encryption was almost exclusively used only by governments and large enterprises until the late 1970s when the Diffie-Hellman key exchange and RSA algorithms were first published and the first personal computers were introduced. By the mid-1990s, both public key and private key encryption were being routinely deployed in web browsers and servers to protect sensitive data.

Encryption is now an important part of many products and services, used in the commercial and consumer realms to protect data both while it is in transit and while it is stored, such as on a hard drive, smartphone or flash drive (data at rest).

Devices like modems, set-top boxes, smartcards and SIM cards all use encryption or rely on protocols like SSH, S/MIME, and SSL/TLS to encrypt sensitive data. Encryption is used to protect data in transit sent from all sorts of devices across all sorts of networks, not just the internet; every time someone uses an ATM or buys something online with a smartphone, makes a mobile phone call or presses a key fob to unlock a car, encryption is used to protect the information being relayed.

Digital rights management systems, which prevent unauthorized use or reproduction of copyrighted material, are yet another example of encryption protecting data.

Cryptographic Hash Functions

Encryption is usually a two-way function, meaning the same algorithm can be used to encrypt plaintext and to decrypt ciphertext. A cryptographic hash function can be viewed as a type of one-way function for encryption, meaning the function output cannot easily be reversed to recover the original input. Hash functions are commonly used in many aspects of security to generate digital signatures and data integrity checks. They take an electronic file, message or block of data and generate a short digital fingerprint of the content called a message digest or hash value. The key properties of a secure cryptographic hash function are:

- Output length is small compared to input.

- Computation is fast and efficient for any input.

- Any change to input affects lots of output bits.

- One-way value the input cannot be determined from the output.

- Strong collision resistance two different inputs can't create the same output.

The ciphers in hash functions are optimized for hashing: They use large keys and blocks, can efficiently change keys every block and have been designed and vetted for resistance to related-key attacks. General-purpose ciphers used for encryption tend to have different design goals. For example, the symmetric-key block cipher AES could also be used for generating hash values, but its key and block sizes make it nontrivial and inefficient.

Backup

In information technology, a backup, or data backup is a copy of computer data taken and stored elsewhere so that it may be used to restore the original after a data loss event. The verb form, referring to the process of doing so, is "back up", whereas the noun and adjective form is "backup". Backups can be used to recover data after its loss from data deletion or corruption, or to recover data from an earlier time. Backups provide a simple form of disaster recovery; however not all backup systems are able to reconstitute a computer system or other complex configuration such as a computer cluster, active directory server, or database server.

A backup system contains at least one copy of all data considered worth saving. The data storage requirements can be large. An information repository model may be used to provide structure to this storage. There are different types of data storage devices used for copying backups of data that is already in secondary storage onto archive files. There are also different ways these devices can be arranged to provide geographic dispersion, data security, and portability.

Data are selected, extracted, and manipulated for storage. The process can include methods for dealing with live data, including open files, as well as compression, encryption, and de-duplication. Additional techniques apply to enterprise client-server backup. Backup schemes may include dry runs that validate the reliability of the data being backed up. There are limitations and human factors involved in any backup scheme.

Storage

A backup strategy requires an information repository, "a secondary storage space for data" that aggregates backups of data "sources". The repository could be as simple as a list of all backup media (DVDs, etc.) and the dates produced, or could include a computerized index, catalog, or relational database.

The backup data needs to be stored, requiring a backup rotation scheme, which is a system of backing up data to computer media that limits the number of backups of different dates retained separately, by appropriate re-use of the data storage media by overwriting of backups no longer needed. The scheme determines how and when each piece of removable storage is used for a backup operation and how long it is retained once it has backup data stored on it.

Backup Methods

Unstructured

An unstructured repository may simply be a stack of tapes, DVD-Rs or external HDDs with minimal information about what was backed up and when. This method is the easiest to implement, but unlikely to achieve a high level of recoverability as it lacks automation.

Full only/System Imaging

A repository using this backup method contains complete source data copies taken at one or more specific points in time. Copying system images, this method is frequently used by computer technicians to record known good configurations. However, imaging is generally more useful as a way of deploying a standard configuration to many systems rather than as a tool for making ongoing backups of diverse systems.

Incremental

An incremental backup stores data changed since a reference point in time. Duplicate copies of unchanged data aren't copied. Typically a full backup of all files is once or at infrequent intervals, serving as the reference point for an incremental repository. Subsequently, a number of incremental backups are made after successive time periods. Restores begin with the last full backup and then apply the incrementals.

Some backup systems can create a synthetic full backup from a series of incrementals, thus providing the equivalent of frequently doing a full backup. When done to modify a single archive file, this speeds restores of recent versions of files.

Near-CDP

True Continuous Data Protection (CDP) refers to a backup that instantly saves a copy of every change made to the data. This allows restoration of data to any point in time and is the most comprehensive and advanced data protection. Near-CDP backup applications (frequently marketed as "CDP") automatically take incremental backups at specific intervals, for example every 15 minutes, one hour, or 24 hours. They can therefore only allow restores at that fixed interval. Near-CDP backup applications use journaling and are typically based on periodic "snapshots", a read-only copy of the data frozen at a particular point in time.

Near-CDP (except for Apple Time Machine) intent-logs every change on the host system, often by saving byte or block-level differences rather than file-level differences. This backup method differs from simple disk mirroring in that it enables a roll-back of the log and thus a restoration of old images of data. Intent-logging allows precautions for the consistency of live data, protecting self-consistent files but requiring applications "be quiesced and made ready for backup."

Near-CDP is more practicable for ordinary personal backup applications, as opposed to true CDP, which must be run in conjunction with a virtual machine or equivalent and is therefore generally used in Enterprise client-server backups.

Reverse Incremental

A Reverse incremental backup method stores a recent archive file "mirror" of the source data and a series of differences between the "mirror" in its current state and its previous states. A reverse incremental backup method starts with a non-image full backup. After the full backup is performed, the system periodically synchronizes the full backup with the live copy, while storing the data necessary to reconstruct older versions. This can either be done using hard links—as Apple Time Machine does, or using binary diffs.

Differential

A differential backup saves only the data that has changed since the last full backup. This means a maximum of two backups from the repository are used to restore the data. However, as time from the last full backup (and thus the accumulated changes in data) increases, so does the time to perform the differential backup. Restoring an entire system requires starting from the most recent full backup and then applying just the last differential backup.

A differential backup copies files that have been created or changed since the last full backup, regardless of whether any other differential backups have been made since, whereas an incremental backup copies files that have been created or changed since the most recent backup of any type (full or incremental). Other variations of incremental backup include multi-level incrementals and block-level incrementals that compare parts of files instead of just entire files.

Storage Media

From left to right, a DVD disc in plastic cover, a USB flash drive and an external hard drive.

Regardless of the repository model that is used, the data has to be copied onto an archive file data storage medium. The medium used is also referred to as the type of backup destination.

Magnetic Tape

Magnetic tape was for a long time the most commonly used medium for bulk data storage, backup, archiving, and interchange. It was previously a less expensive option, but this is no longer the case for smaller amounts of data. Tape is a sequential access medium, so the rate of continuously writing or reading data can be very fast.

Many tape formats have been proprietary or specific to certain markets like mainframes or a particular brand of personal computer. By 2014 LTO had become the primary tape technology. The other remaining viable "super" formats are IBM 3592 (also referred to as the TS11xx series) and Oracle StorageTek T10000.

Hard Disk

The use of hard disk storage has increased over time as it has become progressively cheaper. Hard disks are usually easy to use, widely available, and can be accessed quickly. However, hard disk backups are close-tolerance mechanical devices and may be more easily damaged than tapes, especially while being transported. In the mid-2000s, several drive manufacturers began to produce portable drives employing ramp loading and accelerometer technology (sometimes termed a "shock sensor"), and by 2010 the industry average in drop tests for drives with that technology showed drives remaining intact and working after a 36-inch non-operating drop onto industrial carpeting. Some manufacturers also offer 'ruggedized' portable hard drives, which include a shock-absorbing case around the hard disk, and claim a range of higher drop specifications. Over a period of years the stability of hard disk backups is shorter than that of tape backups.

External hard disks can be connected via local interfaces like SCSI, USB, FireWire, or eSATA, or via longer-distance technologies like Ethernet, iSCSI, or Fibre Channel. Some disk-based backup systems, via Virtual Tape Libraries or otherwise, support data deduplication, which can reduce the amount of disk storage capacity consumed by daily and weekly backup data.

Optical Storage

Optical storage uses lasers to store and retrieve data. Recordable CDs, DVDs, and Blu-ray Discs are commonly used with personal computers and are generally cheap. In the past, the capacities and speeds of these discs have been lower than hard disks or tapes, although advances in optical media are slowly shrinking that gap. Many optical disc formats are WORM type, which makes them useful for archival purposes since the data cannot be changed. Some optical storage systems allow for cataloged data backups without human contact with the discs, allowing for longer data integrity. A French study in 2008 indicated that the lifespan of typically-sold CD-Rs was 2–10 years, but one manufacturer later estimated the longevity of its CD-Rs with a gold-sputtered layer to be as high as 100 years. Sony's Optical Disc Archive can in 2016 reach a read rate of 250MB/s.

Solid-state Drive

Solid-state drives (SSDs) use integrated circuit assemblies to store data. Flash memory, thumb drives, USB flash drives, CompactFlash, SmartMedia, Memory sticks, and Secure Digital card devices are relatively expensive for their low capacity, but convenient for backing up relatively low data volumes. A solid-state drive does not contain any movable parts, making it less susceptible to physical damage, and can have huge throughput of around 500 Mbit/s up to 6 Gbit/s. Available SSDs have become more capacious and cheaper. Flash memory backups are stable for fewer years than hard disk backups.

Remote Backup Service

Remote backup services or cloud backups involve service providers storing data offsite. This has been used to protect against events such as fires, floods, or earthquakes which could destroy locally stored backups. Cloud-based backup provides a layer of data protection. However, the users must trust the provider to maintain the privacy and integrity of their data, with confidentiality enhanced by the use of encryption. Because speed and availability are limited by a user's online connection, users with large amounts of data may need to use cloud seeding and large-scale recovery.

Management

Various methods can be used to manage backup media, striking a balance between accessibility, security and cost. These media management methods are not mutually exclusive and are frequently combined to meet the user's needs. Using on-line disks for staging data before it is sent to a near-line tape library is a common example.

Online

Online backup storage is typically the most accessible type of data storage, and can begin a restore in milliseconds. An internal hard disk or a disk array (maybe connected to SAN) is an example of an online backup. This type of storage is convenient and speedy, but is vulnerable to being deleted or overwritten, either by accident, by malevolent action, or in the wake of a data-deleting virus payload.

Near-line

Nearline storage is typically less accessible and less expensive than online storage, but still useful for backup data storage. A mechanical device is usually used to move media units from storage into a drive where the data can be read or written. Generally it has safety properties similar to on-line storage. An example is a tape library with restore times ranging from seconds to a few minutes.

Off-line

Off-line storage requires some direct action to provide access to the storage media: for example, inserting a tape into a tape drive or plugging in a cable. Because the data are not accessible via any computer except during limited periods in which they are written or read back, they are largely immune to on-line backup failure modes. Access time varies depending on whether the media are on-site or off-site.

Off-site Data Protection

Backup media may be sent to an off-site vault to protect against a disaster or other site-specific problem. The vault can be as simple as a system administrator's home office or as sophisticated as a disaster-hardened, temperature-controlled, high-security bunker with facilities for backup media storage. A data replica can be off-site but also on-line (e.g., an off-site RAID mirror). Such a replica has fairly limited value as a backup.

Backup Site

A backup site or disaster recovery center is used to store data that can enable computer systems and networks to be restored and properly configure in the event of a disaster. Some organisations have heir own data recovery centres, while others contract this out to a third-party. Due to high costs, backing up is rarely considered the preferred method of moving data to a DR site. A more typical way would be remote disk mirroring, which keeps the DR data as up to date as possible.

Selection and Extraction of Data

A backup operation starts with selecting and extracting coherent units of data. Most data on modern computer systems is stored in discrete units, known as files. These files are organized into filesystems. Deciding what to back up at any given time involves tradeoffs. By backing up too much redundant data, the information repository will fill up too quickly. Backing up an insufficient amount of data can eventually lead to the loss of critical information.

Files

- Copying files : Making copies of files is the simplest and most common way to perform a backup. A means to perform this basic function is included in all backup software and all operating systems.

- Partial file copying: A backup may include only the blocks or bytes within a file that have changed in a given period of time. This can substantially reduce needed storage space, but requires higher sophistication to reconstruct files in a restore situation. Some implementations require integration with the source file system.

- Deleted files : To prevent the unintentional restoration of files that have been intentionally deleted, a record of the deletion must be kept.

- Versioning of files : Most backup applications, other than those that do only full only/System imaging, also back up files that have been modified since the last backup. "That way, you can retrieve many different versions of a given file, and if you delete it on your hard disk, you can still find it in your [information repository] archive."

Filesystems

- Filesystem dump: A copy of the whole filesystem in block-level can be made. This is also known as a "raw partition backup" and is related to disk imaging. The process usually involves unmounting the filesystem and running a program like dd (Unix). Because the disk is read sequentially and with large buffers, this type of backup can be faster than reading every file normally, especially when the filesystem contains many small files, is highly fragmented, or is nearly full. But because this method also reads the free disk blocks that contain no useful data, this method can also be slower than conventional reading, especially when the filesystem is nearly empty. Some filesystems, such as XFS, provide a "dump" utility that reads the disk sequentially for high performance while skipping unused sections. The corresponding restore utility can selectively restore individual files or the entire volume at the operator's choice.

- Identification of changes: Some filesystems have an archive bit for each file that says it was recently changed. Some backup software looks at the date of the file and compares it with the last backup to determine whether the file was changed.

- Versioning file system : A versioning filesystem tracks all changes to a file. The NILFS versioning filesystem for Linux is an example.

Live Data

Files that are actively being updated can be called "live" and present a challenge to back up. An effective way to back up live data is to temporarily quiesce them (e.g., close all files), take a "snapshot", and then resume live operations. At this point the snapshot can be backed up through normal methods. A snapshot is an instantaneous function of some filesystems that presents a copy of the filesystem as if it were frozen at a specific point in time, often by a copy-on-write mechanism. Snapshotting a file while it is being changed results in a corrupted file that is unusable. This is also the case across interrelated files, as may be found in a conventional database or in applications such as Microsoft Exchange Server. The term fuzzy backup can be used to describe a backup of live data that looks like it ran correctly, but does not represent the state of the data at a single point in time.

Backup options for data files that cannot be or are not quiesced include:

- Open file backup: Many backup software applications undertake to back up open files in an internally consistent state. Some applications simply check whether open files are in use and try again later. Other applications exclude open files that are updated very frequently. Some low-availability interactive applications can be backed up via natural/induced pausing.

- Interrelated database files backup: Some interrelated database file systems offer a means to generate a "hot backup" of the database while it is online and usable. This may include a snapshot of the data files plus a snapshotted log of changes made while the backup is running. Upon a restore, the changes in the log files are applied to bring the copy of the database up to the point in time at which the initial backup ended. Other low-availability interactive applications can be backed up via coordinated snapshots. However, genuinely-high-availability interactive applications can be only be backed up via *true* Continuous Data Protection.

Metadata

Not all information stored on the computer is stored in files. Accurately recovering a complete system from scratch requires keeping track of this non-file data too.

- System description: System specifications are needed to procure an exact replacement after a disaster.

- Boot sector : The boot sector can sometimes be recreated more easily than saving it. It usually isn›t a normal file and the system won›t boot without it.

- Partition layout: The layout of the original disk, as well as partition tables and filesystem settings, is needed to properly recreate the original system.

- File metadata : Each file›s permissions, owner, group, ACLs, and any other metadata need to be backed up for a restore to properly recreate the original environment.

- System metadata: Different operating systems have different ways of storing configuration information. Microsoft Windows keeps a registry of system information that is more difficult to restore than a typical file.

Manipulation of Data and Dataset Optimization

It is frequently useful or required to manipulate the data being backed up to optimize the backup process. These manipulations can improve backup speed, restore speed, data security, media usage and/or reduced bandwidth requirements.

Automated Data Grooming

Out-of-date data can be automatically deleted, but for personal backup applications—as opposed to enterprise client-server backup applications where automated data "grooming" can be customized—the deletion can at most be globally delayed or be disabled.

Compression

Various schemes can be employed to shrink the size of the source data to be stored so that it uses less storage space. Compression is frequently a built-in feature of tape drive hardware.

Deduplication

Redundancy due to backing up similarly configured workstations can be reduced, thus storing just one copy. This technique can be applied at the file or raw block level. This potentially large reduction is called deduplication. It can occur on a server before any data moves to backup media, sometimes referred to as source/client side deduplication. This approach also reduces bandwidth required to send backup data to its target media. The process can also occur at the target storage device, sometimes referred to as inline or back-end deduplication.

Duplication

Sometimes backups are duplicated to a second set of storage media. This can be done to rearrange the archive files to optimize restore speed, or to have a second copy at a different location or on a different storage medium—as in the disk-to-disk-to-tape capability of Enterprise client-server backup.

Encryption

High-capacity removable storage media such as backup tapes present a data security risk if they are lost or stolen. Encrypting the data on these media can mitigate this problem, however encryption is a CPU intensive process that can slow down backup speeds, and the security of the encrypted backups is only as effective as the security of the key management policy.

Multiplexing

When there are many more computers to be backed up than there are destination storage devices, the ability to use a single storage device with several simultaneous backups can be useful. However cramming the scheduled backup window via "multiplexed backup" is only used for tape destinations.

Refactoring

The process of rearranging the backup sets in an archive file is known as refactoring. For example, if a backup system uses a single tape each day to store the incremental backups for all the protected computers, restoring one of the computers could require many tapes. Refactoring could be used to consolidate all the backups for a single computer onto a single tape, creating a "synthetic full backup". This is especially useful for backup systems that do incrementals forever style backups.

Staging

Sometimes backups are copied to a staging disk before being copied to tape. This process is sometimes referred to as D2D2T, an acronym for Disk to Disk to Tape. It can be useful if there is a problem matching the speed of the final destination device with the source device, as is frequently faced in network-based backup systems. It can also serve as a centralized location for applying other data manipulation techniques.

Objectives

- Recovery point objective (RPO): The point in time that the restarted infrastructure will reflect, expressed as "the maximum targeted period in which data (transactions) might be lost from an IT service due to a major incident". Essentially, this is the roll-back that will be experienced as a result of the recovery. The most desirable RPO would be the point just prior to the data loss event. Making a more recent recovery point achievable requires increasing the frequency of synchronization between the source data and the backup repository.

- Recovery time objective (RTO): The amount of time elapsed between disaster and restoration of business functions.

- Data security: In addition to preserving access to data for its owners, data must be restricted from unauthorized access. Backups must be performed in a manner that does not compromise the original owner›s undertaking. This can be achieved with data encryption and proper media handling policies.

- Data retention period: Regulations and policy can lead to situations where backups are expected to be retained for a particular period, but not any further. Retaining backups after this period can lead to unwanted liability and sub-optimal use of storage media.

- Checksum or hash function validation: Applications that back up to tape archive files need this option to verify that the data was accurately copied.

- Backup process monitoring: Enterprise client-server backup applications need a user interface that allows administrators to monitor the backup process, and proves compliance to regulatory bodies outside the organization; for example, an insurance company in the USA might be required under HIPAA to demonstrate that its client data meet records retention requirements.

- User-initiated backups and restores: To avoid or recover from *minor* disasters, such as inadvertently deleting or overwriting the "good" versions of one or more files, the computer user—rather than an administrator—may initiate backups and restores (from not necessarily the most-recent backup) of files or folders.

Data Masking

Data masking or data obfuscation is the process of hiding original data with modified content (characters or other data.)

The main reason for applying masking to a data field is to protect data that is classified as personal identifiable data, personal sensitive data or commercially sensitive data, however the data must remain usable for the purposes of undertaking valid test cycles. It must also look real and appear consistent. It is more common to have masking applied to data that is represented outside of a corporate production system. In other words, where data is needed for the purpose of application development, building program extensions and conducting various test cycles. It is common practice in enterprise computing to take data from the production systems to fill the data component, required for these non-production environments. However, this practice is not always restricted to non-production environments. In some organizations, data that appears on terminal screens to call centre operators may have masking dynamically applied based on user security permissions (e.g. preventing call centre operators from viewing Credit Card Numbers in billing systems).

The primary concern from a corporate governance perspective is that personnel conducting work in these non-production environments are not always security cleared to operate with the information contained in the production data. This practice represents a security hole where data can be copied by unauthorized personnel and security measures associated with standard production level controls can be easily bypassed. This represents an access point for a data security breach.

The overall practice of Data Masking at an organizational level should be tightly coupled with the Test Management Practice and underlying Methodology and should incorporate processes for the distribution of masked test data subsets.

Data involved in any data-masking or obfuscation must remain meaningful at several levels:

- The data must remain meaningful for the application logic. For example, if elements of addresses are to be obfuscated and city and suburbs are replaced with substitute cities or suburbs, then, if within the application there is a feature that validates postcode or post code lookup, that function must still be allowed to operate without error and operate as expected. The same is also true for credit-card algorithm validation checks and Social Security Number validations.

- The data must undergo enough changes so that it is not obvious that the masked data is from a source of production data. For example, it may be common knowledge in an organisation that there are 10 senior managers all earning in excess of $300K. If a test environment of the organisation's HR System also includes 10 identities in the same earning-bracket, then other information could be pieced together to reverse-engineer a real-life identity. Theoretically, if the data is obviously masked or obfuscated, then it would be reasonable for someone intending a data breach to assume that they could reverse engineer identity-data if they had some degree of knowledge of the identities in the production data-set. Accordingly, data obfuscation or masking of a data-set applies in such a manner as to ensure that identity and sensitive data records are protected - not just the individual data elements in discrete fields and tables.

- The masked values may be required to be consistent across multiple databases within an organization when the databases each contain the specific data element being masked. Applications may initially access one database and later access another one to retrieve related information where the foreign key has been masked (e.g. a call center application first brings up data from a customer master database and, depending on the situation, subsequently accesses one of several other databases with very different financial products.) This requires that the masking applied is repeatable (the same input value to the masking algorithm always yields the same output value) but not able to be reverse engineered to get back to the original value. Additional constraints as mentioned in (1) above may also apply depending on the data element(s) involved. Where different character sets are used across the databases that need to connect in this scenario, a scheme of converting the original values to a common representation will need to be applied, either by the masking algorithm itself or prior to invoking said algorithm.

Techniques

Substitution

Substitution is one of the most effective methods of applying data masking and being able to preserve the authentic look and feel of the data records.

It allows the masking to be performed in such a manner that another authentic looking value can be substituted for the existing value. There are several data field types where this approach provides optimal benefit in disguising the overall data sub set as to whether or not it is a masked data set. For example, if dealing with source data which contains customer records, real life surname or first name can be randomly substituted from a supplied or customised look up file. If the first pass of the substitution allows for applying a male first name to all first names, then the second pass would need to allow for applying a female first name to all first names where gender equals "F". Using this approach we could easily maintain the gender mix within the data structure, apply anonymity to the data records but also maintain a realistic looking database which could not easily be identified as a database consisting of masked data.

This substitution method needs to be applied for many of the fields that are in DB structures across the world, such as telephone numbers, zip codes and postcodes, as well as credit card numbers and other card type numbers like Social Security numbers and Medicare numbers where these numbers actually need to conform to a checksum test of the Luhn algorithm.

In most cases, the substitution files will need to be fairly extensive so having large substitution datasets as well the ability to apply customized data substitution sets should be a key element of the evaluation criteria for any data masking solution.

Shuffling

The shuffling method is a very common form of data obfuscation. It is similar to the substitution method but it derives the substitution set from the same column of data that is being masked. In very simple terms, the data is randomly shuffled within the column. However, if used in isolation, anyone with any knowledge of the original data can then apply a "What If" scenario to the data set and then piece back together a real identity. The shuffling method is also open to being reversed if the shuffling algorithm can be deciphered.

Shuffling, however, has some real strengths in certain areas. If for instance, the end of year figures for financial information in a test data base, one can mask the names of the suppliers and then shuffle the value of the accounts throughout the masked database. It is highly unlikely that anyone, even someone with intimate knowledge of the original data could derive a true data record back to its original values.

Number and Date Variance

The numeric variance method is very useful for applying to financial and date driven information fields. Effectively, a method utilising this manner of masking can still leave a meaningful range in a financial data set such as payroll. If the variance applied is around +/- 10% then it is still a very meaningful data set in terms of the ranges of salaries that are paid to the recipients.

The same also applies to the date information. If the overall data set needs to retain demographic and actuarial data integrity then applying a random numeric variance of +/- 120 days to date fields would preserve the date distribution but still prevent traceability back to a known entity based on their known actual date or birth or a known date value of whatever record is being masked.

Encryption

Encryption is often the most complex approach to solving the data masking problem. The encryption algorithm often requires that a "key" be applied to view the data based on user rights. This often sounds like the best solution but in practice the key may then be given out to personnel without the proper rights to view the data and this then defeats the purpose of the masking exercise. Old databases may then be copied with the original credentials of the supplied key and the same uncontrolled problem lives on.

Recently, the problem of encrypting data while preserving the properties of the entities got a recognition and newly acquired interest among the vendors and academia. New challenge gave birth to algorithms called FPE (format preserving encryption). They are based on the accepted AES algorithmic mode that makes them being recognized by NIST.

Nulling Out or Deletion

Sometimes a very simplistic approach to masking is adopted through applying a null value to a particular field. The null value approach is really only useful to prevent visibility of the data element.

In almost all cases it lessens the degree of data integrity that is maintained in the masked data set. It is not a realistic value and will then fail any application logic validation that may have been applied in the front end software that is in the system under test. It also highlights to anyone that wishes to reverse engineer any of the identity data that data masking has been applied to some degree on the data set.

Masking Out

Character scrambling or masking out of certain fields is also another simplistic yet very effective method of preventing sensitive information to be viewed. It is really an extension of the previous method of nulling out but there is greater emphasis on keeping the data real and not fully masked all together.

This is commonly applied to credit card data in production systems. For instance, an operator in a Call Centre might bill an item to a customer's credit card. They then quote a billing reference to the card with the last 4 digits of XXXX XXXX xxxx 6789. As an operator they can only see the last 4 digits of the card number, but once the billing system passes the customer's details for charging, the full number is revealed to the payment gateway systems.

This system is not very effective for test systems but is very useful for the billing scenario detailed above. It is also commonly known as a dynamic data masking method.

Additional Complex Rules

Additional rules can also be factored into any masking solution regardless of how the masking methods are constructed. Product agnostic White Papers are a good source of information for exploring some of the more common complex requirements for enterprise masking solutions which include Row Internal Synchronisation Rules, Table Internal Synchronisation Rules and Table to Table Synchronisation Rules.

Different Types

Data masking is tightly coupled with building test data. Two major types of data masking are static and on-the-fly data masking.

Static Data Masking

Static Data Masking is usually performed on the golden copy of the database, but can also be applied to values in other sources, including files. In DB environments, production DBAs will typically load table backups to a separate environment, reduce the dataset to a subset that holds the data necessary for a particular round of testing (a technique called "subsetting"), apply data masking rules while data is in stasis, apply necessary code changes from source control, and/or and push data to desired environment.

Statistical Data Obfuscation

There are also alternatives to the static data masking that rely on stochastic perturbations of the data that preserve some of the statistical properties of the original data. Examples of statistical data obfuscation methods include differential privacy and the *DataSifter* method.

On-the-fly Data Masking

On-the-Fly Data Masking happens in the process of transferring data from environment to environment without data touching the disk on its way. The same technique is applied to "Dynamic Data Masking" but one record at a time. This type of data masking is most useful for environments that do continuous deployments as well as for heavily integrated applications. Organizations that employ continuous deployment or continuous delivery practices do not have the time necessary to create a backup and load it to the golden copy of the database. Thus, continuously sending smaller subsets (deltas) of masked testing data from production is important. In heavily integrated applications, developers get feeds from other production systems at the very onset of development and masking of these feeds is either overlooked and not budgeted until later, making organizations non-compliant. Having on-the-fly data masking in place becomes essential.

Dynamic Data Masking

Dynamic Data Masking is similar to On-the-Fly Data Masking but it differs in the sense that On-the-Fly Data Masking is about copying data from one source to another source so that the latter can be shared. Dynamic data masking happens at runtime, dynamically, and on-demand so that there doesn't need to be a second data source where to store the masked data dynamically.

Dynamic data masking enables several scenarios, many of which revolve around strict privacy regulations e.g. the Singapore Monetary Authority or the Privacy regulations in Europe.

Dynamic data masking is attribute-based and policy-driven. Policies include:

- Doctors can view the medical records of patients they are assigned to (data filtering)

- Doctors cannot view the SSN field inside a medical record (data masking).

Dynamic data masking can also be used to encrypt or decrypt values on the fly especially when using format-preserving encryption.

Several standards have emerged in recent years to implement dynamic data filtering and masking. For instance, XACML policies can be used to mask data inside databases.

There are five possible technologies to apply Dynamic data masking:

- In the Database: Database receives the SQL and applies rewrite to returned masked result set. Applicable for developers & DBAs but not for applications (because connection pools, application caching and data-bus hide the application user identity from the database and can also cause application data corruption).

- Network Proxy between the application and the database: Captures the SQL and applies rewrite on the select request. Applicable for developers & DBAs with simple 'select'requests but not for stored procedures (which the proxy only identifies the exec.) and applications (because connection pools, application caching and data-bus hide the application user identity from the database and can also cause application data corruption).

- Network Proxy between the end-user and the application: identifying text strings and replacing them. This method is not applicable for complex applications as it will easily cause corruption when the real-time string replacement is unintentionally applied.

- Code changes in the applications & XACML: code changes are hard to perform, impossible to maintain and not applicable for packaged applications.

- Within the application run-time: By instrumenting the application run-time, policies are defined to rewrite the result set returned from the data sources, while having full visibility to the application user. This method is the only applicable way to dynamically mask complex applications as it enables control to the data request, data result and user result.

- Supported by a browser plugin: In the case of SaaS or local web applications, browser add-ons can be configured to mask data fields corresponding to precise CSS Selectors. This can either be accomplished by marking sensitive fields in the application, for example by a HTML class or by finding the right selectors that identify the fields to be obfuscated or masked.

Data Masking and the Cloud

In latest years, organizations develop their new applications in the cloud more and more often, regardless of whether final applications will be hosted in the cloud or on- premises. The cloud solutions as of now allow organizations to use Infrastructure as a Service or IaaS, Platform as a Service or PaaS, and Software as a Service or SaaS. There are various modes of creating test data and moving it from on-premises databases to the cloud, or between different environments within the cloud. Data masking invariably becomes the part of these processes in SDLC as the development environments' SLAs are usually not as stringent as the production environments' SLAs regardless of whether application is hosted in the cloud or on-premises.

Data Erasure

Data erasure (sometimes referred to as data clearing, data wiping, or data destruction) is a software-based method of overwriting the data that aims to completely destroy all electronic data residing on a hard disk drive or other digital media by using zeros and ones to overwrite data onto all sectors of the device. By overwriting the data on the storage device, the data is rendered unrecoverable and achieves data sanitization.

Ideally, software designed for data erasure should:

- Allow for selection of a specific standard, based on unique needs, and

- Verify the overwriting method has been successful and removed data across the entire device.

Permanent data erasure goes beyond basic file deletion commands, which only remove direct pointers to the data disk sectors and make the data recovery possible with common software tools. Unlike degaussing and physical destruction, which render the storage media unusable, data erasure removes all information while leaving the disk operable. New flash memory-based media implementations, such as solid-state drives or USB flash drives, can cause data erasure techniques to fail allowing remnant data to be recoverable.

Software-based overwriting uses a software application to write a stream of zeros, ones or meaningless pseudorandom data onto all sectors of a hard disk drive. There are key differentiators between data erasure and other overwriting methods, which can leave data intact and raise the risk of data breach, identity theft or failure to achieve regulatory compliance. Many data eradication programs also provide multiple overwrites so that they support recognized government and industry standards, though a single-pass overwrite is widely considered to be sufficient for modern hard disk drives. Good software should provide verification of data removal, which is necessary for meeting certain standards.

To protect the data on lost or stolen media, some data erasure applications remotely destroy the data if the password is incorrectly entered. Data erasure tools can also target specific data on a disk for routine erasure, providing a hacking protection method that is less time-consuming than software encryption. Hardware/firmware encryption built into the drive itself or integrated controllers is a popular solution with no degradation in performance at all.

Encryption

When encryption is in place, data erasure acts as a complement to crypto-shredding, or the practice of 'deleting' data by (only) deleting or overwriting the encryption keys. Presently, dedicated hardware/firmware encryption solutions can perform a 256-bit full AES encryption faster than the drive electronics can write the data. Drives with this capability are known as self-encrypting drives (SEDs); they are present on most modern enterprise-level laptops and are increasingly used in the enterprise to protect the data. Changing the encryption key renders inaccessible all data stored on a SED, which is an easy and very fast method for achieving a 100% data erasure. Theft of an SED results in a physical asset loss, but the stored data is inaccessible without the decryption key that is not stored on a SED, assuming there are no effective attacks against AES or its implementation in the drive hardware.

Importance

Information technology assets commonly hold large volumes of confidential data. Social security numbers, credit card numbers, bank details, medical history and classified information are often stored on computer hard drives or servers. These can inadvertently or intentionally make their way onto other media such as printers, USB, flash, Zip, Jaz, and REV drives.

Data Breach

Increased storage of sensitive data, combined with rapid technological change and the shorter lifespan of IT assets, has driven the need for permanent data erasure of electronic devices as they are retired or refurbished. Also, compromised networks and laptop theft and loss, as well as that of other portable media, are increasingly common sources of data breaches.

If data erasure does not occur when a disk is retired or lost, an organization or user faces a possibility that the data will be stolen and compromised, leading to identity theft, loss of corporate reputation, threats to regulatory compliance and financial impacts. Companies spend large amounts of money to make sure their data is erased when they discard disks. High-profile incidents of data theft include:

- CardSystems Solutions (2005-06-19): Credit card breach exposes 40 million accounts.

- Lifeblood (2008-02-13): Missing laptops contain personal information including dates of birth and some Social Security numbers of 321,000.

- Hannaford (2008-03-17): Breach exposes 4.2 million credit, debit cards.

- Compass Bank (2008-03-21): Stolen hard drive contains 1,000,000 customer records.

- University of Florida College of Medicine, Jacksonville (2008-05-20): Photographs and identifying information of 1,900 on improperly disposed computer.

- Oklahoma Corporation Commission (2008-05-21): Server sold at auction compromises more than 5,000 Social Security numbers.

- Department of Finance, the Australian Electoral Commission and National Disability Insurance Agency (2017-11-02) - 50,000 Australians and 5000 Federal Public servant records.

Regulatory Compliance

Strict industry standards and government regulations are in place that force organizations to mitigate the risk of unauthorized exposure of confidential corporate and government data. Regulations in the United States include HIPAA (Health Insurance Portability and Accountability Act); FACTA (The Fair and Accurate Credit Transactions Act of 2003); GLB (Gramm-Leach Bliley); Sarbanes-Oxley Act (SOx); and Payment Card Industry Data Security Standards (PCI DSS) and the Data Protection Act in the United Kingdom. Failure to comply can result in fines and damage to company reputation, as well as civil and criminal liability.

Preserving Assets and the Environment

Data erasure offers an alternative to physical destruction and degaussing for secure removal of all the disk data. Physical destruction and degaussing destroy the digital media, requiring disposal and contributing to electronic waste while negatively impacting the carbon footprint of individuals and companies. Hard drives are nearly 100% recyclable and can be collected at no charge from a variety of hard drive recyclers after they have been sanitized.

Limitations

Data erasure may not work completely on flash based media, such as Solid State Drives and USB Flash Drives, as these devices can store remnant data which is inaccessible to the erasure technique, and data can be retrieved from the individual flash memory chips inside the device. Data erasure through overwriting only works on hard drives that are functioning and writing to all sectors. Bad sectors cannot usually be overwritten, but may contain recoverable information. Bad sectors, however, may be invisible to the host system and thus to the erasing software. Disk encryption before use prevents this problem. Software-driven data erasure could also be compromised by malicious code.

Differentiators

Software-based data erasure uses a disk accessible application to write a combination of ones, zeroes and any other alpha numeric character also known as the "mask" onto each hard disk drive sector. The level of security when using software data destruction tools are increased dramatically by pre-testing hard drives for sector abnormalities and ensuring that the drive is 100% in working order. The number of wipes has become obsolete with the more recent inclusion of a "verify pass" which scans all sectors of the disk and checks against what character should be there i.e.; 1 Pass of AA has to fill every writable sector of the hard disk. This makes any more than 1 Pass an unnecessary and certainly a more damaging act especially as drives have passed the 1TB mark.

Full Disk Overwriting

While there are many overwriting programs, only those capable of complete data erasure offer full security by destroying the data on all areas of a hard drive. Disk overwriting programs that cannot access the entire hard drive, including hidden/locked areas like the host protected area (HPA), device configuration overlay (DCO), and remapped sectors, perform an incomplete erasure, leaving some of the data intact. By accessing the entire hard drive, data erasure eliminates the risk of data remanence.

Data erasure can also bypass the Operating System (OS). Overwriting programs that operate through the OS will not always perform a complete erasure because they cannot modify the contents of the hard drive that are actively in use by that OS. Because of this, many data erasure programs like DBAN are provided in a bootable format, where you run off of a live CD that has all of the necessary software to erase the disk.

Hardware Support

Data erasure can be deployed over a network to target multiple PCs rather than having to erase each one sequentially. In contrast with DOS-based overwriting programs that may not detect all network hardware, Linux-based data erasure software supports high-end server and storage area network (SAN) environments with hardware support for Serial ATA, Serial Attached SCSI (SAS) and Fibre Channel disks and remapped sectors. It operates directly with sector sizes such as 520, 524, and 528, removing the need to first reformat back to 512 sector size. WinPE has now overtaken Linux as the environment of choice since drivers can be added with little effort. This also helps with data destruction of tablets and other handheld devices that require pure UEFI environments without hardware NIC's installed and/or are lacking UEFI network stack support.

Standards

Many government and industry standards exist for software-based overwriting that removes the data. A key factor in meeting these standards is the number of times the data is overwritten. Also, some standards require a method to verify that all the data have been removed from the entire hard drive and to view the overwrite pattern. Complete data erasure should account for hidden areas, typically DCO, HPA and remapped sectors.

The 1995 edition of the National Industrial Security Program Operating Manual (DoD 5220.22-M) permitted the use of overwriting techniques to sanitize some types of media by writing all address-able locations with a character, its complement, and then a random character. This provision was removed in a 2001 change to the manual and was never permitted for Top Secret media, but it is still listed as a technique by many providers of the data erasure software.

Data erasure software should provide the user with a validation certificate indicating that the over-writing procedure was completed properly. Data erasure software should also comply with re-quirements to erase hidden areas, provide a defects log list and list bad sectors that could not be overwritten.

Data can sometimes be recovered from a broken hard drive. However, if the platters on a hard drive are damaged, such as by drilling a hole through the drive (and the platters inside), then the data can only theoretically be recovered by bit-by-bit analysis of each platter with advanced foren-sic technology.

Number of Overwrites Needed

Data on floppy disks can sometimes be recovered by forensic analysis even after the disks have been overwritten once with zeros (or random zeros and ones). This is not the case with modern hard drives:

- According to the 2014 NIST Special Publication: "For storage devices containing magnetic media, a single overwrite pass with a fixed pattern such as binary zeros typically hinders recovery of data even if state of the art laboratory techniques are applied to attempt to re-trieve the data." It recommends cryptographic erase as a more general mechanism.

- According to the University of California, San Diego Center for Magnetic Recording Research's (now its Center for Memory and Recording Research) "Tutorial on Disk Drive Data Sanitization": "Secure erase does a single on-track erasure of the data on the disk drive. The U.S. National Security Agency published an Information Assurance Ap-proval of single-pass overwrite, after technical testing at CMRR showed that multiple on-track overwrite passes gave no additional erasure." "Secure erase" is a utility built into modern ATA hard drives that overwrites all data on a disk, including remapped (error) sectors.

- Further analysis by Wright et al. seems to also indicate that one overwrite is all that is gen-erally required.

Data Loss Prevention Software

Data loss prevention software detects potential data breaches/data ex-filtration transmissions and prevents them by monitoring, detecting and blocking sensitive data while in use (endpoint ac-tions), in motion (network traffic), and at rest (data storage).

The terms "data loss" and "data leak" are related and are often used interchangeably. Data loss incidents turn into data leak incidents in cases where media containing sensitive information is lost and subsequently acquired by an unauthorized party. However, a data leak is possible without losing the data on the originating side. Other terms associated with data leakage prevention are information leak detection and prevention (ILDP), information leak prevention (ILP), content monitoring and filtering (CMF), information protection and control (IPC) and extrusion prevention system (EPS), as opposed to intrusion prevention system.

Categories

The technological means employed for dealing with data leakage incidents can be divided into categories: standard security measures, advanced/intelligent security measures, access control and encryption and designated DLP systems.

Standard Measures

Standard security measures, such as firewalls, intrusion detection systems (IDSs) and antivirus software, are commonly available products that guard computers against outsider and insider attacks. The use of a firewall, for example, prevents the access of outsiders to the internal network and an intrusion detection system detects intrusion attempts by outsiders. Inside attacks can be averted through antivirus scans that detect Trojan horses that send confidential information, and by the use of thin clients that operate in a client-server architecture with no personal or sensitive data stored on a client device.

Advanced Measures

Advanced security measures employ machine learning and temporal reasoning algorithms for detecting abnormal access to data (e.g., databases or information retrieval systems) or abnormal email exchange, honeypots for detecting authorized personnel with malicious intentions and activity-based verification (e.g., recognition of keystroke dynamics) and user activity monitoring for detecting abnormal data access.

Designated Systems

Designated systems detect and prevent unauthorized attempts to copy or send sensitive data, intentionally or unintentionally, mainly by personnel who are authorized to access the sensitive information. In order to classify certain information as sensitive, these use mechanisms, such as exact data matching, structured data fingerprinting, statistical methods, rule and regular expression matching, published lexicons, conceptual definitions and keywords.

Types

Network

Network (data in motion) technology is typically installed at network egress points near the perimeter. It analyzes network traffic to detect sensitive data that is being sent in violation of information security policies. Multiple security control points may report activity to be analyzed by a central management server.

Endpoint

Endpoint (data in use) systems run on internal end-user workstations or servers. Like network-based systems, endpoint-based technology can address internal as well as external communications. it can therefore be used to control information flow between groups or types of users (e.g. 'Chinese walls'). They can also control email and Instant Messaging communications before they reach the corporate archive, such that a blocked communication (i.e., one that was never sent, and therefore not subject to retention rules) will not be identified in a subsequent legal discovery situation. Endpoint systems have the advantage that they can monitor and control access to physical devices (such as mobile devices with data storage capabilities) and in some cases can access information before it is encrypted. Some endpoint-based systems provide application controls to block attempted transmissions of confidential information and provide immediate user feedback. They must be installed on every workstation in the network, cannot be used on mobile devices (e.g., cell phones and PDAs) or where they cannot be practically installed (for example on a workstation in an Internet café).

Data Identification

DLP includes techniques for identifying confidential or sensitive information. Sometimes confused with discovery, data identification is a process by which organizations use a DLP technology to determine what to look for.

Data is classified as either structured or unstructured. Structured data resides in fixed fields within a file such as a spreadsheet, while unstructured data refers to free-form text or media in text documents, PDF files and video. An estimated 80% of all data is unstructured and 20% structured. Data classification is divided into content analysis, focused on structured data and contextual analysis which looks at the place of origin or the application or system that generated the data.

Methods for describing sensitive content are abundant. They can be divided into both precise and imprecise methods. Precise methods involve content registration and trigger almost zero false positive incidents. All other methods are imprecise and can include: keywords, lexicons, regular expressions, extended regular expressions, meta data tags, Bayesian analysis and statistical analysis techniques such as machine learning, behavior analytics, hierarchical threat modeling, predefined DLP (templates), etc.

The strength of the analysis engine directly relates to its accuracy. The accuracy of DLP identification is important to lowering/avoiding false positives and negatives. Accuracy can depend on many variables, some of which may be situational or technological. Testing for accuracy is recommended to ensure virtually zero false positives/negatives. High false positive rates cause the system to be considered DLD not DLP.

Data Leak Detection

Sometimes a data distributor gives sensitive data to one or more third parties. Sometime later, some of the data is found in an unauthorized place (e.g., on the web or on a user's laptop). The distributor must then investigate the source of the leak.

Data at Rest

"Data at rest" specifically refers to old archived information. This information is of great concern to businesses and government institutions simply because the longer data is left unused in storage, the more likely it might be retrieved by unauthorized individuals. Protecting such data involves methods such as access control, data encryption and data retention policies.

Data in use

"Data in use" refers to data that the user is currently interacting with. DLP systems that protect data in-use may monitor and flag unauthorized activities. These activities include screen-capture, copy/paste, print and fax operations involving sensitive data. It can be intentional or unintentional attempts to transmit sensitive data over communication channels.

Data in Motion

"Data in motion" is data that is traversing through a network to an endpoint

Networks can be internal or external. DLP systems that protect data in-motion monitor sensitive data traveling across a network through various communication channels.

USB Flash Drive Security

Secure USB flash drives protect the data stored on them from access by unauthorized users. USB flash drive products have been on the market since 2000, and their use is increasing exponentially. As both consumers and businesses have increased demand for these drives, manufacturers are producing faster devices with greater data storage capacities.

An increasing number of portable devices are used in business, such as laptops, notebooks, personal digital assistants (PDA), smartphones, USB flash drives and other mobile devices.

Companies in particular are at risk when sensitive data are stored on unsecured USB flash drives by employees who use the devices to transport data outside the office. The consequences of losing drives loaded with such information can be significant, including the loss of customer data, financial information, business plans and other confidential information, with the associated risk of reputation damage.

Major dangers of USB drives

USB flash drives pose two major challenges to information system security: data leakage owing to their small size and ubiquity and system compromise through infections from computer viruses, malware and spyware.

Data Leakage

The large storage capacity of USB flash drives relative to their small size and low cost means that using them for data storage without adequate operational and logical controls may pose a serious threat to information availability, confidentiality and integrity. The following factors should be taken into consideration for securing important assets:

- Storage: USB flash drives are hard to track physically, being stored in bags, backpacks, laptop cases, jackets, trouser pockets or left at unattended workstations.

- Usage: Tracking corporate data stored on personal flash drives is a significant challenge; the drives are small, common and constantly moving. While many enterprises have strict management policies toward USB drives and some companies ban them outright to minimize risk, others seem unaware of the risks these devices pose to system security.

The average cost of a data breach from any source (not necessarily a flash drive) ranges from less than $100,000 to about $2.5 million.

A SanDisk survey characterized the data corporate end users most frequently copy:

- Customer data (25%),

- Financial information (17%),

- Business plans (15%),

- Employee data (13%),

- Marketing plans (13%),

- Intellectual property (6%),

- Source code (6%).

Examples of security breaches resulting from USB drives include:

- In the UK:

  ○ HM Revenue & Customs lost personal details of 6,500 private pension holders.

- In the United States:

  ○ A USB drive was stolen with names, grades, and social security numbers of 6,500 former students.

  ○ USB flash drives with US Army classified military information were up for sale at a bazaar outside Bagram, Afghanistan.

Malware Infections

In the early days of computer viruses, malware, and spyware, the primary means of transmission and infection was the floppy disk. Today, USB flash drives perform the same data and software storage and transfer role as the floppy disk, often used to transfer files between computers which may be on different networks, in different offices, or owned by different people. This has made USB flash drives a leading form of information system infection. When a piece of malware gets onto a USB flash drive, it may infect the devices into which that drive is subsequently plugged.

The prevalence of malware infection by means of USB flash drive was documented in a 2011 Microsoft study analyzing data from more than 600 million systems worldwide in the first half of 2011. The study found that 26 percent of all malware infections of Windows system were due to USB flash drives exploiting the AutoRun feature in Microsoft Windows. That finding was in line with other statistics, such as the monthly reporting of most commonly detected malware by antivirus company ESET, which lists abuse of autorun.inf as first among the top ten threats in 2011.

The Windows autorun.inf file contains information on programs meant to run automatically when removable media (often USB flash drives and similar devices) are accessed by a Windows PC user. The default Autorun setting in Windows versions prior to Windows 7 will automatically run a program listed in the autorun.inf file when you access many kinds of removable media. Many types of malware copy themselves to removable storage devices: while this is not always the program's primary distribution mechanism, malware authors often build in additional infection techniques.

Examples of malware spread by USB flash drives include:

- The Duqu collection of computer malware.
- The Flame modular computer malware.
- The Stuxnet malicious computer worm.

Since the security of the physical drive cannot be guaranteed without compromising the benefits of portability, security measures are primarily devoted to making the data on a compromised drive inaccessible to unauthorized users and unauthorized processes, such as may be executed by malware. One common approach is to encrypt the data for storage and routinely scan USB flash drives for computer viruses, malware and spyware with an antivirus program, although other methods are possible.

Software Encryption

Software solutions such as BitLocker, DiskCryptor and the popular VeraCrypt allow the contents of a USB drive to be encrypted automatically and transparently. Also, Windows 7 Enterprise, Windows 7 Ultimate and Windows Server 2008 R2 provide USB drive encryption using BitLocker to Go. The Apple Computer Mac OS X operating system has provided software for disc data encryption since Mac OS X Panther was issued in 2003.

Additional software can be installed on an external USB drive to prevent access to files in case the drive becomes lost or stolen. Installing software on company computers may help track and minimize risk by recording the interactions between any USB drive and the computer and storing them in a centralized database.

Hardware Encryption

Some USB drives utilize hardware encryption in which microchips within the USB drive provide automatic and transparent encryption. Some manufacturers offer drives that require a pin code to be entered into a physical keypad on the device before allowing access to the drive. The cost of these USB drives can be significant but is starting to fall due to this type of USB drive gaining popularity.

Hardware systems may offer additional features, such as the ability to automatically overwrite the contents of the drive if the wrong password is entered more than a certain number of times. This type of functionality cannot be provided by a software system since the encrypted data can simply be copied from the drive. However, this form of hardware security can result in data loss if activated accidentally by legitimate users and strong encryption algorithms essentially make such functionality redundant.

As the encryption keys used in hardware encryption are typically never stored in the computer's memory, *technically* hardware solutions are less subject to "cold boot" attacks than software-based systems. In reality however, "cold boot" attacks pose little (if any) threat, assuming basic, rudimentary, security precautions are taken with software-based systems.

Compromised Systems

The security of encrypted flash drives is constantly tested by individual hackers as well as professional security firms. At times (as in January 2010) flash drives that have been positioned as secure were found to have been poorly designed such that they provide little or no actual security, giving access to data without knowledge of the correct password.

Flash drives that have been compromised (and claimed to now be fixed) include:

- SanDisk Cruzer Enterprise.

- Kingston DataTraveler BlackBox.

- Verbatim Corporate Secure USB Flash Drive.

- Trek Technology ThumbDrive CRYPTO.

All of the above companies reacted immediately, Kingston offered replacement drives with a different security architecture. SanDisk, Verbatim, and Trek released patches.

Remote Management

In commercial environments, where most secure USB drives are used, a central/remote management system may provide organizations with an additional level of IT asset control, significantly reducing the risks of a harmful data breach. This can include initial user deployment and ongoing management, password recovery, data backup, remote tracking of sensitive data and termination of any issued secure USB drives. Such management systems are available as software as a service (SaaS), where Internet connectivity is allowed, or as behind-the-firewall solutions.

Data-centric Security

Data-centric security is a fundamentally different approach for protecting sensitive data from theft or misuse.

Most security technology focuses on where data is— protecting, for example, all the data stored on a specific laptop or server, or all the data that crosses a specific network. The problem with this approach is that as soon as data moves somewhere else, another solution is required, or data is left unprotected.

Data-centric security, on the other hand, focuses on what needs to be protected—the files containing sensitive information—and applying the appropriate form of protection no matter where the data happens to be.

The defining characteristic of data-centric security is that protection is applied to data itself, independent of the data's location. To be effective, this must happen automatically—sensitive information should identified as soon as it enters an organization's IT ecosystem, and should be secured with policy-based protection that lasts throughout the data lifecycle.

A typical implementation of data-centric security consists of software agents installed on every IT asset where sensitive data might be created or stored—laptops, desktops, servers, mainframes, mobile devices, and elsewhere. These agents are controlled by a centralized management console, where administrators define the appropriate form of protection for each data type and use case.

Each time a file is created or modified, the system scans the file to determine whether it contains sensitive information, and automatically applies the appropriate protection. End users may be given the ability to modify these actions manually, but are otherwise not involved in the process. Protected data remains available to authorized users, but cannot be accessed by unauthorized users, even when files travel outside the company network.

When implemented on an organization-wide scale, data-centric security reduces or eliminates the impact when network and device protections inevitably fail, while at the same time removing data silos and other internal obstacles.

Key Principles of Data-centric Security

Each organization requires a unique solution—one tailored to fit the company's threat exposure and business needs. However, all successful implementations of data-centric security have certain characteristics in common: they're tightly controlled from a centralized management system, they provide coverage across the entire organization without security gaps, they rely on automation rather than manual intervention, and they're adaptable enough to grow and change along with the organization.

Every data-centric security solution must be designed with these key principles in mind, or the finished product will fall short of its goals.

Centralized Control

Centralized management is essential to ensure that data is protected according to the organization's security policies, and that data remains available for appropriate use.

Most organizations, even those that have not adopted the data-centric model, already have some data-level protection in place. Typically, this takes the form of user-applied file encryption—when employees encrypt files with passwords before sharing them with colleagues or external recipients.

Though very common, this approach creates three significant problems:

- Employees might neglect to apply protection when it's needed, or might choose methods that don't provide adequate protection.

- When they do encrypt their files, employees must then find a way to share the passwords (the encryption keys) with the recipients, which typically requires the use of unencrypted email or another unsecure method.

- User-applied encryption leaves employees, rather than administrators, in control of encryption keys. When keys are not available (for example, when employees fail to share them, forget them, or leave the company without providing them), the organization can permanently lose access to critical data.

When properly implemented, data-centric security gives the organization complete control over its sensitive data from the moment that each file or database record is created. Access to protected data can be granted or revoked at any time, and all activity is logged for auditing and reporting.

Gapless Protection

Network-centric and device-centric security strategies inevitably leave gaps between protected systems, because data has to be decrypted or otherwise stripped of protection before it can be transferred between operating systems or platforms. Even experienced security managers can be unaware that sensitive information is being sent or stored without protection. Hackers and malicious insiders, however, are adept at finding and exploiting these gaps.

Effective data-centric security eliminates security gaps, keeping sensitive information protected everywhere it's shared or stored. This is only possible when a data protection solution provides both of the following:

- Persistent protection that travels with files, even when they are sent outside the company network.

- Cross-platform operability that allows the organization to protect files (and make them available for authorized use) on every operating system within its IT architecture.

Automation

Automated workflows are the key to success in data-centric security. End users do have a part to play in protecting an organization's information, but they should not be expected to shoulder the burden of evaluating and securing the large and constantlygrowing volumes of data they handle each day.

Automation takes user error out of the equation, and allows employees to do their jobs without interruption and without jeopardizing the company's data.

An organization's security technology must apply its data protection policies in real time, across the entire enterprise, without user intervention. This requires technology that continuously monitors file activity, and automatically applies the appropriate protection as soon as sensitive data appears.

Adaptability

Data-centric security is not a "one size fits all" proposition. Within a single organization, there can be dozens of security policies, hundreds of data types, and thousands of use cases. Some data might require encryption, while other data may need to be masked, deleted, quarantined, or left as is.

An effective security strategy will be tailored to meet the organization's unique requirements, while accommodating changes in those requirements over time. Organizations must have confidence that they can add and remove infrastructure, change business processes, and create new partnerships, without having to rebuild their data security solution each time.

References

- Boudriga, Noureddine (2010). Security of mobile communications. Boca Raton: CRC Press. Pp. 32–33. ISBN 978-0849379420

- Overview-of-information-security-management, itil: invensislearning.com, Retrieved 8 April, 2019

- Tim Boyles (2010). CCNA Security Study Guide: Exam 640-553. John Wiley and Sons. P. 249. ISBN 978-0-470-52767-2. Retrieved 29 June 2010

- Unifying identity management and access control". Sourcesecurity.com. Retrieved 15 July 2013

- Brucker, Achim D.; Petritsch, Helmut (2009). "Extending Access Control Models with Break-glass.". ACM symposium on access control models and technologies (SACMAT). ACM Press. Pp. 197–206. Doi:10.1145/1542207.1542239

- Thomas Chen, Jean-Marc Robert (2004). "The Evolution of Viruses and Worms". Archived from the original on May 17, 2009. Retrieved February 16, 2009

- Szor, Peter (February 13, 2005). The Art of Computer Virus Research and Defense. Addison-Wesley Professional. ISBN 978-0321304544 – via Amazon

- Encryption, definition: techtarget.com, Retrieved 16 August, 2010

- Evers, Joris (19 June 2005). "Credit card breach exposes 40 million accounts". ZDNET. CNET News. Retrieved 20 July2010

- Secure USB flash drives. European Union Agency for Network and Information Security. 5 June 2008. ISBN 978-92-9204-011-6. Retrieved 21 July 2014

5
Cryptography

Cryptography refers to the study and practice of techniques to ensure secure communication in the presence of third parties known as adversaries. Some of the algorithms used in cryptography are cryptographic primitives and symmetric-key algorithm. The diverse aspects of cryptography have been carefully analyzed in this chapter.

Cryptography is a method of protecting information and communications through the use of codes so that only those for whom the information is intended can read and process it. The pre-fix "crypt" means "hidden" or "vault" and the suffix "graphy" stands for "writing."

In computer science, cryptography refers to secure information and communication techniques derived from mathematical concepts and a set of rule-based calculations called algorithms to transform messages in ways that are hard to decipher. These deterministic algorithms are used for cryptographic key generation and digital signing and verification to protect data privacy, web browsing on the internet and confidential communications such as credit card transactions and email.

Cryptography Techniques

Cryptography is closely related to the disciplines of cryptology and cryptanalysis. It includes techniques such as microdots, merging words with images, and other ways to hide information in storage or transit. However, in today's computer-centric world, cryptography is most often associated with scrambling plaintext (ordinary text, sometimes referred to as cleartext) into ciphertext (a process called encryption), then back again (known as decryption). Individuals who practice this field are known as cryptographers.

Modern cryptography concerns itself with the following four objectives:

1. Confidentiality: The information cannot be understood by anyone for whom it was unintended.

2. Integrity: The information cannot be altered in storage or transit between sender and intended receiver without the alteration being detected.

3. Non-repudiation: The creator/sender of the information cannot deny at a later stage his or her intentions in the creation or transmission of the information.

4. Authentication: The sender and receiver can confirm each other's identity and the origin/destination of the information.

Procedures and protocols that meet some or all of the above criteria are known as cryptosystems. Cryptosystems are often thought to refer only to mathematical procedures and computer programs; however, they also include the regulation of human behavior, such as choosing hard-to-guess passwords, logging off unused systems, and not discussing sensitive procedures with outsiders.

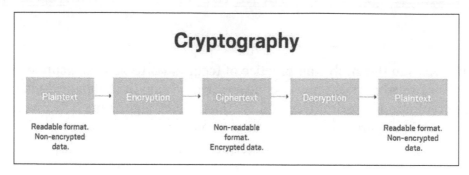

Cryptographic Algorithms

Cryptosystems use a set of procedures known as cryptographic algorithms, or ciphers, to encrypt and decrypt messages to secure communications among computer systems, devices such as smartphones, and applications. A cipher suite uses one algorithm for encryption, another algorithm for message authentication and another for key exchange. This process, embedded in protocols and written in software that runs on operating systems and networked computer systems, involves public and private key generation for data encryption/decryption, digital signing and verification for message authentication, and key exchange.

Types of Cryptography

Single-key or symmetric-key encryption algorithms create a fixed length of bits known as a block cipher with a secret key that the creator/sender uses to encipher data (encryption) and the receiver uses to decipher it. Types of symmetric-key cryptography include the Advanced Encryption Standard (AES), a specification established in November 2001 by the National Institute of Standards and Technology as a Federal Information Processing Standard (FIPS 197), to protect sensitive information. The standard is mandated by the U.S. government and widely used in the private sector.

In June 2003, AES was approved by the U.S. government for classified information. It is a royalty-free specification implemented in software and hardware worldwide. AES is the successor to the Data Encryption Standard (DES) and DES3. It uses longer key lengths (128-bit, 192-bit, 256-bit) to prevent brute force and other attacks.

Public-key or asymmetric-key encryption algorithms use a pair of keys, a public key associated with the creator/sender for encrypting messages and a private key that only the originator knows (unless it is exposed or they decide to share it) for decrypting that information. The types of public-key cryptography include RSA, used widely on the internet; Elliptic Curve Digital Signature

Algorithm (ECDSA) used by Bitcoin; Digital Signature Algorithm (DSA) adopted as a Federal Information Processing Standard for digital signatures by NIST in FIPS 186-4; and Diffie-Hellman key exchange.

To maintain data integrity in cryptography, hash functions, which return a deterministic output from an input value, are used to map data to a fixed data size. Types of cryptographic hash functions include SHA-1 (Secure Hash Algorithm 1), SHA-2 and SHA-3.

Cryptographic Primitive

Cryptographic primitives are well-established, low-level cryptographic algorithms that are frequently used to build cryptographic protocols for computer security systems. These routines include, but are not limited to, one-way hash functions and encryption functions.

When creating cryptographic systems, designers use cryptographic primitives as their most basic building blocks. Because of this, cryptographic primitives are designed to do one very specific task in a precisely defined and highly reliable fashion.

Since cryptographic primitives are used as building blocks, they must be very reliable, i.e. perform according to their specification. For example, if an encryption routine claims to be only breakable with X number of computer operations, then if it can be broken with significantly fewer than X operations, that cryptographic primitive is said to fail. If a cryptographic primitive is found to fail, almost every protocol that uses it becomes vulnerable. Since creating cryptographic routines is very hard, and testing them to be reliable takes a long time, it is essentially never sensible (nor secure) to design a new cryptographic primitive to suit the needs of a new cryptographic system. The reasons include:

- The designer might not be competent in the mathematical and practical considerations involved in cryptographic primitives.

- Designing a new cryptographic primitive is *very* time-consuming and *very* error prone, even for experts in the field.

- Since algorithms in this field are not only required to be designed well, but also need to be tested well by the cryptologist community, even if a cryptographic routine looks good from a design point of view it might still contain errors. Successfully withstanding such scrutiny gives some confidence (in fact, so far, the only confidence) that the algorithm is indeed secure enough to use; security proofs for cryptographic primitives are generally not available.

Cryptographic primitives are similar in some ways to programming languages. A computer programmer rarely invents a new programming language while writing a new program; instead, they will use one of the already established programming languages to program in.

Cryptographic primitives are one of the building blocks of every crypto system, e.g., TLS, SSL, SSH, etc. Crypto system designers, not being in a position to definitively prove their security, must take the primitives they use as secure. Choosing the best primitive available for use in a protocol usually provides the best available security. However, compositional weaknesses are possible in any crypto system and it is the responsibility of the designer(s) to avoid them.

Commonly used Primitives

- One-way hash function, sometimes also called as one-way compression function: Compute a reduced hash value for a message (e.g., SHA-256).

- Authentication.

- Symmetric key cryptography: Compute a ciphertext decodable with the same key used to encode (e.g., AES).

- Public key cryptography: Compute a ciphertext decodable with a different key used to encode (e.g., RSA).

- Digital signatures: Confirm the author of a message.

- Mix network: Pool communications from many users to anonymize what came from whom.

- Private information retrieval: Get database information without server knowing which item was requested.

- Commitment scheme: Allows one to commit to a chosen value while keeping it hidden to others, with the ability to reveal it later.

- Cryptographically secure pseudorandom number generator.

Combining Cryptographic Primitives

Cryptographic primitives, on their own, are quite limited. They cannot be considered, properly, to be a cryptographic system. For instance, a bare encryption algorithm will provide no authentication mechanism, nor any explicit message integrity checking. Only when combined in security protocols, can more than one security requirement be addressed. For example, to transmit a message that is not only encoded but also protected from tinkering (i.e. it is confidential and integrity-protected), an encoding routine, such as DES, and a hash-routine such as SHA-1 can be used in combination. If the attacker does not know the encryption key, he can not modify the message such that message digest value would be valid.

Combining cryptographic primitives to make a security protocol is itself an entire specialization. Most exploitable errors (i.e., insecurities in crypto systems) are due not to design errors in the primitives (assuming always that they were chosen with care), but to the way they are used, i.e. bad protocol design and buggy or not careful enough implementation. Mathematical analysis of protocols is, at the time of this writing, not mature. There are some basic properties that can be verified with automated methods, such as BAN logic. There are even methods for full verification (e.g. the SPI calculus) but they are extremely cumbersome and cannot be automated. Protocol design is an art requiring deep knowledge and much practice; even then mistakes are common.

Cryptographic Protocol

A security protocol (cryptographic protocol or encryption protocol) is an abstract or concrete protocol that performs a security-related function and applies cryptographic methods, often as sequences of cryptographic primitives. A protocol describes how the algorithms should be used. A sufficiently detailed protocol includes details about data structures and representations, at which point it can be used to implement multiple, interoperable versions of a program.

Cryptographic protocols are widely used for secure application-level data transport. A cryptographic protocol usually incorporates at least some of these aspects:

- Key agreement or establishment.

- Entity authentication.

- Symmetric encryption and message authentication material construction.

- Secured application-level data transport.

- Non-repudiation methods.

- Secret sharing methods.

- Secure multi-party computation.

For example, Transport Layer Security (TLS) is a cryptographic protocol that is used to secure web (HTTPS) connections. It has an entity authentication mechanism, based on the X.509 system; a key setup phase, where a symmetric encryption key is formed by employing public-key cryptography; and an application-level data transport function. These three aspects have important interconnections. Standard TLS does not have non-repudiation support.

There are other types of cryptographic protocols as well, and even the term itself has various readings; Cryptographic *application* protocols often use one or more underlying key agreement methods, which are also sometimes themselves referred to as "cryptographic protocols". For instance, TLS employs what is known as the Diffie–Hellman key exchange, which although it is only a part of TLS *per se*, Diffie–Hellman may be seen as a complete cryptographic protocol in itself for other applications.

Advanced Cryptographic Protocols

A wide variety of cryptographic protocols go beyond the traditional goals of data confidentiality, integrity, and authentication to also secure a variety of other desired characteristics of computer-mediated collaboration. Blind signatures can be used for digital cash and digital credentials to prove that a person holds an attribute or right without revealing that person's identity or the identities of parties that person transacted with. Secure digital timestamping can be used to prove that data (even if confidential) existed at a certain time. Secure multiparty computation can be used to compute answers (such as determining the highest bid in an auction) based on confidential data (such as private bids), so that when the protocol is complete the participants know only their own input and the answer. End-to-end auditable voting systems provide sets of desirable privacy and auditability properties for conducting e-voting. Undeniable signatures include interactive protocols that allow the signer to prove a forgery and limit who can verify the signature. Deniable encryption augments standard encryption by making it impossible for an attacker to mathematically prove the existence of a plain text message. Digital mixes create hard-to-trace communications.

Formal Verification

Cryptographic protocols can sometimes be verified formally on an abstract level. When it is done, there is a necessity to formalize the environment in which the protocol operates in order to identify threats. This is frequently done through the Dolev-Yao model.

Logics, concepts and calculi used for formal reasoning of security protocols:

- Burrows–Abadi–Needham logic (BAN logic).

- Dolev–Yao model.

- π-calculus.

- Protocol composition logic (PCL).

- Strand space.

Research projects and tools used for formal verification of security protocols:

- Automated Validation of Internet Security Protocols and Applications (AVISPA) and follow-up project AVANTSSAR.

  ◦ Constraint Logic-based Attack Searcher (CL-AtSe).

  ◦ Open-Source Fixed-Point Model-Checker (OFMC).

  ◦ SAT-based Model-Checker (SATMC).

- Casper.

- CryptoVerif.

- Cryptographic Protocol Shapes Analyzer (CPSA).

- Knowledge In Security protocolS (KISS).

- Maude-NRL Protocol Analyzer (Maude-NPA).

- ProVerif.

- Scyther.

- Tamarin Prover.

Notion of Abstract Protocol

To formally verify a protocol it is often abstracted and modelled using Alice & Bob notation. A simple example is the following:

$$A \to B : \{X\}_{K_{A,B}}$$

This states that Alice A intends a message for Bob B consisting of a message X encrypted under shared key $K_{A,B}$.

Examples:

- Internet Key Exchange,

- IPsec,

- Kerberos,

- Off-the-Record Messaging,

- Point to Point Protocol,

- Secure Shell (SSH),

- Signal Protocol,

- Transport Layer Security,

- ZRTP.

Asymmetric Cryptography

Asymmetric cryptography, also known as public key cryptography, uses public and private keys to encrypt and decrypt data. The keys are simply large numbers that have been paired together but are not identical (asymmetric). One key in the pair can be shared with everyone; it is called the public key. The other key in the pair is kept secret; it is called the private key. Either of the keys can be used to encrypt a message; the opposite key from the one used to encrypt the message is used for decryption.

Many protocols like SSH, OpenPGP, S/MIME, and SSL/TLS rely on asymmetric cryptography for encryption and digital signature functions. It is also used in software programs, such as browsers, which need to establish a secure connection over an insecure network like the Internet or need to validate a digital signature. Encryption strength is directly tied to key size and doubling the key length delivers an exponential increase in strength, although it does impair performance. As computing power increases and more efficient factoring algorithms are discovered, the ability to factor larger and larger numbers also increases.

For asymmetric encryption to deliver confidentiality, integrity, authenticity and non-repudiability, users and systems need to be certain that a public key is authentic, that it belongs to the person or entity claimed and that it has not been tampered with nor replaced by a malicious third party. There is no perfect solution to this public key authentication problem. A public key infrastructure (PKI) where trusted certificate authorities certify ownership of key pairs and certificates is the most common approach, but encryption products based on the Pretty Good Privacy (PGP) model including OpenPGP rely on a decentralized authentication model called a web of trust, which relies on individual endorsements of the link between user and public key.

Asymmetric encryption algorithms use a mathematically-related key pair for encryption and decryption; one is the public key and the other is the private key. If the public key is used for encryption, the related private key is used for decryption and if the private key is used for encryption, the related public key is used for decryption.

Only the user or computer that generates the key pair has the private key. The public key can be distributed to anyone who wants to send encrypted data to the holder of the private key. It's impossible to determine the private key with the public one.

The two participants in the asymmetric encryption workflow are the sender and the receiver. First, the sender obtains the receiver's public key. Then the plaintext is encrypted with the asymmetric encryption algorithm using the recipient's public key, creating the ciphertext. The ciphertext is then sent to the receiver, who decrypts the ciphertext with his private key so he can access the sender's plaintext.

Because of the one-way nature of the encryption function, one sender is unable to read the messages of another sender, even though each has the public key of the receiver.

Examples of Asymmetric Cryptography

RSA (Rivest-Shamir-Adleman) the most widely used asymmetric algorithm is embedded in the SSL/TSL protocols which is used to provide communications security over a computer network. RSA derives its security from the computational difficulty of factoring large integers that are the product of two large prime numbers.

Multiplying two large primes is easy, but the difficulty of determining the original numbers from the product factoring forms the basis of public key cryptography security. The time it takes to factor the product of two sufficiently large primes is considered to be beyond the capabilities of most attackers, excluding nation-state actors who may have access to sufficient computing power. RSA keys are typically 1024- or 2048-bits long, but experts believe that 1024-bit keys could be broken in the near future, which is why government and industry are moving to a minimum key length of 2048-bits.

Elliptic Curve Cryptography (ECC) is gaining favor with many security experts as an alternative to RSA for implementing public key cryptography. ECC is a public key encryption technique based on elliptic curve theory that can create faster, smaller, and more efficient cryptographic keys. ECC generates keys through the properties of the elliptic curve equation.

To break ECC, one must compute an elliptic curve discrete logarithm, and it turns out that this is a significantly more difficult problem than factoring. As a result, ECC key sizes can be significantly smaller than those required by RSA yet deliver equivalent security with lower computing power and battery resource usage making it more suitable for mobile applications than RSA.

Uses of Asymmetric Cryptography

The typical application for asymmetric cryptography is authenticating data through the use of digital signatures. Based on asymmetric cryptography, digital signatures can provide assurances of evidence to the origin, identity and status of an electronic document, transaction or message, as well as acknowledging informed consent by the signer.

To create a digital signature, signing software such as an email program creates a one-way hash of the electronic data to be signed. The user's private key is then used to encrypt the hash, returning a value that is unique to the hashed data. The encrypted hash, along with other information such as the hashing algorithm, forms the digital signature. Any change in the data, even to a single bit, results in a different hash value.

This attribute enables others to validate the integrity of the data by using the signer's public key to decrypt the hash. If the decrypted hash matches a second computed hash of the same data, it proves that the data hasn't changed since it was signed. If the two hashes don't match, the data has either been tampered with in some way indicating a failure of integrity or the signature was created with a private key that doesn't correspond to the public key presented by the signer indicating a failure of authentication.

A digital signature also makes it difficult for the signing party to deny having signed something the property of non-repudiation. If a signing party denies a valid digital signature, their private key has either been compromised or they are being untruthful. In many countries, including the United States, digital signatures have the same legal weight as more traditional forms of signatures.

Asymmetric cryptography can be applied to systems in which many users may need to encrypt and decrypt messages, such as encrypted email, in which a public key can be used to encrypt a message, and a private key can be used to decrypt it.

The SSL/TSL cryptographic protocols for establishing encrypted links between websites and browsers also make use of asymmetric encryption.

Additionally, Bitcoin and other cryptocurrencies rely on asymmetric cryptography as users have public keys that everyone can see and private keys that are kept secret. Bitcoin uses a cryptographic algorithm to ensure that only the legitimate owners can spend the funds.

In the case of the Bitcoin ledger, each unspent transaction output (UTXO) is typically associated with a public key. So if user X, who has an UTXO associated with his public key, wants to send the money to user Y, user X uses his private key to sign a transaction that spends the UTXO and creates a new UTXO that's associated with user Y's public key.

Benefits and Disadvantages of Asymmetric Cryptography

The benefits of asymmetric cryptography include:

- The key distribution problem is eliminated because there's no need for exchanging keys.

- Security is increased as the private keys don't ever have to be transmitted or revealed to anyone.

- The use of digital signatures is enabled so that a recipient can verify that a message comes from a particular sender.

- It allows for non-repudiation so the sender can't deny sending a message.

Disadvantages include:

- It's a slow process compared to symmetric crytography, so it's not appropriate for decrypting bulk messages.

- If an individual loses his private key, he can't decrypt the messages he receives.

- Since the public keys aren't authenticated, no one really knows if a public key belongs to the person specified. Consequently, users have to verify that their public keys belong to them.

- If a hacker identifies a person's private key, the attacker can read all of that individual's messages.

Symmetric-key Algorithm

Symmetric-key algorithms are algorithms for cryptography that use the same cryptographic keys for both encryption of plaintext and decryption of ciphertext. The keys may be identical or there may be a simple transformation to go between the two keys. The keys, in practice, represent a shared secret between two or more parties that can be used to maintain a private information link. This requirement that both parties have access to the secret key is one of the main drawbacks of symmetric key encryption, in comparison to public-key encryption (also known as asymmetric key encryption).

Cryptographic Primitives based on Symmetric Ciphers

Symmetric ciphers are commonly used to achieve other cryptographic primitives than just encryption.

Encrypting a message does not guarantee that this message is not changed while encrypted. Hence often a message authentication code is added to a ciphertext to ensure that changes to the cipher-text will be noted by the receiver. Message authentication codes can be constructed from symmetric ciphers (e.g. CBC-MAC).

However, symmetric ciphers cannot be used for non-repudiation purposes except by involving additional parties.

Another application is to build hash functions from block ciphers.

Construction of Symmetric Ciphers

Many modern block ciphers are based on a construction proposed by Horst Feistel. Feistel's construction makes it possible to build invertible functions from other functions that are themselves not invertible.

Security of Symmetric Ciphers

Symmetric ciphers have historically been susceptible to known-plaintext attacks, chosen-plaintext attacks, differential cryptanalysis and linear cryptanalysis. Careful construction of the functions for each round can greatly reduce the chances of a successful attack.

Key Establishment

Symmetric-key algorithms require both the sender and the recipient of a message to have the same secret key. All early cryptographic systems required one of those people to somehow receive a copy of that secret key over a physically secure channel.

Nearly all modern cryptographic systems still use symmetric-key algorithms internally to encrypt the bulk of the messages, but they eliminate the need for a physically secure channel by using Diffie–Hellman key exchange or some other public-key protocol to securely come to agreement on a fresh new secret key for each message (forward secrecy).

Key Generation

When used with asymmetric ciphers for key transfer, pseudorandom key generators are nearly always used to generate the symmetric cipher session keys. However, lack of randomness in those generators or in their initialization vectors is disastrous and has led to cryptanalytic breaks in the past. Therefore, it is essential that an implementation uses a source of high entropy for its initialization.

Reciprocal Cipher

A reciprocal cipher is a cipher where, just as one enters the plaintext into the cryptography system to get the ciphertext, one could enter the ciphertext into the same place in the system to get the plaintext. A reciprocal cipher is also sometimes referred as self-reciprocal cipher. Examples of reciprocal ciphers include:

- Beaufort cipher,
- Enigma machine,
- ROT13,
- XOR cipher,
- Vatsyayana cipher.

Stream Cipher

A stream cipher is a symmetric key cipher where plaintext digits are combined with a pseudorandom cipher digit stream (keystream). In a stream cipher, each plaintext digit is encrypted one at a time with the corresponding digit of the keystream, to give a digit of the ciphertext stream. Since encryption of each digit is dependent on the current state of the cipher, it is also known as state cipher. In practice, a digit is typically a bit and the combining operation an exclusive-or (XOR).

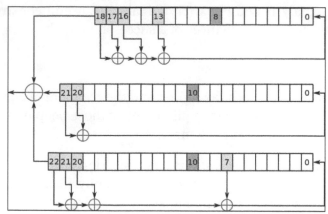

The operation of the keystream generator in A5/1, an LFSR-based stream cipher used to encrypt mobile phone conversations.

The pseudorandom keystream is typically generated serially from a random seed value using digital shift registers. The seed value serves as the cryptographic key for decrypting the ciphertext stream. Stream ciphers represent a different approach to symmetric encryption from block ciphers. Block ciphers operate on large blocks of digits with a fixed, unvarying transformation. This distinction is not always clear-cut: in some modes of operation, a block cipher primitive is used in such a way that it acts effectively as a stream cipher. Stream ciphers typically execute at a higher speed than block ciphers and have lower hardware complexity. However, stream ciphers can be susceptible to serious security problems if used incorrectly; in particular, the same starting state (seed) must never be used twice.

Stream ciphers can be viewed as approximating the action of a proven unbreakable cipher, the one-time pad (OTP), sometimes known as the Vernam cipher. A one-time pad uses a keystream of completely random digits. The keystream is combined with the plaintext digits one at a time to form the ciphertext. This system was proved to be secure by Claude E. Shannon in 1949. However, the keystream must be generated completely at random with at least the same length as the plaintext and cannot be used more than once. This makes the system cumbersome to implement in many practical applications, and as a result the one-time pad has not been widely used, except for the most critical applications. Key generation, distribution and management are critical for those applications.

A stream cipher makes use of a much smaller and more convenient key such as 128 bits. Based on this key, it generates a pseudorandom keystream which can be combined with the plaintext digits in a similar fashion to the one-time pad. However, this comes at a cost. The keystream is now pseudorandom and so is not truly random. The proof of security associated with the one-time pad no longer holds. It is quite possible for a stream cipher to be completely insecure.

Types

A stream cipher generates successive elements of the keystream based on an internal state. This state is updated in essentially two ways: if the state changes independently of the plaintext or ciphertext messages, the cipher is classified as a synchronous stream cipher. By contrast, self-synchronising stream ciphers update their state based on previous ciphertext digits.

Synchronous Stream Ciphers

Lorenz SZ cipher machine as used by the German military during World War II.

In a synchronous stream cipher a stream of pseudo-random digits is generated independently of the plaintext and ciphertext messages, and then combined with the plaintext (to encrypt) or the ciphertext (to decrypt). In the most common form, binary digits are used (bits), and the keystream is combined with the plaintext using the exclusive or operation (XOR). This is termed a binary additive stream cipher.

In a synchronous stream cipher, the sender and receiver must be exactly in step for decryption to be successful. If digits are added or removed from the message during transmission, synchronisation is lost. To restore synchronisation, various offsets can be tried systematically to obtain the correct decryption. Another approach is to tag the ciphertext with markers at regular points in the output.

If, however, a digit is corrupted in transmission, rather than added or lost, only a single digit in the plaintext is affected and the error does not propagate to other parts of the message. This property is useful when the transmission error rate is high; however, it makes it less likely the error would be detected without further mechanisms. Moreover, because of this property, synchronous stream ciphers are very susceptible to active attacks: if an attacker can change a digit in the ciphertext, he might be able to make predictable changes to the corresponding plaintext bit; for example, flipping a bit in the ciphertext causes the same bit to be flipped in the plaintext.

Self-synchronizing Stream Ciphers

Another approach uses several of the previous N ciphertext digits to compute the keystream. Such schemes are known as self-synchronizing stream ciphers, asynchronous stream ciphers or ciphertext autokey (CTAK). The idea of self-synchronization was patented in 1946, and has the advantage that the receiver will automatically synchronise with the keystream generator after receiving N ciphertext digits, making it easier to recover if digits are dropped or added to the message stream. Single-digit errors are limited in their effect, affecting only up to N plaintext digits.

An example of a self-synchronising stream cipher is a block cipher in cipher feedback (CFB) mode.

Based on linear-feedback Shift Registers

Binary stream ciphers are often constructed using linear-feedback shift registers (LFSRs) because they can be easily implemented in hardware and can be readily analysed mathematically. The use of LFSRs on their own, however, is insufficient to provide good security. Various schemes have been proposed to increase the security of LFSRs.

Non-linear Combining Functions

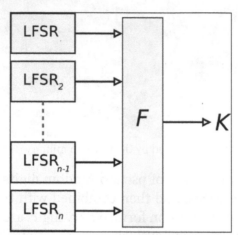

One approach is to use n LFSRs in parallel, their outputs combined using an n-input binary Boolean function (F).

Because LFSRs are inherently linear, one technique for removing the linearity is to feed the outputs of several parallel LFSRs into a non-linear Boolean function to form a combination generator. Various properties of such a combining function are critical for ensuring the security of the resultant scheme, for example, in order to avoid correlation attacks.

Clock-controlled Generators

Normally LFSRs are stepped regularly. One approach to introducing non-linearity is to have the LFSR clocked irregularly, controlled by the output of a second LFSR. Such generators include the stop-and-go generator, the alternating step generator and the shrinking generator.

An alternating step generator comprises three LFSRs, which we will call LFSR0, LFSR1 and LFSR2 for convenience. The output of one of the registers decides which of the other two is to be used; for instance if LFSR2 outputs a 0, LFSR0 is clocked, and if it outputs a 1, LFSR1 is clocked instead. The output is the exclusive OR of the last bit produced by LFSR0 and LFSR1. The initial state of the three LFSRs is the key.

The stop-and-go generator consists of two LFSRs. One LFSR is clocked if the output of a second is a 1, otherwise it repeats its previous output. This output is then (in some versions) combined with the output of a third LFSR clocked at a regular rate.

The shrinking generator takes a different approach. Two LFSRs are used, both clocked regularly. If the output of the first LFSR is 1, the output of the second LFSR becomes the output of the generator. If the first LFSR outputs 0, however, the output of the second is discarded, and no bit is output by the generator. This mechanism suffers from timing attacks on the second generator, since the speed of the output is variable in a manner that depends on the second generator's state. This can be alleviated by buffering the output.

Filter Generator

Another approach to improving the security of an LFSR is to pass the entire state of a single LFSR into a non-linear filtering function.

Other Designs

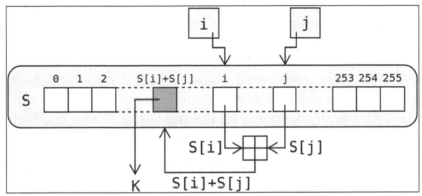

RC4 is one of the most widely used stream cipher designs.

Instead of a linear driving device, one may use a nonlinear update function. For example, Klimov and Shamir proposed triangular functions (T-functions) with a single cycle on n-bit words.

Security

For a stream cipher to be secure, its keystream must have a large period and it must be impossible to recover the cipher's key or internal state from the keystream. Cryptographers also demand that the keystream be free of even subtle biases that would let attackers distinguish a stream from random noise, and free of detectable relationships between keystreams that correspond to related keys or related cryptographic nonces. That should be true for all keys (there should be no weak keys), even if the attacker can know or choose some plaintext or ciphertext.

As with other attacks in cryptography, stream cipher attacks can be certificational so they are not necessarily practical ways to break the cipher but indicate that the cipher might have other weaknesses.

Securely using a secure synchronous stream cipher requires that one never reuse the same keystream twice. That generally means a different nonce or key must be supplied to each invocation of the cipher. Application designers must also recognize that most stream ciphers provide not authenticity but privacy: encrypted messages may still have been modified in transit.

Short periods for stream ciphers have been a practical concern. For example, 64-bit block ciphers like DES can be used to generate a keystream in output feedback (OFB) mode. However, when not using full feedback, the resulting stream has a period of around 2^{32} blocks on average; for many applications, the period is far too low. For example, if encryption is being performed at a rate of 8 megabytes per second, a stream of period 2^{32} blocks will repeat after about a half an hour.

Some applications using the stream cipher RC4 are attackable because of weaknesses in RC4's key setup routine; new applications should either avoid RC4 or make sure all keys are unique and ideally unrelated (such as generated by a well-seeded CSPRNG or a cryptographic hash function) and that the first bytes of the keystream are discarded.

Usage

Stream ciphers are often used for their speed and simplicity of implementation in hardware, and in applications where plaintext comes in quantities of unknowable length like a secure wireless connection. If a block cipher (not operating in a stream cipher mode) were to be used in this type of application, the designer would need to choose either transmission efficiency or implementation complexity, since block ciphers cannot directly work on blocks shorter than their block size. For example, if a 128-bit block cipher received separate 32-bit bursts of plaintext, three quarters of the data transmitted would be padding. Block ciphers must be used in ciphertext stealing or residual block termination mode to avoid padding, while stream ciphers eliminate this issue by naturally operating on the smallest unit that can be transmitted (usually bytes).

Another advantage of stream ciphers in military cryptography is that the cipher stream can be generated in a separate box that is subject to strict security measures and fed to other devices such as a radio set, which will perform the xor operation as part of their function. The latter device can then be designed and used in less stringent environments.

ChaCha is becoming the most widely used stream cipher in software; others include: RC4, A5/1, A5/2, Chameleon, FISH, Helix, ISAAC, MUGI, Panama, Phelix, Pike, SEAL, SOBER, SOBER-128, and WAKE.

Block Cipher

In cryptography, a block cipher is a deterministic algorithm operating on fixed-length groups of bits, called blocks, with an unvarying transformation that is specified by a symmetric key. Block ciphers operate as important elementary components in the design of many cryptographic protocols, and are widely used to implement encryption of bulk data.

The modern design of block ciphers is based on the concept of an iterated product cipher. In his seminal 1949 publication, Communication Theory of Secrecy Systems, Claude Shannon analyzed product ciphers and suggested them as a means of effectively improving security by combining simple operations such as substitutions and permutations. Iterated product ciphers carry out encryption in multiple rounds, each of which uses a different subkey derived from the original key. One widespread implementation of such ciphers, named a Feistel network after Horst Feistel, is notably implemented in the DES cipher. Many other realizations of block ciphers, such as the AES, are classified as substitution–permutation networks.

The publication of the DES cipher by the United States National Bureau of Standards (subsequently the U.S. National Institute of Standards and Technology, NIST) in 1977 was fundamental in the public understanding of modern block cipher design. It also influenced the academic development of cryptanalytic attacks. Both differential and linear cryptanalysis arose out of studies on the DES design. As of 2016 there is a palette of attack techniques against which a block cipher must be secure, in addition to being robust against brute-force attacks.

Even a secure block cipher is suitable only for the encryption of a single block under a fixed key. A multitude of modes of operation have been designed to allow their repeated use in a secure way, commonly to achieve the security goals of confidentiality and authenticity. However, block ciphers may also feature as building blocks in other cryptographic protocols, such as universal hash functions and pseudo-random number generators.

A block cipher consists of two paired algorithms, one for encryption, E, and the other for decryption, D. Both algorithms accept two inputs: an input block of size n bits and a key of size k bits; and both yield an n-bit output block. The decryption algorithm D is defined to be the inverse function of encryption, i.e., $D = E^{-1}$. More formally, a block cipher is specified by an encryption function:

$$E_K(P) := E(K,P) : \{0,1\}^k \times \{0,1\}^n \to \{0,1\}^n,$$

which takes as input a key K of bit length k, called the *key size*, and a bit string P of length n, called the *block size*, and returns a string C of n bits. P is called the plaintext, and C is termed the ciphertext. For each K, the function $E_K(P)$ is required to be an invertible mapping on $\{0,1\}^n$. The inverse for E is defined as a function:

$$E_K^{-1}(C) := D_K(C) = D(K,C) : \{0,1\}^k \times \{0,1\}^n \to \{0,1\}^n,$$

taking a key K and a ciphertext C to return a plaintext value P, such that:

$$\forall K : D_K(E_K(P)) = P.$$

For example, a block cipher encryption algorithm might take a 128-bit block of plaintext as input, and output a corresponding 128-bit block of ciphertext. The exact transformation is controlled using a second input – the secret key. Decryption is similar: the decryption algorithm takes, in this example, a 128-bit block of ciphertext together with the secret key, and yields the original 128-bit block of plain text.

For each key K, E_K is a permutation (a bijective mapping) over the set of input blocks. Each key selects one permutation from the set of $(2^n)!$ possible permutations.

Design

Iterated Block Ciphers

Most block cipher algorithms are classified as *iterated block ciphers* which means that they transform fixed-size blocks of plaintext into identical size blocks of ciphertext, via the repeated application of an invertible transformation known as the *round function*, with each iteration referred to as a *round*.

Usually, the round function R takes different *round keys* K_i as second input, which are derived from the original key:

$$M_i = R_{K_i}(M_{i-1})$$

where M_0 is the plaintext and M_r the ciphertext, with r being the number of rounds.

Frequently, key whitening is used in addition to this. At the beginning and the end, the data is modified with key material (often with XOR, but simple arithmetic operations like adding and subtracting are also used):

$$M_0 = M \oplus K_0$$

$$M_i = R_{K_i}(M_{i-1}) \, ; \, i = 1 \dots r$$

$$C = M_r \oplus K_{r+1}$$

Given one of the standard iterated block cipher design schemes, it is fairly easy to construct a block cipher that is cryptographically secure, simply by using a large number of rounds. However, this will make the cipher inefficient. Thus, efficiency is the most important additional design criterion for professional ciphers. Further, a good block cipher is designed to avoid side-channel attacks, such as input-dependent memory accesses that might leak secret data via the cache state or the execution time. In addition, the cipher should be concise, for small hardware and software implementations. Finally, the cipher should be easily cryptanalyzable, such that it can be shown how many rounds the cipher needs to be reduced to, so that the existing cryptographic attacks would work – and, conversely, that it can be shown that the number of actual rounds is large enough to protect against them.

Substitution–permutation Networks

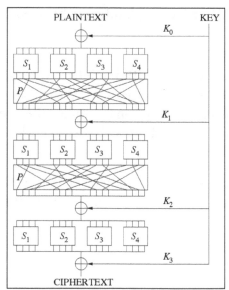

A sketch of a substitution–permutation network with 3 rounds, encrypting a plaintext block of 16 bits into a ciphertext block of 16 bits. The S-boxes are the S_i, the P-boxes are the same P, and the round keys are the K_i.

One important type of iterated block cipher known as a *substitution–permutation network (SPN)* takes a block of the plaintext and the key as inputs, and applies several alternating rounds consisting of a substitution stage followed by a permutation stage—to produce each block of ciphertext output. The non-linear substitution stage mixes the key bits with those of the plaintext, creating Shannon's *confusion*. The linear permutation stage then dissipates redundancies, creating *diffusion*.

A substitution box (S-box) substitutes a small block of input bits with another block of output bits. This substitution must be one-to-one, to ensure invertibility (hence decryption). A secure S-box will have the property that changing one input bit will change about half of the output bits on average, exhibiting what is known as the avalanche effect—i.e. it has the property that each output bit will depend on every input bit.

A permutation box (P-box) is a permutation of all the bits: it takes the outputs of all the S-boxes of one round, permutes the bits, and feeds them into the S-boxes of the next round. A good P-box has the property that the output bits of any S-box are distributed to as many S-box inputs as possible.

At each round, the round key (obtained from the key with some simple operations, for instance, using S-boxes and P-boxes) is combined using some group operation, typically XOR.

Decryption is done by simply reversing the process (using the inverses of the S-boxes and P-boxes and applying the round keys in reversed order).

Feistel Ciphers

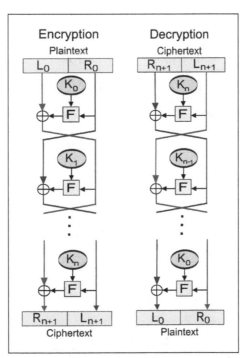

Many block ciphers, such as DES and Blowfish utilize structures known as *Feistel ciphers*.

In a *Feistel cipher*, the block of plain text to be encrypted is split into two equal-sized halves. The round function is applied to one half, using a subkey, and then the output is XORed with the other half. The two halves are then swapped.

Let F be the round function and let $K_0, K_1, \ldots, K_n$ be the sub-keys for the rounds $0, 1, \ldots, n$ respectively.

Then the basic operation is as follows:

Split the plaintext block into two equal pieces, (L_0, R_0)

For each round $i = 0, 1, \ldots, n$, compute,

$$L_{i+1} = R_i$$

$$R_{i+1} = L_i \oplus F(R_i, K_i).$$

Then the ciphertext is (R_{n+1}, L_{n+1}).

Decryption of a ciphertext (R_{n+1}, L_{n+1}) is accomplished by computing for $i = n, n-1, \ldots, 0$

$$R_i = L_{i+1}$$

$$L_i = R_{i+1} \oplus F(L_{i+1}, K_i).$$

Then (L_0, R_0) is the plaintext again.

One advantage of the Feistel model compared to a substitution–permutation network is that the round function F does not have to be invertible.

Lai–Massey Ciphers

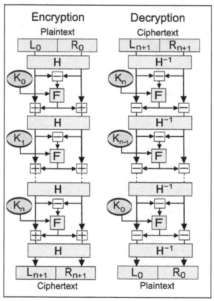

The Lai–Massey scheme. The archetypical cipher utilizing it is IDEA.

The Lai–Massey scheme offers security properties similar to those of the Feistel structure. It also shares its advantage that the round function F does not have to be invertible. Another similarity is that is also splits the input block into two equal pieces. However, the round function is applied to the difference between the two, and the result is then added to both half blocks.

Let F be the round function and H a half-round function and let $K_0, K_1, \ldots, K_n$ be the sub-keys for the rounds $0, 1, \ldots, n$ respectively.

Then the basic operation is as follows:

Split the plaintext block into two equal pieces, (L_0, R_0)

For each round $i = 0, 1, \ldots, n$, compute,

$$(L'_{i+1}, R'_{i+1}) = H(L_{i'} + T_i, R'_i + T_i)$$

where $T_i = F(L'_i - R'_i, K_i)$ and $(L'_0, R'_0) = H(L_0, R_0)$

Then the ciphertext is $(L_{n+1}, R_{n+1}) = (L'_{n+1}, R'_{n+1})$. .

Decryption of a ciphertext (L_{n+1}, R_{n+1}) is accomplished by computing for $i = n, n-1, \ldots, 0$

$$(L'_i, R'_i) = H^{-1}(L'_{i+1} - T_i, R'_{i+1} - T_i)$$

where $T_i = F(L'_{i+1} - R'_{i+1}, K_i)$ and $(L'_{n+1}, R'_{n+1}) = H^{-1}(L_{n+1}, R_{n+1})$

Then (L_0, R_0) (L'_0, R'_0) is the plaintext again.

Operations

ARX (Add–rotate–xor)

Many modern block ciphers and hashes are ARX algorithms—their round function involves only three operations: modular addition, rotation with fixed rotation amounts, and XOR (ARX). Examples include ChaCha20, Speck, XXTEA, and BLAKE. Many authors draw an ARX network, a kind of data flow diagram, to illustrate such a round function.

These ARX operations are popular because they are relatively fast and cheap in hardware and software, and also because they run in constant time, and are therefore immune to timing attacks. The rotational cryptanalysis technique attempts to attack such round functions.

Other Operations

Other operations often used in block ciphers include data-dependent rotations as in RC5 and RC6, a substitution box implemented as a lookup table as in Data Encryption Standard and Advanced Encryption Standard, a permutation box, and multiplication as in IDEA.

Modes of Operation

A block cipher by itself allows encryption only of a single data block of the cipher's block length. For a variable-length message, the data must first be partitioned into separate cipher blocks. In the simplest case, known as the Electronic Codebook (ECB) mode, a message is first split into separate blocks of the cipher's block size (possibly extending the last block with padding bits), and then each block is encrypted and decrypted independently. However, such a naive method is generally insecure because equal plaintext blocks will always generate equal ciphertext blocks (for the same key), so patterns in the plaintext message become evident in the ciphertext output.

To overcome this limitation, several so called block cipher modes of operation have been designed and specified in national recommendations such as NIST 800-38A and BSI TR-02102 and international standards such as ISO/IEC 10116. The general concept is to use randomization of the plaintext data based on an additional input value, frequently called an initialization vector, to create what is termed probabilistic encryption. In the popular cipher block chaining (CBC) mode, for encryption to be secure the initialization vector passed along with the plaintext message must be a random or pseudo-random value, which is added in an exclusive-or manner to the first plaintext block before it is being encrypted. The resultant ciphertext block is then used as the new initialization vector for the next plaintext block. In the cipher feedback (CFB) mode, which emulates a self-synchronizing stream cipher, the initialization vector is first encrypted and then added to the plaintext block. The output feedback (OFB) mode repeatedly encrypts the initialization vector to create a key stream for the emulation of a synchronous stream cipher. The newer counter (CTR) mode similarly creates a key stream, but has the advantage of only needing unique and not (pseudo-)random values as initialization vectors; the needed randomness is derived internally by using the initialization vector as a block counter and encrypting this counter for each block.

Insecure encryption of an image as a result of Electronic Codebook (ECB) mode encoding.

From a security-theoretic point of view, modes of operation must provide what is known as semantic security. Informally, it means that given some ciphertext under an unknown key one cannot practically derive any information from the ciphertext (other than the length of the message) over what one would have known without seeing the ciphertext. It has been shown that all of the modes discussed above, with the exception of the ECB mode, provide this property under so-called chosen plaintext attacks.

Padding

Some modes such as the CBC mode only operate on complete plaintext blocks. Simply extending the last block of a message with zero-bits is insufficient since it does not allow a receiver to easily distinguish messages that differ only in the amount of padding bits. More importantly, such a simple solution gives rise to very efficient padding oracle attacks. A suitable padding scheme is therefore needed to extend the last plaintext block to the cipher's block size. While many popular schemes described in standards and in the literature have been shown to be vulnerable to padding oracle attacks, a solution which adds a one-bit and then extends the last block with zero-bits, standardized as "padding method 2" in ISO/IEC 9797-1, has been proven secure against these attacks.

Cryptanalysis

Brute-force Attacks

This property results in the cipher's security degrading quadratically, and needs to be taken into account when selecting a block size. There is a trade-off though as large block sizes can result in the algorithm becoming inefficient to operate. Earlier block ciphers such as the DES have typically selected a 64-bit block size, while newer designs such as the AES support block sizes of 128 bits or more, with some ciphers supporting a range of different block sizes.

Differential Cryptanalysis

Linear Cryptanalysis

Linear cryptanalysis is a form of cryptanalysis based on finding affine approximations to the action of a cipher. Linear cryptanalysis is one of the two most widely used attacks on block ciphers; the other being differential cryptanalysis.

The discovery is attributed to Mitsuru Matsui, who first applied the technique to the FEAL cipher.

Integral Cryptanalysis

Integral cryptanalysis is a cryptanalytic attack that is particularly applicable to block ciphers based on substitution–permutation networks. Unlike differential cryptanalysis, which uses pairs of chosen plaintexts with a fixed XOR difference, integral cryptanalysis uses sets or even multisets of chosen plaintexts of which part is held constant and another part varies through all possibilities. For example, an attack might use 256 chosen plaintexts that have all but 8 of their bits the same, but all differ in those 8 bits. Such a set necessarily has an XOR sum of 0, and the XOR sums of the corresponding sets of ciphertexts provide information about the cipher's operation. This contrast between the differences of pairs of texts and the sums of larger sets of texts inspired the name "integral cryptanalysis", borrowing the terminology of calculus.

Other Techniques

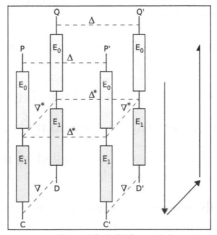

The development of the boomerang attack enabled differential cryptanalysis techniques to be applied to many ciphers that had previously been deemed secure against differential attacks.

In addition to linear and differential cryptanalysis, there is a growing catalog of attacks: truncated differential cryptanalysis, partial differential cryptanalysis, integral cryptanalysis, which encompasses square and integral attacks, slide attacks, boomerang attacks, the XSL attack, impossible differential cryptanalysis and algebraic attacks. For a new block cipher design to have any credibility, it must demonstrate evidence of security against known attacks.

Provable Security

When a block cipher is used in a given mode of operation, the resulting algorithm should ideally be about as secure as the block cipher itself. ECB (discussed above) emphatically lacks this property: regardless of how secure the underlying block cipher is, ECB mode can easily be attacked. On the other hand, CBC mode can be proven to be secure under the assumption that the underlying block cipher is likewise secure. Note, however, that making statements like this requires formal mathematical definitions for what it means for an encryption algorithm or a block cipher to "be secure". This topic describes two common notions for what properties a block cipher should have. Each corresponds to a mathematical model that can be used to prove properties of higher level algorithms, such as CBC.

This general approach to cryptography – proving higher-level algorithms (such as CBC) are secure under explicitly stated assumptions regarding their components (such as a block cipher) – is known as *provable security*.

Standard Model

Informally, a block cipher is secure in the standard model if an attacker cannot tell the difference between the block cipher (equipped with a random key) and a random permutation.

To be a bit more precise, let E be an n-bit block cipher. We imagine the following game:

- The person running the game flips a coin.

  - If the coin lands on heads, he chooses a random key K and defines the function $f = E_K$.

  - If the coin lands on tails, he chooses a random permutation π on the set of n-bit strings, and defines the function $f = \pi$.

- The attacker chooses an n-bit string X, and the person running the game tells him the value of $f(X)$.

- Step 2 is repeated a total of q times. (Each of these q interactions is a *query*.)

- The attacker guesses how the coin landed. He wins if his guess is correct.

The attacker, which we can model as an algorithm, is called an *adversary*. The function f (which the adversary was able to query) is called an *oracle*.

Note that an adversary can trivially ensure a 50% chance of winning simply by guessing at random (or even by, for example, always guessing "heads"). Therefore, let $P_E(A)$ denote the probability that the adversary A wins this game against E, and define the *advantage* of A as $2(P_E(A) - 1/2)$. It follows that if A guesses randomly, its advantage will be 0; on the other hand, if A always wins, then its advantage is 1. The block cipher E is a *pseudo-random permutation* (PRP) if no adversary has an advantage significantly greater than 0, given specified restrictions on q and the adversary's running time. If in Step 2 above adversaries have the option of learning $f^{-1}(X)$ instead of $f(X)$ (but still have only small advantages) then E is a *strong* PRP (SPRP). An adversary is *non-adaptive* if it chooses all q values for X before the game begins (that is, it does not use any information gleaned from previous queries to choose each X as it goes).

These definitions have proven useful for analyzing various modes of operation. For example, one can define a similar game for measuring the security of a block cipher-based encryption algorithm, and then try to show (through a reduction argument) that the probability of an adversary winning this new game is not much more than $P_E(A)$ for some A. (The reduction typically provides limits on q and the running time of A.) Equivalently, if $P_E(A)$ is small for all relevant A, then no attacker has a significant probability of winning the new game. This formalizes the idea that the higher-level algorithm inherits the block cipher's security.

Ideal Cipher Model

Practical Evaluation

Block ciphers may be evaluated according to multiple criteria in practice. Common factors include:

- Key parameters, such as its key size and block size, both of which provide an upper bound on the security of the cipher.

- The estimated security level, which is based on the confidence gained in the block cipher design after it has largely withstood major efforts in cryptanalysis over time, the design's mathematical soundness, and the existence of practical or certificational attacks.

- The cipher's complexity and its suitability for implementation in hardware or software. Hardware implementations may measure the complexity in terms of gate count or energy consumption, which are important parameters for resource-constrained devices.

- The cipher's performance in terms of processing throughput on various platforms, including its memory requirements.

- The cost of the cipher, which refers to licensing requirements that may apply due to intellectual property rights.

- The flexibility of the cipher, which includes its ability to support multiple key sizes and block lengths.

Notable Block Ciphers

Lucifer / DES

Lucifer is generally considered to be the first civilian block cipher, developed at IBM in the 1970s based on work done by Horst Feistel. A revised version of the algorithm was adopted as a U.S. government Federal Information Processing Standard: FIPS PUB 46 Data Encryption Standard (DES). It was chosen by the U.S. National Bureau of Standards (NBS) after a public invitation for submissions and some internal changes by NBS (and, potentially, the NSA). DES was publicly released in 1976 and has been widely used.

DES was designed to, among other things, resist a certain cryptanalytic attack known to the NSA and rediscovered by IBM, though unknown publicly until rediscovered again and published by Eli Biham and Adi Shamir in the late 1980s. The technique is called differential cryptanalysis and remains one of the few general attacks against block ciphers; linear cryptanalysis is another, but may have been unknown even to the NSA, prior to its publication by Mitsuru Matsui. DES prompted a large amount of other work and publications in cryptography and cryptanalysis in the open community and it inspired many new cipher designs.

DES has a block size of 64 bits and a key size of 56 bits. 64-bit blocks became common in block cipher designs after DES. Key length depended on several factors, including government regulation. Many observers in the 1970s commented that the 56-bit key length used for DES was too short. As time went on, its inadequacy became apparent, especially after a special purpose machine designed to break DES was demonstrated in 1998 by the Electronic Frontier Foundation. An extension to DES, Triple DES, triple-encrypts each block with either two independent keys (112-bit key and 80-bit security) or three independent keys (168-bit key and 112-bit security). It was widely adopted as a replacement. As of 2011, the three-key version is still considered secure, though the National Institute of Standards and Technology (NIST) standards no longer permit the use of the two-key version in new applications, due to its 80-bit security level.

IDEA

The International Data Encryption Algorithm (IDEA) is a block cipher designed by James Massey of ETH Zurich and Xuejia Lai; it was first described in 1991, as an intended replacement for DES.

IDEA operates on 64-bit blocks using a 128-bit key, and consists of a series of eight identical transformations (a round) and an output transformation (the half-round). The processes for encryption and decryption are similar. IDEA derives much of its security by interleaving operations from different groups – modular addition and multiplication, and bitwise exclusive or (XOR) – which are algebraically "incompatible" in some sense.

The designers analysed IDEA to measure its strength against differential cryptanalysis and concluded that it is immune under certain assumptions. No successful linear or algebraic weaknesses have been reported. As of 2012, the best attack which applies to all keys can break full 8.5-round IDEA using a narrow-bicliques attack about four times faster than brute force.

RC5

RC5 is a block cipher designed by Ronald Rivest in 1994 which, unlike many other ciphers, has a variable block size (32, 64 or 128 bits), key size (0 to 2040 bits) and number of rounds (0 to 255). The original suggested choice of parameters were a block size of 64 bits, a 128-bit key and 12 rounds.

A key feature of RC5 is the use of data-dependent rotations; one of the goals of RC5 was to prompt the study and evaluation of such operations as a cryptographic primitive. RC5 also consists of a number of modular additions and XORs. The general structure of the algorithm is a Feistel-like network. The encryption and decryption routines can be specified in a few lines of code. The key schedule, however, is more complex, expanding the key using an essentially one-way function with the binary expansions of both e and the golden ratio as sources of "nothing up my sleeve numbers". The tantalising simplicity of the algorithm together with the novelty of the data-dependent rotations has made RC5 an attractive object of study for cryptanalysts.

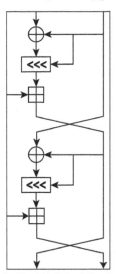

One round (two half-rounds) of the RC5 block cipher.

12-round RC5 (with 64-bit blocks) is susceptible to a differential attack using 2^{44} chosen plaintexts. 18–20 rounds are suggested as sufficient protection.

Rijndael / AES

The *Rijndael* cipher developed by Belgian cryptographers, Joan Daemen and Vincent Rijmen was one of the competing designs to replace DES. It won the 5-year public competition to become the AES, (Advanced Encryption Standard).

Adopted by NIST in 2001, AES has a fixed block size of 128 bits and a key size of 128, 192, or 256 bits, whereas Rijndael can be specified with block and key sizes in any multiple of 32 bits, with a minimum of 128 bits. The blocksize has a maximum of 256 bits, but the keysize has no theoretical maximum. AES operates on a 4×4 column-major order matrix of bytes, termed the *state* (versions of Rijndael with a larger block size have additional columns in the state).

Blowfish

Blowfish is a block cipher, designed in 1993 by Bruce Schneier and included in a large number of cipher suites and encryption products. Blowfish has a 64-bit block size and a variable key length from 1 bit up to 448 bits. It is a 16-round Feistel cipher and uses large key-dependent S-boxes. Notable features of the design include the key-dependent S-boxes and a highly complex key schedule.

It was designed as a general-purpose algorithm, intended as an alternative to the ageing DES and free of the problems and constraints associated with other algorithms. At the time Blowfish was released, many other designs were proprietary, encumbered by patents or were commercial/government secrets. Schneier has stated that, "Blowfish is unpatented, and will remain so in all countries. The algorithm is hereby placed in the public domain, and can be freely used by anyone."

The same applies to Twofish, a successor algorithm from Schneier.

Generalizations

Tweakable Block Ciphers

M. Liskov, R. Rivest, and D. Wagner have described a generalized version of block ciphers called "tweakable" block ciphers. A tweakable block cipher accepts a second input called the *tweak* along with its usual plaintext or ciphertext input. The tweak, along with the key, selects the permutation computed by the cipher. If changing tweaks is sufficiently lightweight (compared with a usually fairly expensive key setup operation), then some interesting new operation modes become possible. The disk encryption theory article describes some of these modes.

Format-preserving Encryption

Block ciphers traditionally work over a binary alphabet. That is, both the input and the output are binary strings, consisting of n zeroes and ones. In some situations, however, one may wish to have a block cipher that works over some other alphabet; for example, encrypting 16-digit credit card numbers in such a way that the ciphertext is also a 16-digit number might facilitate adding an encryption layer to legacy software. This is an example of format-preserving encryption. More generally, format-preserving encryption requires a keyed permutation on some finite language. This makes format-preserving encryption schemes a natural generalization of (tweakable) block ciphers. In contrast, traditional encryption schemes, such as CBC, are not permutations because the same plaintext can encrypt to multiple different ciphertexts, even when using a fixed key.

Cryptanalysis

Close-up of the rotors in a Fialka cipher machine.

Cryptanalysis is the study of analyzing information systems in order to study the hidden aspects of the systems. Cryptanalysis is used to breach cryptographic security systems and gain access to the contents of encrypted messages, even if the cryptographic key is unknown.

In addition to mathematical analysis of cryptographic algorithms, cryptanalysis includes the study of side-channel attacks that do not target weaknesses in the cryptographic algorithms themselves, but instead exploit weaknesses in their implementation.

Even though the goal has been the same, the methods and techniques of cryptanalysis have changed drastically through the history of cryptography, adapting to increasing cryptographic complexity, ranging from the pen-and-paper methods of the past, through machines like the British Bombes and Colossus computers at Bletchley Park in World War II, to the mathematically advanced computerized schemes of the present. Methods for breaking modern cryptosystems often involve solving carefully constructed problems in pure mathematics, the best-known being integer factorization.

Given some encrypted data ("ciphertext"), the goal of the cryptanalyst is to gain as much information as possible about the original, unencrypted data ("plaintext"). It is useful to consider two aspects of achieving this. The first is breaking the system — that is discovering how the encipherment process works. The second is solving the key that is unique for a particular encrypted message or group of messages.

Amount of Information Available to the Attacker

Attacks can be classified based on what type of information the attacker has available. As a basic starting point it is normally assumed that, for the purposes of analysis, the general algorithm is known; this is Shannon's Maxim "the enemy knows the system" — in its turn, equivalent to Kerckhoffs' principle. This is a reasonable assumption in practice — throughout history, there are countless examples of secret algorithms falling into wider knowledge, variously through espionage, betrayal and reverse engineering. (And on occasion, ciphers have been broken through pure deduction; for example, the German Lorenz cipher and the Japanese Purple code, and a variety of classical schemes):

- Ciphertext-only: The cryptanalyst has access only to a collection of ciphertexts or codetexts.

- Known-plaintext: The attacker has a set of ciphertexts to which he knows the corresponding plaintext.

- Chosen-plaintext (chosen-ciphertext): The attacker can obtain the ciphertexts (plaintexts) corresponding to an arbitrary set of plaintexts (ciphertexts) of his own choosing.

- Adaptive chosen-plaintext: Like a chosen-plaintext attack, except the attacker can choose subsequent plaintexts based on information learned from previous encryptions. Similarly Adaptive chosen ciphertext attack.

- Related-key attack: Like a chosen-plaintext attack, except the attacker can obtain ciphertexts encrypted under two different keys. The keys are unknown, but the relationship between them is known; for example, two keys that differ in the one bit.

Computational Resources Required

Attacks can also be characterised by the resources they require. Those resources include:

- Time: The number of computation steps (e.g., test encryptions) which must be performed.

- Memory: The amount of *storage* required to perform the attack.

- Data: The quantity and type of *plaintexts and ciphertexts* required for a particular approach.

It's sometimes difficult to predict these quantities precisely, especially when the attack isn't practical to actually implement for testing. But academic cryptanalysts tend to provide at least the estimated *order of magnitude* of their attacks' difficulty, saying, for example, "SHA-1 collisions now."

Bruce Schneier notes that even computationally impractical attacks can be considered breaks: "Breaking a cipher simply means finding a weakness in the cipher that can be exploited with a complexity less than brute force. Never mind that brute-force might require 2^{128} encryptions; an attack requiring 2^{110} encryptions would be considered a break simply put, a break can just be a certificational weakness: evidence that the cipher does not perform as advertised."

Partial Breaks

The results of cryptanalysis can also vary in usefulness. For example, cryptographer Lars Knudsen classified various types of attack on block ciphers according to the amount and quality of secret information that was discovered:

- Total break: The attacker deduces the secret key.

- Global deduction: The attacker discovers a functionally equivalent algorithm for encryption and decryption, but without learning the key.

- Instance (local) deduction: The attacker discovers additional plaintexts (or ciphertexts) not previously known.

- Information deduction: The attacker gains some Shannon information about plaintexts (or ciphertexts) not previously known.

- Distinguishing algorithm: The attacker can distinguish the cipher from a random permutation.

Academic attacks are often against weakened versions of a cryptosystem, such as a block cipher or hash function with some rounds removed. Many, but not all, attacks become exponentially more difficult to execute as rounds are added to a cryptosystem, so it's possible for the full cryptosystem to be strong even though reduced-round variants are weak. Nonetheless, partial breaks that come close to breaking the original cryptosystem may mean that a full break will follow; the successful attacks on DES, MD5, and SHA-1 were all preceded by attacks on weakened versions.

In academic cryptography, a *weakness* or a *break* in a scheme is usually defined quite conservatively: it might require impractical amounts of time, memory, or known plaintexts. It also might require the attacker be able to do things many real-world attackers can't: for example, the attacker may need to choose particular plaintexts to be encrypted or even to ask for plaintexts to be encrypted using several keys related to the secret key. Furthermore, it might only reveal a small amount of information, enough to prove the cryptosystem imperfect but too little to be useful to real-world attackers. Finally, an attack might only apply to a weakened version of cryptographic tools, like a reduced-round block cipher, as a step towards breaking of the full system.

Differential Cryptanalysis

Differential cryptanalysis is a general form of cryptanalysis applicable primarily to block ciphers, but also to stream ciphers and cryptographic hash functions. In the broadest sense, it is the study of how differences in information input can affect the resultant difference at the output. In the case of a block cipher, it refers to a set of techniques for tracing differences through the network of transformation, discovering where the cipher exhibits non-random behavior, and exploiting such properties to recover the secret key (cryptography key).

Attack Mechanics

Differential cryptanalysis is usually a chosen plaintext attack, meaning that the attacker must be able to obtain ciphertexts for some set of plaintexts of their choosing. There are, however, extensions that would allow a known plaintext or even a ciphertext-only attack. The basic method uses pairs of plaintext related by a constant *difference*; difference can be defined in several ways, but the eXclusive OR (XOR) operation is usual. The attacker then computes the differences of the corresponding ciphertexts, hoping to detect statistical patterns in their distribution. The resulting pair of differences is called a differential. Their statistical properties depend upon the nature of the S-boxes used for encryption, so the attacker analyses differentials (Δ_X, Δ_Y), where $\Delta_Y = S(X, \Delta_X)$, $S(X)$ (and, denotes exclusive or) for each such S-box S. In the basic attack, one particular ciphertext difference is expected to be especially frequent; in this way, the cipher can be distinguished from random. More sophisticated variations allow the key to be recovered faster than exhaustive search.

In the most basic form of key recovery through differential cryptanalysis, an attacker requests the ciphertexts for a large number of plaintext pairs, then assumes that the differential holds for at least $r - 1$ rounds, where r is the total number of rounds. The attacker then deduces which round keys (for the final round) are possible, assuming the difference between the blocks before the final round is fixed. When round keys are short, this can be achieved by simply exhaustively decrypting the ciphertext pairs one round with each possible round key. When one round key has been deemed a potential round key considerably more often than any other key, it is assumed to be the correct round key.

For any particular cipher, the input difference must be carefully selected for the attack to be successful. An analysis of the algorithm's internals is undertaken; the standard method is to trace a path of highly probable differences through the various stages of encryption, termed a *differential characteristic*.

Since differential cryptanalysis became public knowledge, it has become a basic concern of cipher designers. New designs are expected to be accompanied by evidence that the algorithm is resistant to this attack, and many, including the Advanced Encryption Standard, have been proven secure against the attack.

The attack relies primarily on the fact that a given input/output difference pattern only occurs for certain values of inputs. Usually the attack is applied in essence to the non-linear components as if they were a solid component (usually they are in fact look-up tables or *S-boxes*). Observing the desired output difference (between two chosen or known plaintext inputs) *suggests* possible key values.

For example, if a differential of 1 => 1 (implying a difference in the least significant bit (LSB) of the input leads to an output difference in the LSB) occurs with probability of 4/256 (possible with the non-linear function in the AES cipher for instance) then for only 4 values (or 2 pairs) of inputs is that differential possible. Suppose we have a non-linear function where the key is XOR'ed before evaluation and the values that allow the differential are {2,3} and {4,5}. If the attacker sends in the values of {6, 7} and observes the correct output difference it means the key is either $6 \oplus K = 2$, or $6 \oplus K = 4$, meaning the key K is either 2 or 4.

In essence, for an n-bit non-linear function one would ideally seek as close to $2^{-(n-1)}$ as possible to achieve *differential uniformity*. When this happens, the differential attack requires as much work to determine the key as simply brute forcing the key.

The AES non-linear function has a maximum differential probability of 4/256 (most entries however are either 0 or 2). Meaning that in theory one could determine the key with half as much work as brute force, however, the high branch of AES prevents any high probability trails from existing over multiple rounds. In fact, the AES cipher would be just as immune to differential and linear attacks with a much *weaker* non-linear function. The incredibly high branch (active S-box count) of 25 over 4R means that over 8 rounds no attack involves fewer than 50 non-linear transforms, meaning that the probability of success does not exceed Pr[attack] ≤ Pr[best attack on S-box]^{50}. For example, with the current S-box AES emits no fixed differential with a probability higher than $(4/256)^{50}$ or 2^{-300} which is far lower than the required threshold of 2^{-128} for a 128-bit block cipher. This would have allowed room for a more efficient S-box, even if it is 16-uniform the probability of attack would have still been 2^{-200}.

There exist no bijections for even sized inputs/outputs with 2-uniformity. They exist in odd fields (such as $GF(2^7)$) using either cubing or inversion (there are other exponents that can be used as well). For instance $S(x) = x^3$ in any odd binary field is immune to differential and linear cryptanalysis. This is in part why the MISTY designs use 7- and 9-bit functions in the 16-bit non-linear function. What these functions gain in immunity to differential and linear attacks they lose to algebraic attacks. That is, they are possible to describe and solve via a SAT solver. This is in part why AES (for instance) has an affine mapping after the inversion.

Linear Cryptanalysis

In cryptography, linear cryptanalysis is a general form of cryptanalysis based on finding affine approximations to the action of a cipher. Attacks have been developed for block ciphers and stream ciphers. Linear cryptanalysis is one of the two most widely used attacks on block ciphers; the other being differential cryptanalysis.

The discovery is attributed to Mitsuru Matsui, who first applied the technique to the FEAL cipher. Subsequently, Matsui published an attack on the Data Encryption Standard (DES), eventually leading to the first experimental cryptanalysis of the cipher reported in the open community. The attack on DES is not generally practical, requiring 2^{47} known plaintexts.

A variety of refinements to the attack have been suggested, including using multiple linear approximations or incorporating non-linear expressions, leading to a generalized partitioning cryptanalysis. Evidence of security against linear cryptanalysis is usually expected of new cipher designs.

There are two parts to linear cryptanalysis. The first is to construct linear equations relating plaintext, ciphertext and key bits that have a high bias; that is, whose probabilities of holding (over the space of all possible values of their variables) are as close as possible to 0 or 1. The second is to use these linear equations in conjunction with known plaintext-ciphertext pairs to derive key bits.

Constructing Linear Equations

For the purposes of linear cryptanalysis, a linear equation expresses the equality of two expressions which consist of binary variables combined with the exclusive-or (XOR) operation. For example, the following equation, from a hypothetical cipher, states the XOR sum of the first and third plaintext bits (as in a block cipher's block) and the first ciphertext bit is equal to the second bit of the key:

$$P_1 \oplus P_3 \oplus C_1 = K_2.$$

In an ideal cipher, any linear equation relating plaintext, ciphertext and key bits would hold with probability 1/2. Since the equations dealt with in linear cryptanalysis will vary in probability, they are more accurately referred to as linear *approximations*.

The procedure for constructing approximations is different for each cipher. In the most basic type of block cipher, a substitution-permutation network, analysis is concentrated primarily on the S-boxes, the only nonlinear part of the cipher (i.e. the operation of an S-box cannot be encoded in a linear equation). For small enough S-boxes, it is possible to enumerate every possible linear equation relating the S-box's input and output bits, calculate their biases and choose the best ones. Linear approximations for S-boxes then must be combined with the cipher's other actions, such as permutation and key mixing, to arrive at linear approximations for the entire cipher. The piling-up lemma is a useful tool for this combination step. There are also techniques for iteratively improving linear approximations.

Deriving Key Bits

Having obtained a linear approximation of the form:

$$P_{i_1} \oplus P_{i_2} \oplus \cdots \oplus C_{j_1} \oplus C_{j_2} \oplus \cdots = K_{k_1} \oplus K_{k_2} \oplus \cdots$$

we can then apply a straightforward algorithm, using known plaintext-ciphertext pairs, to guess at the values of the key bits involved in the approximation.

For each set of values of the key bits on the right-hand side (referred to as a *partial key*), count how many times the approximation holds true over all the known plaintext-ciphertext pairs; call this count T. The partial key whose T has the greatest absolute difference from half the number of plaintext-ciphertext pairs is designated as the most likely set of values for those key bits. This is because it is assumed that the correct partial key will cause the approximation to hold with a high bias. The magnitude of the bias is significant here, as opposed to the magnitude of the probability itself.

This procedure can be repeated with other linear approximations, obtaining guesses at values of key bits, until the number of unknown key bits is low enough that they can be attacked with brute force.

Digital Rights Management

Digital rights management (DRM) is a way to protect copyrights for digital media. This approach includes the use of technologies that limit the copying and use of copyrighted works and proprietary software.

In a way, digital rights management allows publishers or authors to control what paying users can do with their works. For companies, implementing digital rights management systems or processes can help to prevent users from accessing or using certain assets, allowing the organization to avoid legal issues that arise from unauthorized use. Today, DRM is playing a growing role in data security.

With the rise of peer-to-peer file exchange services such as torrent sites, online piracy has been the bane of copyrighted material. DRM technologies do not catch those who engage in piracy. Instead, they make it impossible to steal or share the content in the first place.

Most of the time, digital rights management includes codes that prohibit copying, or codes that limit the time or number of devices on which a certain product can be accessed.

Publishers, authors, and other content creators use an application that encrypts media, data, e-book, content, software, or any other copyrighted material. Only those with the decryption keys can access the material. They can also use tools to limit or restrict what users are able to do with their materials.

There are many ways to protect the content, software, or product. DRM allows one to:

- Restrict or prevent users from editing or saving the content.

- Restrict or prevent users from sharing or forwarding the product or content.

- Restrict or prevent users from printing the content. For some, the document or artwork may only be printed up to a limited number of times.

- Disallow users from creating screenshots or screen grabs of the content.

- Set an expiry date on the document or media, after which the user will no longer be able to access it. This could also be done by limiting the number of uses that a user has. For instance, a document may be revoked after the user has listened ten times or opened and printed the PDF 20 times.

- Lock access only to certain IP addresses, locations, or devices. This means that if the media is only available to US residents, then it will not be accessible to people in other countries.

- Watermark artworks and documents in order to establish ownership and identity.

Digital rights management also allows publishers and authors to access a log of people and times when certain media, content, or software was used. For instance, one can see when a particular e-book was downloaded or printed and who accessed it.

In today's digital world, digital rights management is increasingly important, not only for digital content creators but also for companies and individuals that make use of digital assets licensed or purchased from third-party creators. Here are a few common use cases for digital rights management:

- Digital rights management allows authors, musicians, movie professionals, and other creators to prevent unauthorized use of their content. It can also protect their bottom lines and control the distribution of their products.

- Digital rights management can help companies control access to confidential information. They can use these technologies to restrict access to sensitive data, while at the same time allowing it to be shared securely. Furthermore, having DRM technologies makes it easier for auditors to investigate and identify leaks. When used in a business setting, digital rights management may be called by a different name, such as information rights management or enterprise rights management. Healthcare organizations and financial services companies turn to DRM to meet data protection regulations such as HIPAA or GLBA.

- Digital rights management ensures that digital work remains unaltered. Creators often want their work to be distributed in its original form to serve its intended purposes. The FDIC uses digital rights management to prevent the unauthorized redistribution of sensitive digital information, for example.

Challenges of Digital Rights Management

Not everybody agrees with digital rights management. For instance, users who pay for music on iTunes would love to be able to listen to the song on any device or use it in whatever way they wish.

On the other hand, businesses that pay thousands of dollars for a high-value industry report are willing to use DRM so that their competitors are unable to get the same report for free. Some critics of DRM have pointed out that this creates an unfair advantage for businesses that have money to burn because smaller operations may not be able to afford the information that they need to grow their businesses.

However, DRM technology is not a perfect solution. Even if copywrite holders incorporate digital rights management code into their product, the public may discover a way to work around it. For instance, if they make their content playable only on one player, some users will inevitably try to figure out the decryption keys and then create another player that can play the copyrighted content. Users then download the new player in the hopes of circumventing the DRM encryption. There are also free tools to remove DRM codes, which – while unethical – are readily available online.

Benefits of Digital Rights Management

Digital rights management can protect copyright holders from piracy, but when tools that can easily remove DRM code from digital works are readily available, why do content creators continue to bother with it? Despite its shortcomings, digital rights management still offers numerous benefits:

- Digital rights management educates users about copyright and intellectual property. Most people are not concerned with copyrights and are passive when it comes to DRM. As long as they can access the content they like, they have no issue with smaller details. With DRM in place, companies can communicate to users what they can and cannot do with respect to digital content.

- DRM helps make way for better licensing agreements and technologies. Digital rights management technologies are aimed at restricting the ways in which users interact with content, such as listening to music on multiple devices or sharing content with friends with family. Users who do not want to be restrained by DRM codes are able to support vendors who offer and sell DRM-free content, thus encouraging vendors to look for other technologies that are better at licensing than DRM.

- Digital rights management helps authors retain ownership of their works. It is very easy for a company or user to copy content from someone else's e-book and rebrand it as their own. With DRM, it is possible to stop anybody from altering content. This also applies to scientists who rely on DRM to protect their inventions.

- Digital rights management helps protect income streams. Video and moviemakers spend money to create their videos in the hopes that they will be able to recoup their investments once it hits screens, or when it streams or is distributed online. DRM can help ensure that only paying users are able to watch the video or movie. It also ensures that the video is only accessible to a certain audience. For instance, videos with adult-oriented content should only be accessible to adults who can verify their age.

- Digital rights management can help secure files and keep them private. DRM effectively prevents unauthorized users from seeing or reading confidential files.

References

- Menezes, Alfred J : Handbook of applied cryptography, CRC Press, ISBN 0-8493-8523-7, October 2006, 816 pages

- Cryptography, definition: techtarget.com, Retrieved 23 July, 2014

- "Automated Validation of Internet Security Protocols and Applications (AVISPA)". Archived from the original on 2016-09-22. Retrieved 2016-10-07

- Asymmetric-cryptography, definition: techtarget.com, Retrieved 7 February, 2009

- Levy, Steven (2001). Crypto: How the Code Rebels Beat the Government — Saving Privacy in the Digital Age. Penguin Books. Pp. 55–56. ISBN 0-14-024432-8

- What-digital-rights-management: digitalguardian.com, Retrieved 19 August, 2019

Permissions

Index

Printed in the USA
CPSIA information can be obtained
at www.ICGtesting.com
JSHW051413221024
72173JS00006B/1357